IMAGES of America
SHELBY

ON THE COVER: This image from around 1910 depicts a family on the north side of Cleveland County Court Square. (Courtesy of the author.)

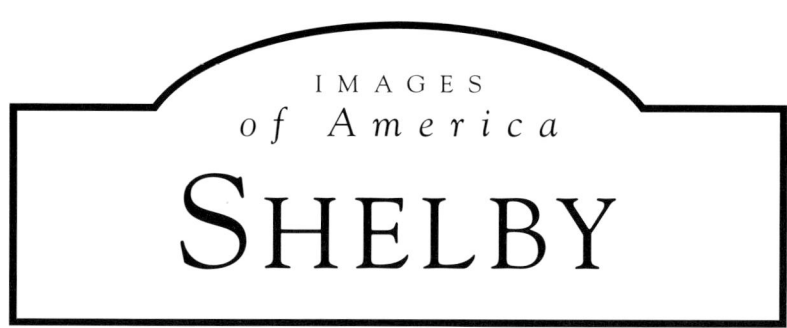

Images of America
SHELBY

U. L. "Rusty" Patterson
and Barry Hambright

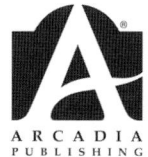

Copyright © 2007 by U. L. "Rusty" Patterson and Barry Hambright
ISBN 978-0-7385-5291-0

Published by Arcadia Publishing
Charleston SC, Chicago IL, Portsmouth NH, San Francisco CA

Printed in the United States of America

Library of Congress Catalog Card Number: 2007928064

For all general information contact Arcadia Publishing at:
Telephone 843-853-2070
Fax 843-853-0044
E-mail sales@arcadiapublishing.com
For customer service and orders:
Toll-Free 1-888-313-2665

Visit us on the Internet at www.arcadiapublishing.com

Contents

Acknowledgments		6
Introduction		7
1.	Shelby: 1841–1920	9
2.	People and Places: 1921–1970	31
3.	The All-America City	69
4.	Shelby City Schools	89
5.	The Sports Town	111

ACKNOWLEDGMENTS

The authors wish to thank those people who have helped make this publication possible. Many people throughout the community continue to generously and enthusiastically provide photographs, names, dates, timelines, stories, and background information. Unless otherwise noted, all images are from the U. L. Patterson collection. Several publications have been instrumental in the production of this work. A history of Shelby would not be possible if not for the work of Lee B. Weathers's 1956 book *The Living Past of Cleveland County*. Other works of note include *A History of Cleveland County* by Henry Weathers, local newspaper the *Star* (originally the *Shelby Daily Star*), *The Heritage of Cleveland County* by the Cleveland County Historical Association, *Architectural Perspectives of Cleveland County, North Carolina* by Brian R. Eades and J. Daniel Pezzoni, the *Shelby Daily Star 75th Anniversary Special*, *A History of First Baptist Church* by Grace Hamrick, *Tracks through Time* by Dave Baity, and the Shelby High School annual *Cruiser*.

We wish to thank Robert "Bob" Arey, Stough Wray, Charles Wray, Reid Bridges, Cleveland County Archives, Alan Ford, Judith Parker-Procter, Brendan Camp LeGrand, U.S. Department of the Interior, the National Park Service, Julie Greene Burch, Catherine Blanton Freedberg, Alison Gilbert, Bryon Gragg, Allison Gragg, Chandler Poole and Uptown Shelby Association, Tommy Forney, Jo Ann Surratt, Tom Bridges, Millie Keeter Holbrook, Patrick McMurry, Jim and Linda Horn, Jay Morgan, Jim Morgan, Larry Ware, David Grose, David Allen, Dr. Will Plaster, and June Albright for their contributions.

Access to the works of professional photographers Floyd Willis and Ellis Studios and the Lloyd Hamrick Photograph Collection have again proven a valuable resource, as have postcard images from T. W. Hamrick Company and Austin and Clontz 5, 10, and 25¢ Store. Thank you to Mary Emma Hambright and Frankie Patterson for their patience and support. And a special thank you to Marion Patterson and Margaret Patterson for their moral and technical support in the publishing of the book.

A reasonable effort has been made to gather accurate information about each image within the deadlines provided by the publisher. All of these people have helped make this publication possible. None of them are responsible for the errors, which are the authors' alone.

INTRODUCTION

As we have written books on various aspects of Shelby and Cleveland County, we have seen a love of local history that is shared by many. People respond to pictures that bring back memories of the past. People in every town or city possess pictures that constitute a great resource in preserving local history. Gradually these images are being lost or discarded by those who do not comprehend their value. Also, the history and stories that make these images valuable need to be recorded. Arcadia Publishing's Images of America series is helping save the memories of hundreds of communities across the nation.

In our first book on Shelby, we collected pictures that were easily available. Since then, we have tried to seek out pictures that are significant in portraying the people and places in Shelby's past. In this work we have included pictures of early, key figures all the way back to Col. Isaac Shelby, for whom the city is named.

This work has its focus on Shelby, the county seat of Cleveland County. The county was formed by an act of the North Carolina Legislature on January 11, 1841, and two years later, in 1843, the legislature chartered Shelby as a town. The law creating Cleveland County stated that the county seat must be within four miles of the Cleveland Springs. Shelby, just west of the spring, satisfied that requirement. The name Shelby was in honor of one of the many heroes of the famous Revolutionary War battle at nearby Kings Mountain in 1781. Col. Isaac Shelby would become the first governor of Kentucky and have several towns and cities named for him.

We open this volume with a look at people and places in the early history of Shelby. In this first chapter and a follow up one on Shelby in the middle of the 20th century, we seek to use new views of the city and include people who made contributions to the growth and development of the city. We go beyond obvious leaders such as Governors O. Max Gardner and Clyde R. Hoey. We strongly believe that a city is built and sustained by hundreds of solid, hard-working citizens, and we try to show many of these people.

We feature two areas of Shelby's life that have been a key party of the city's history. First the Shelby Public School System is remembered. This system served for 100 years and produced most of the city's leaders and the authors of this book. Images of elementary schools are not easy to find, but we try to show the main schools and some of their pupils. Then we look at Shelby's proud sporting heritage, which includes high school championships in football (including 2005 and 2006), ranked and well-known tennis players on all levels, and several state championships in American Legion Baseball. In 1945, Shelby won the National American Legion Baseball Championship. Because of the city's excellent job of hosting the 2002 Legion regional playoffs, Shelby will be host in August 2008 to both the regional and national championship playoffs.

We once again hope many will enjoy this book of memories of days gone by and can relate personally to the sites and people pictured inside.

One

SHELBY
1841–1920

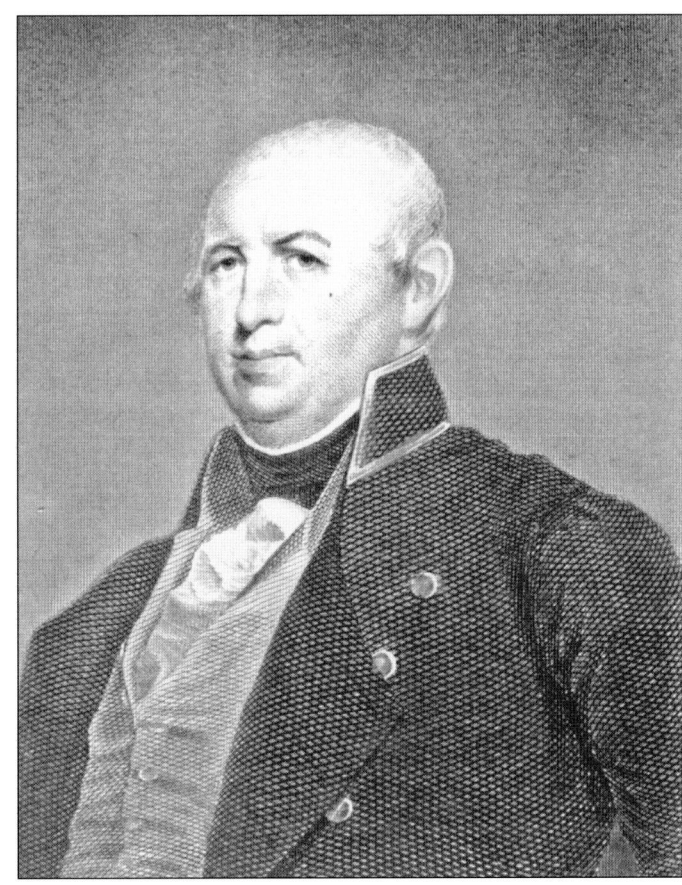

The town of Shelby is named for Isaac Shelby (1750–1826), a Revolutionary War hero of the Battle of Kings Mountain. The town was formed in 1841 and officially incorporated by an act of the North Carolina Legislature on January 25, 1843. The original town limits extended one-quarter mile in a circular direction from the public square.

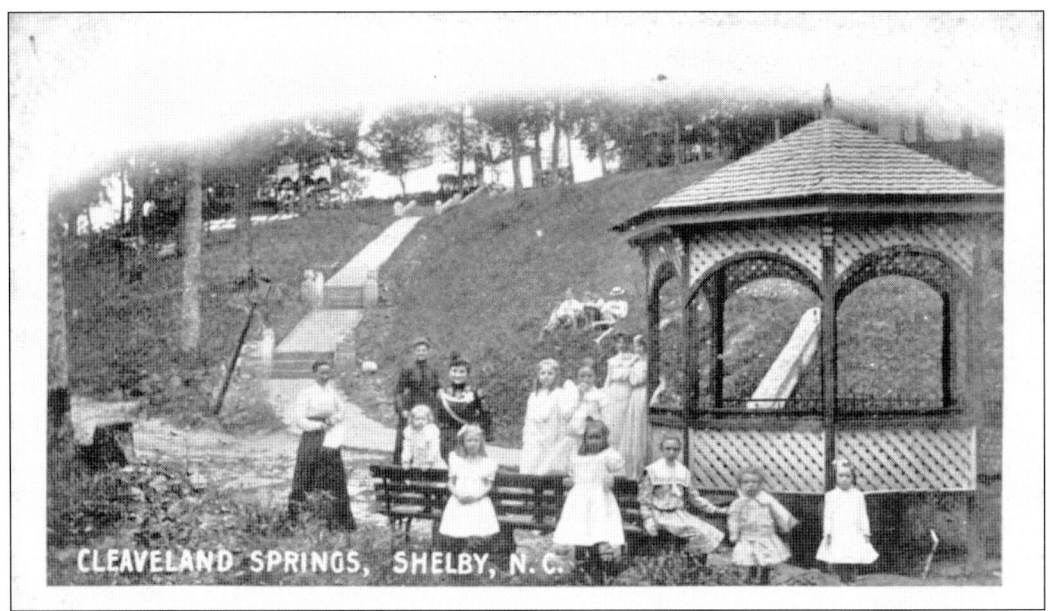

Cleveland County was formed by an act of the state legislature on January 11, 1841. Named for another Revolutionary War hero, Col. Benjamin Cleaveland (1738–1806), the act called for the county seat to be located "not more than four miles from the Wilson (later Cleveland) Mineral Springs." This postcard view shows guests of the Cleaveland Springs Hotel in 1905. When Grover Cleveland was elected president of the United States, the spelling of Cleaveland was changed to avoid confusion.

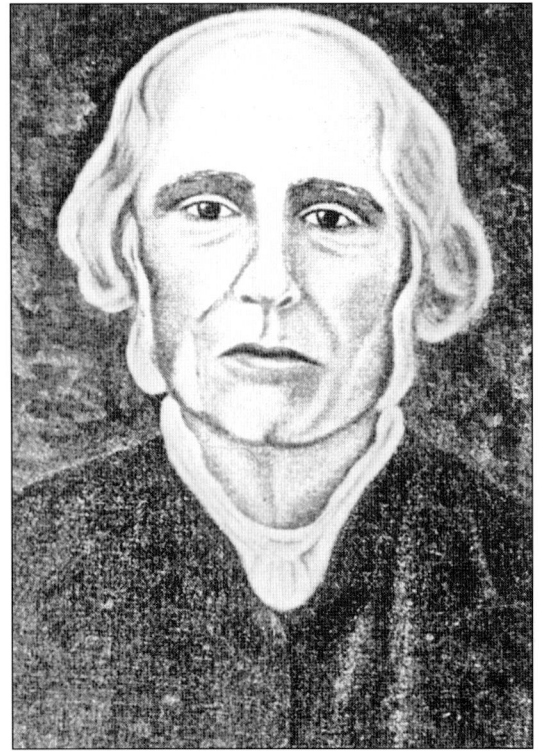

This early image depicts James Love (1796–1884) who in 1841, along with his wife, Susan, gave 147 acres of land upon which the city of Shelby is located. In the same year, William Forbes (1799–1851) gave an additional 50 acres for the formation of the county seat. Love requested that four lots be reserved for the construction of churches and two lots reserved as school sites. Love designated lots for the use of the Baptist, Methodist, Presbyterian, and Episcopal congregations. Only the Methodist congregation built its church opposite the public square as Love had intended. The Baptists and Presbyterians built on their present sites in uptown Shelby, and the Episcopalians built their first church near the intersection of Graham and Lafayette Streets.

John R. Logan (1811–1884), James Love, and S. L. Gidney had visited Washington, D.C., and were impressed with the width of the streets. A surveyor by trade, Logan was appointed engineer to make the first map of the city and "lay out the streets and parcel up the lots for business and home sites," according to *The Heritage of Cleveland County*. The main streets in uptown Shelby were named for Revolutionary War heroes Gen. George Washington, Lt. Col. Francis Marion, Marquis de Lafayette, Gen. Baron Johan DeKalb, Maj. Gen. Joseph Warren, Gen. Daniel Morgan, Col. Joseph Graham, and Gen. Thomas Sumter. (*The Heritage of Cleveland County*.)

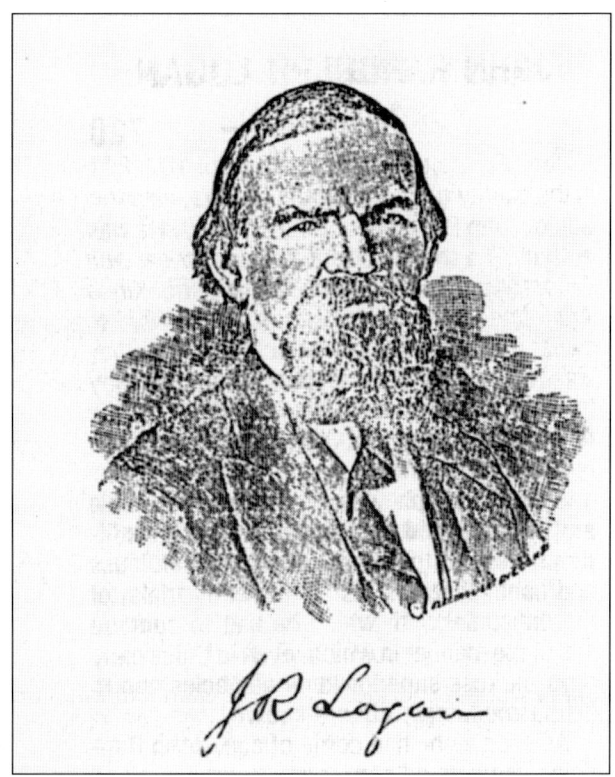

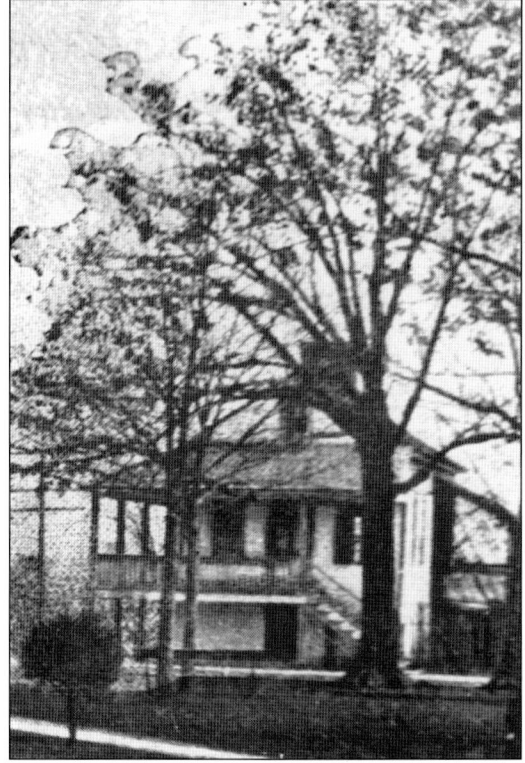

The first house built in Shelby was the home of Dr. Thomas Williams, a civic leader and Shelby's first medical doctor. The home was located on North Washington Street across from the square on the site of the present Central United Methodist Church. Shelby was slow to grow in its early years. Only a few wooden-frame structures were built in the uptown for homes and businesses. Most families lived on farms away from the center of town. The uptown did not begin to flourish until the 1880s.

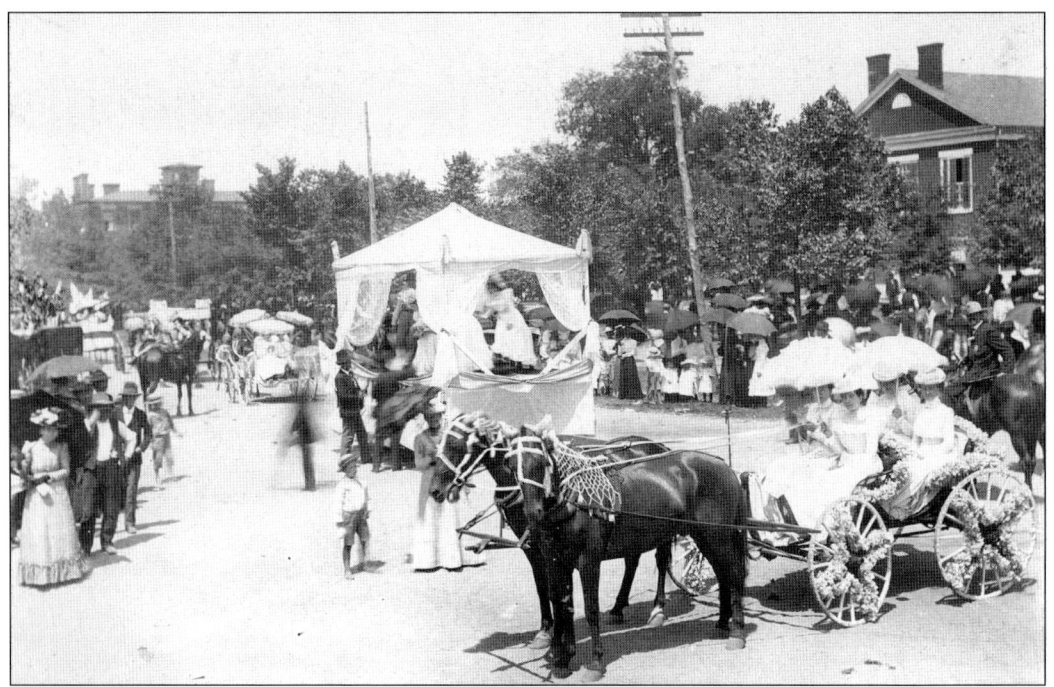
This c. 1890 photograph shows a crowd gathering for a Fourth of July parade at the intersection of Washington and Warren Streets. The building to the right is the first courthouse on the square, and the building in the left background is the First National Bank building.

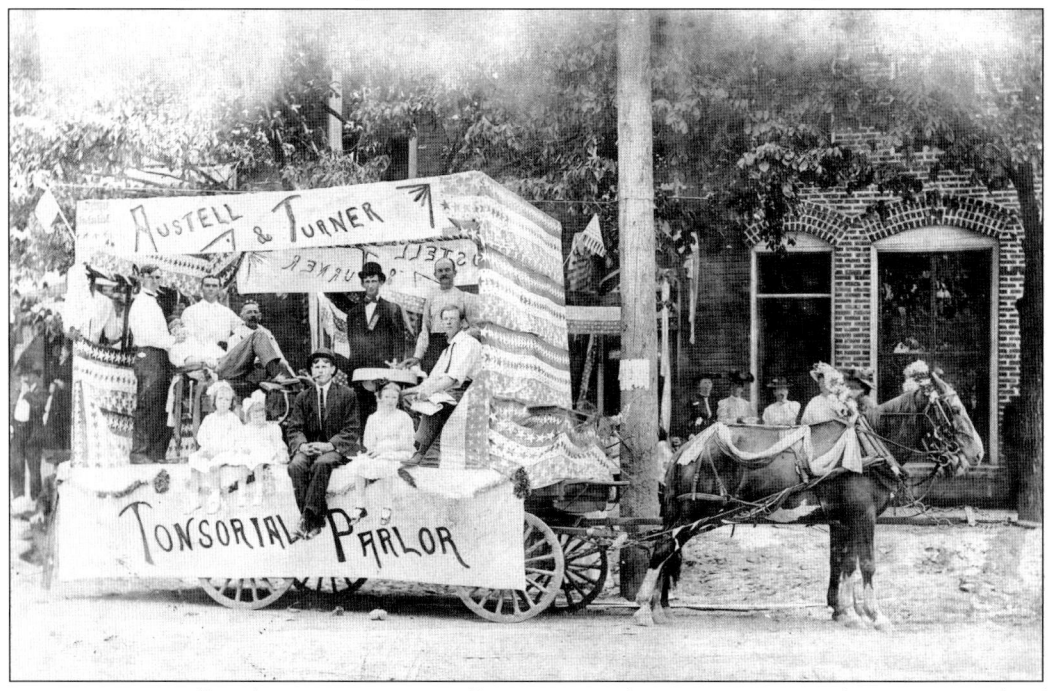
Mary Jane Austell and James Petty Austell are among the participants in the 1904 Fourth of July parade in uptown Shelby. The Austell and Turner Tonsorial Parlor sponsored the horse-drawn float.

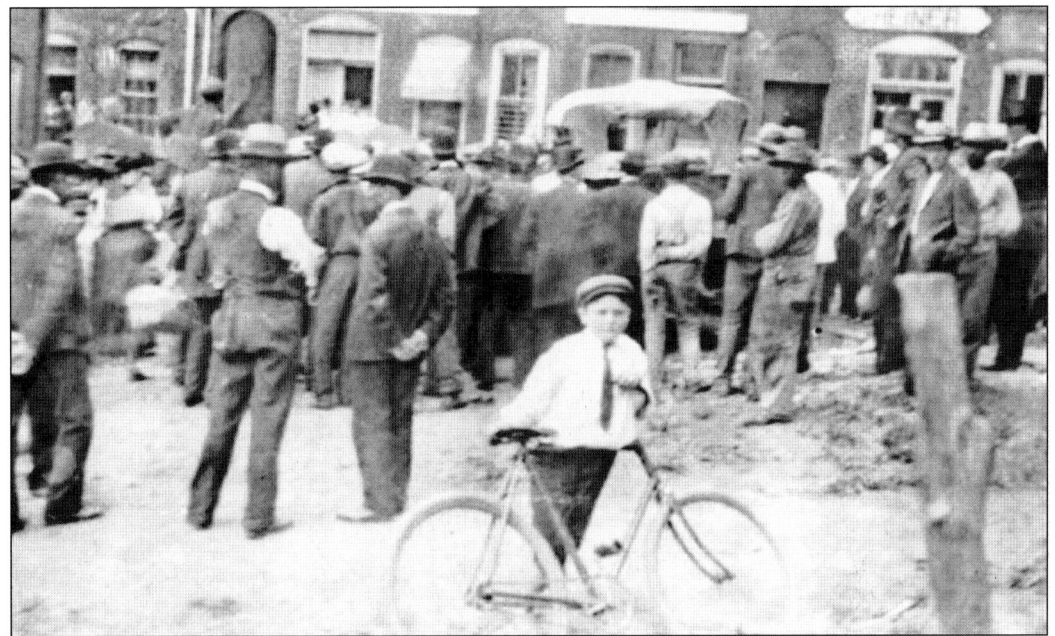

This June 1, 1906, photograph from the U.S. Department of the Interior National Park Services shows the crowd gathering in uptown Shelby for a visit by Thomas Edison. Edison often vacationed in Western North Carolina and is reported to have visited Cleveland County on several occasions. Edison had a keen interest in mineral mines in the area. (U.S. Department of the Interior National Park Services.)

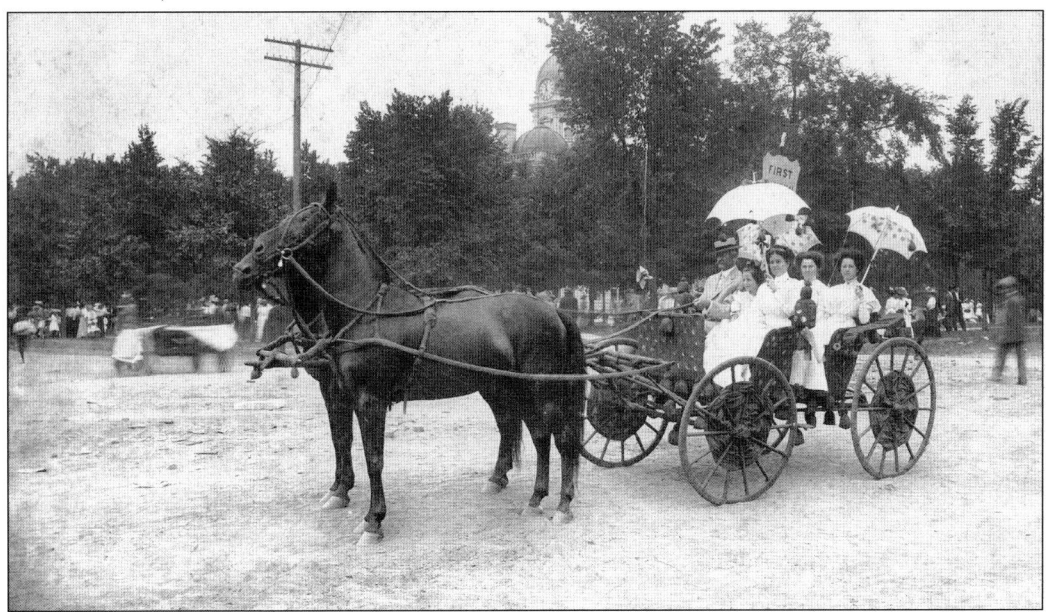

C. C. Blanton is seen driving a carriage sponsored by First National Bank in the 1909 Fourth of July parade. Riding with Blanton are, from left to right, Millicent Blanton (Mrs. W. A. Thompson), Madge Webb Riley, Agnes McBrayer, and Mrs. Carl B. Thompson. Time was spent decorating carriages for the parade; the First National carriage was described as being colored with gold ribbon. (Catherine Freedberg.)

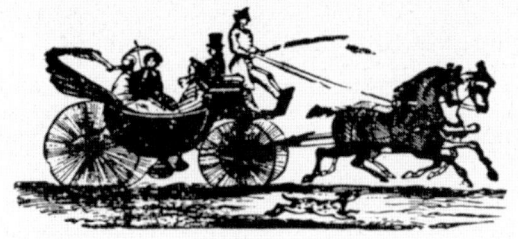

Pictured above is an advertisement for the Wray and Suttle Livery Stables from the 1880s. Shelby supported several livery businesses, many close to the railway station on Morgan Street. Horse-and-carriage was the popular form of transportation from the rail station to the community's many hotels and resorts.

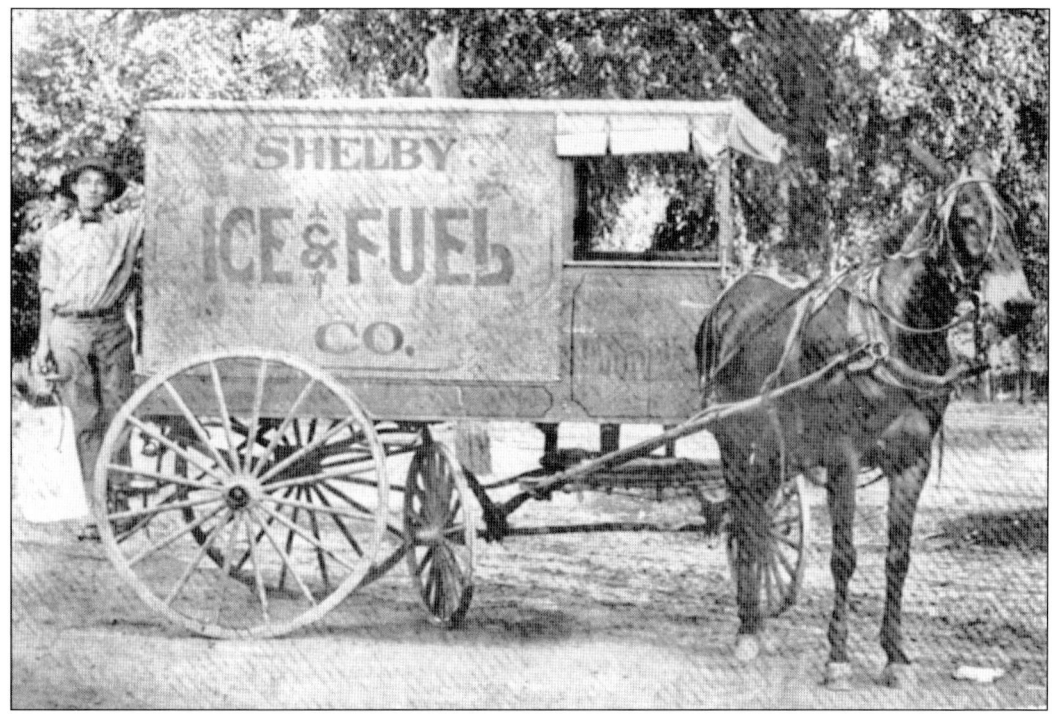
Paul Wellmon poses with a block of ice in hand next to his Shelby Ice and Fuel Company wagon in this early-20th-century photograph. (Uptown Shelby Association.)

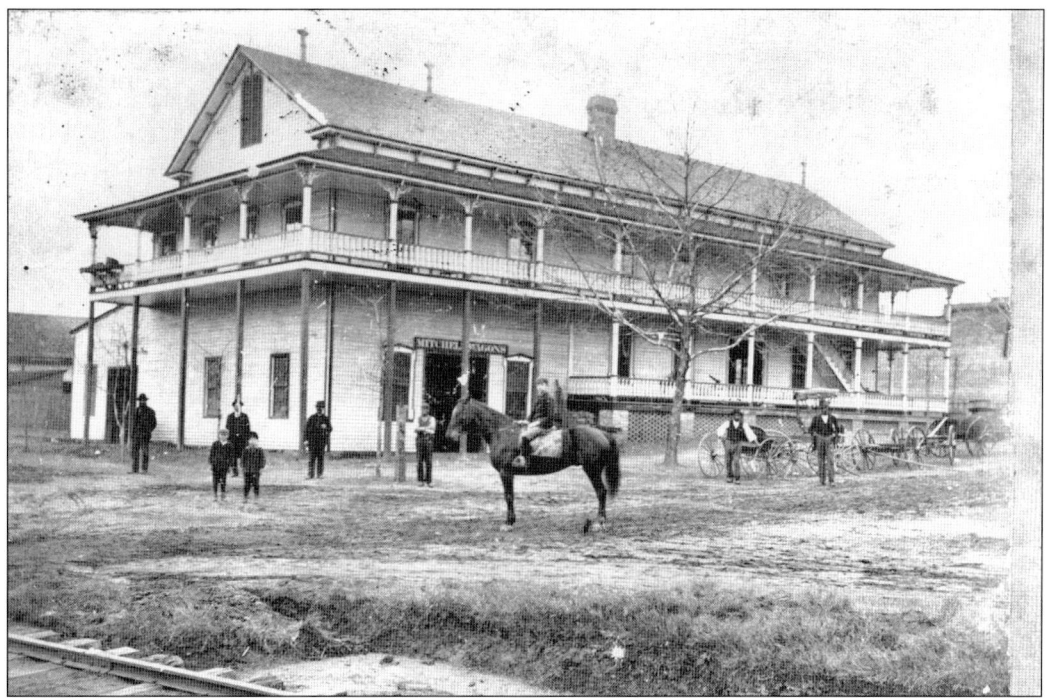
The Eskridge Livery was located at Marion and Morgan Streets by the railroad tracks. The second floor served as a hotel and boardinghouse for train passengers.

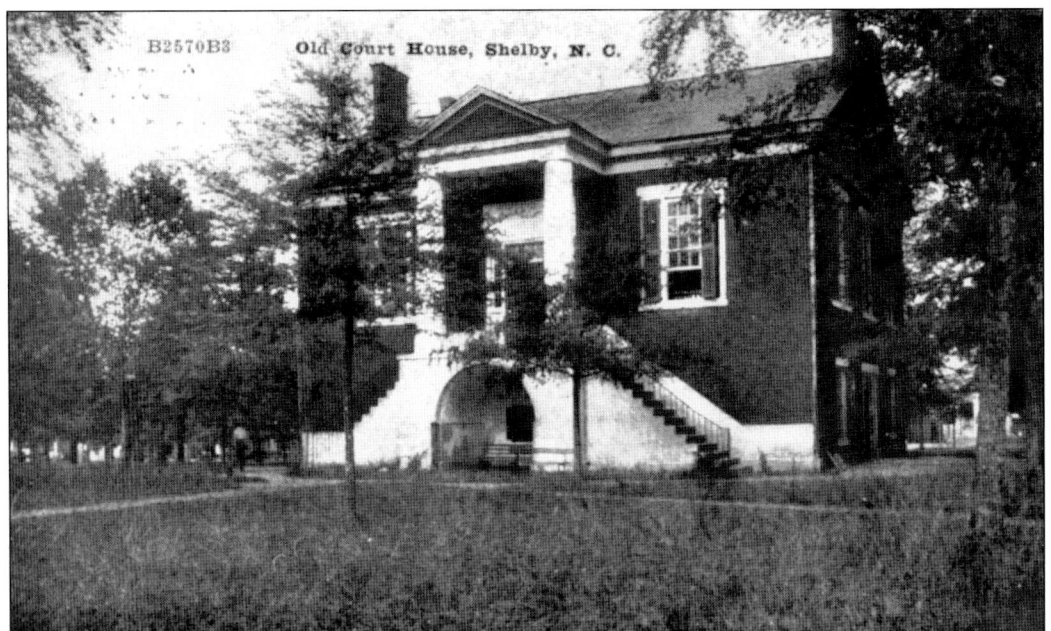

This early-1900s postcard shows the red-brick courthouse that was built on the square in 1845. A cornfield and pasture for cattle had occupied the land where the courthouse and First National Bank buildings were built. Sidewalks were poured in 1907–1909. Streets would not begin to be paved until 1917.

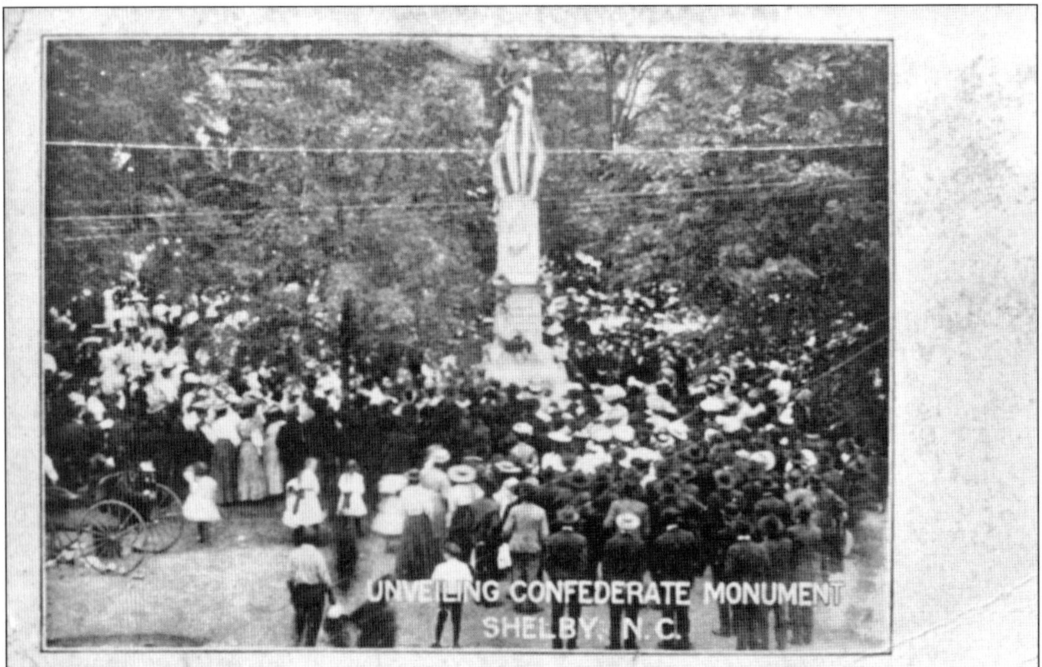

The Confederate War Memorial was dedicated on November 22, 1906. The old courthouse would soon be razed to make way for the current building on the square.

This postcard view is an architectural rendering of how the new courthouse might have looked. Fortunately the fathers chose to incorporate a large lawn with trees around the square.

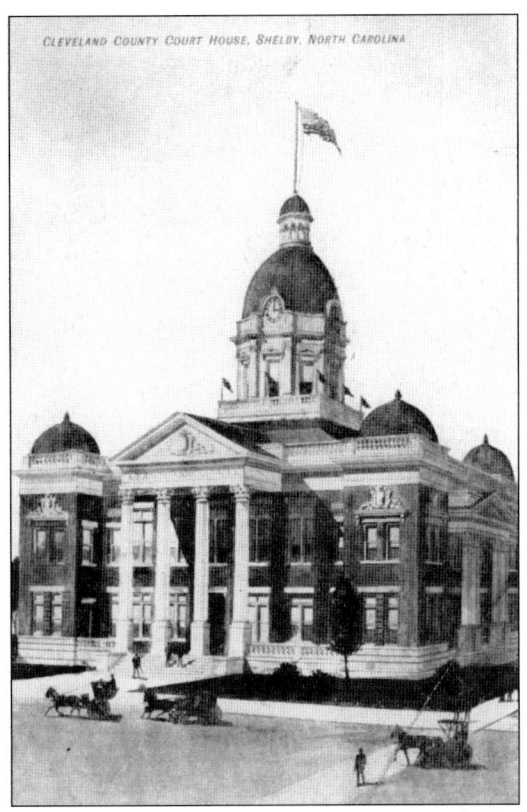

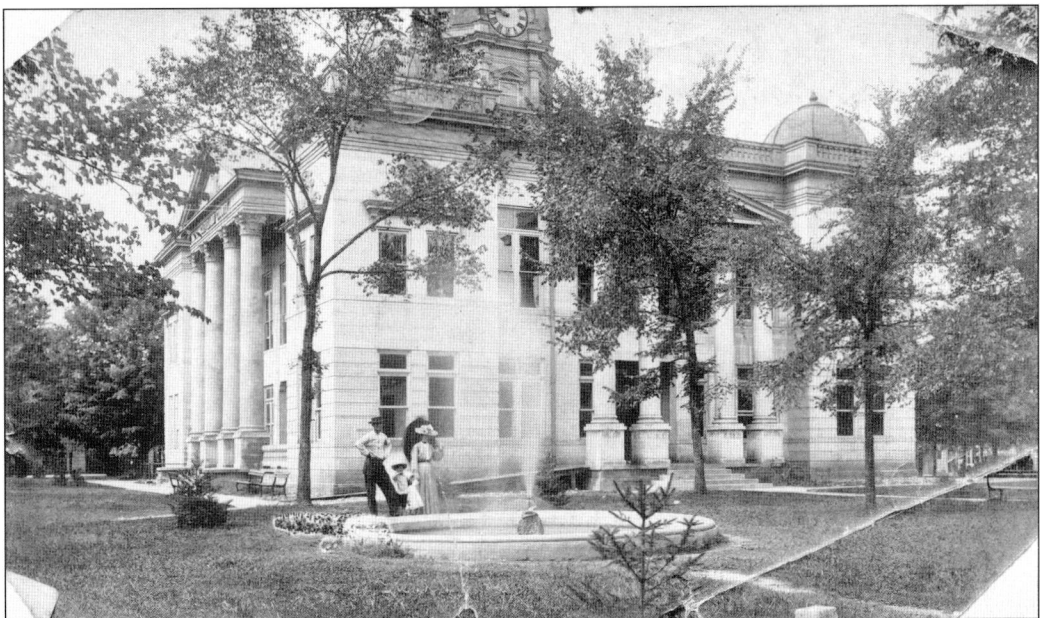

The image used for the cover of the book shows a couple walking with a child in front of a fountain on the north side of the courthouse. Over the years, there have been at least five wells or fountains on the square. Beck Quinn sold lithia water on the square that was pumped from Lithia Spring, north of town.

17

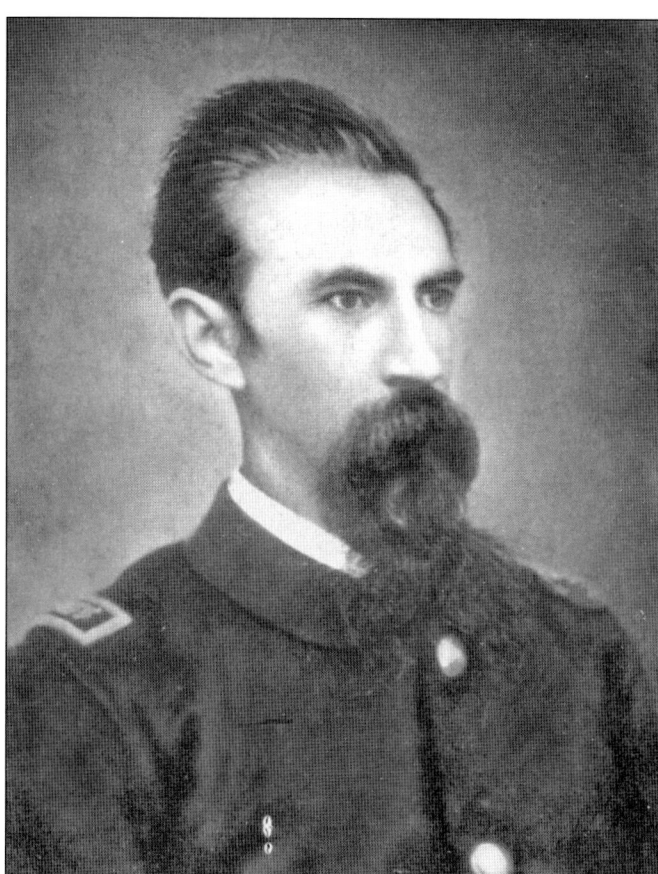

Capt. William Bell is credited with beginning the first school in Shelby. The Shelby Military Academy was established in the 1880s on the site of the first graded school on West Marion Street. A monument stands today to the right of the former school to honor Captain Bell, a graduate of the University of Virginia. (*Tracks though Time.*)

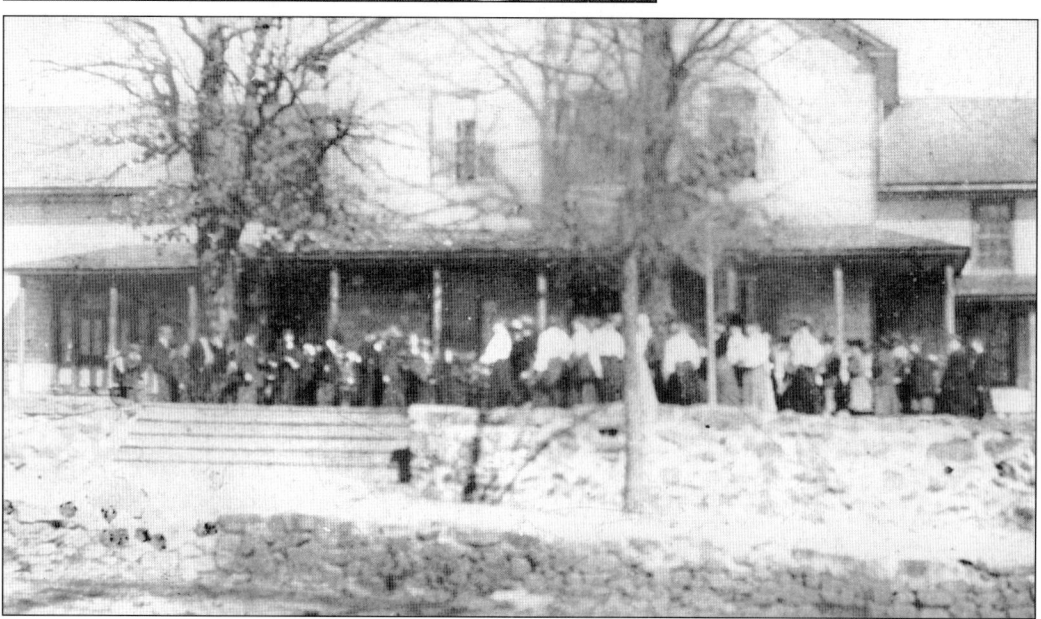

The photograph shows the Shelby Military Academy as it appeared in the late 1880s. The school would later be used as the first Shelby Graded School.

Mrs. John McDonald was named an instructor at Shelby Female Academy in 1887 and elected president of the college in 1889. McDonald had served as an instructor at Peace Institute in Raleigh before accepting the position in Shelby.

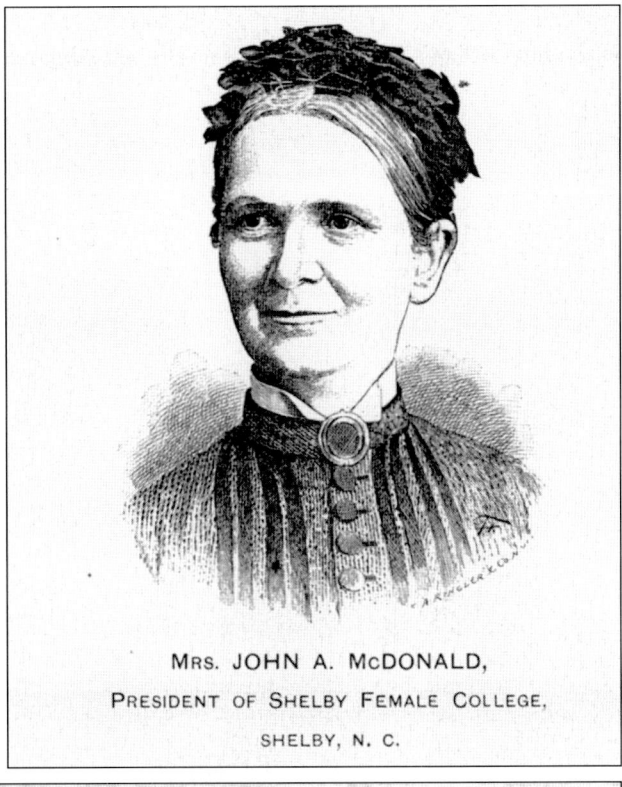

Mrs. JOHN A. McDONALD,
President of Shelby Female College,
SHELBY, N. C.

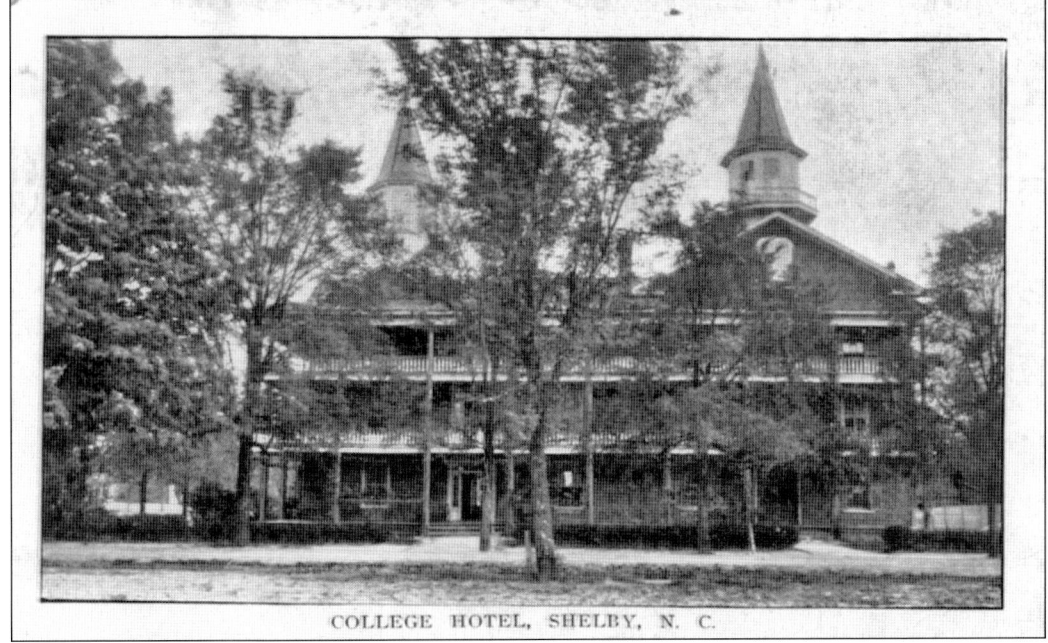

COLLEGE HOTEL, SHELBY, N. C.

The Shelby Female College (also know as Shelby Female Academy) was built on the southwest corner of Washington and Graham Streets on the site of the present city hall. The school operated as a boarding school in the 1880s and 1890s. The structure was later used as a hotel and served as Shelby's first hospital. The hotel was torn down in the 1930s to make way for city hall.

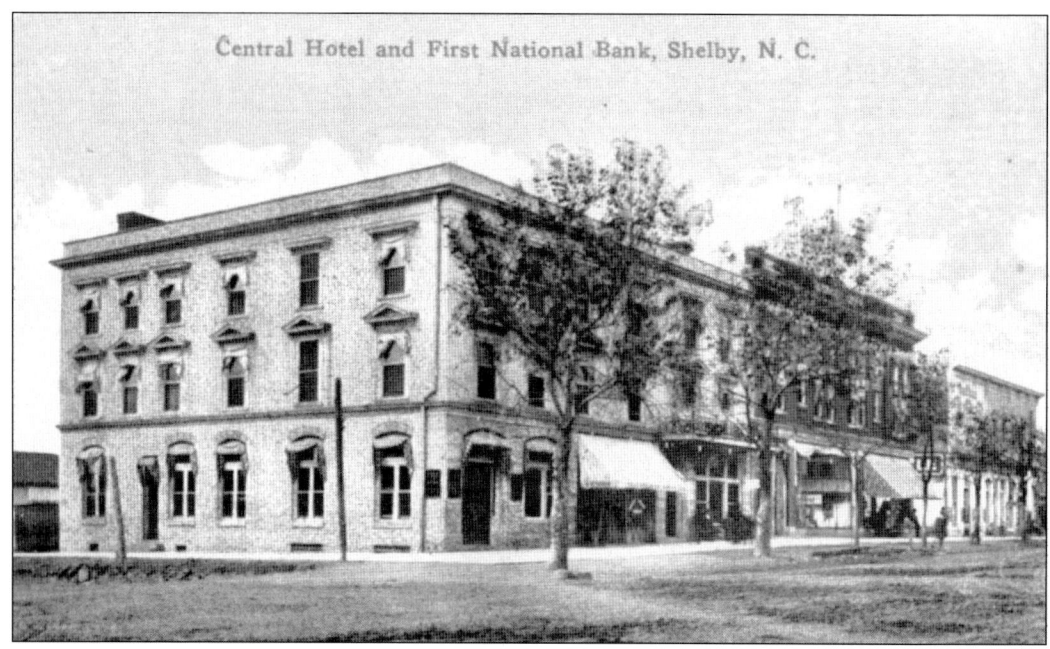

This c. 1910 postcard shows the Central Hotel and First National Bank at the corner of Lafayette and Warren Streets. The bank had first occupied an office inside the hotel lobby but with time grew to occupy most of the first floor of the hotel.

AMERICAN PLAN   RATES $2.00, $2.50 AND $3.00

CENTRAL HOTEL
MRS. P. A. WARE, Proprietress

Hot and Cold Running Water   Private and Public Baths

Bell Service:

1 Ring, Bell Boy;   2 Rings, Ice Water;   3 Rings, Hot Water
4 Rings, Prop.

Meal Hours:

Breakfast, 7:00 to 9:00   Dinner, 12:20 to 1:30   Supper, 6:20 to 8:00

NOTICE

THE RULES AND REGULATIONS of this hotel are such as prevail in all first-class hotels. The co-operation of our guests is kindly requested that all may be better served. By reporting to the management any lack of service or inattention on part of any employee a favor will be confered.

The management will not be responsible for goods or valuables left in rooms. All valuables should be left at office.

Please do not spit on floors, walls, woodwork of rooms or hallways of this hotel.

Please do not scratch matches or paste stickers on walls or woodwork of this hotel.

This advertisement for the Central Hotel was published in 1917. Note the rules and regulations for staying in a first-class hotel.

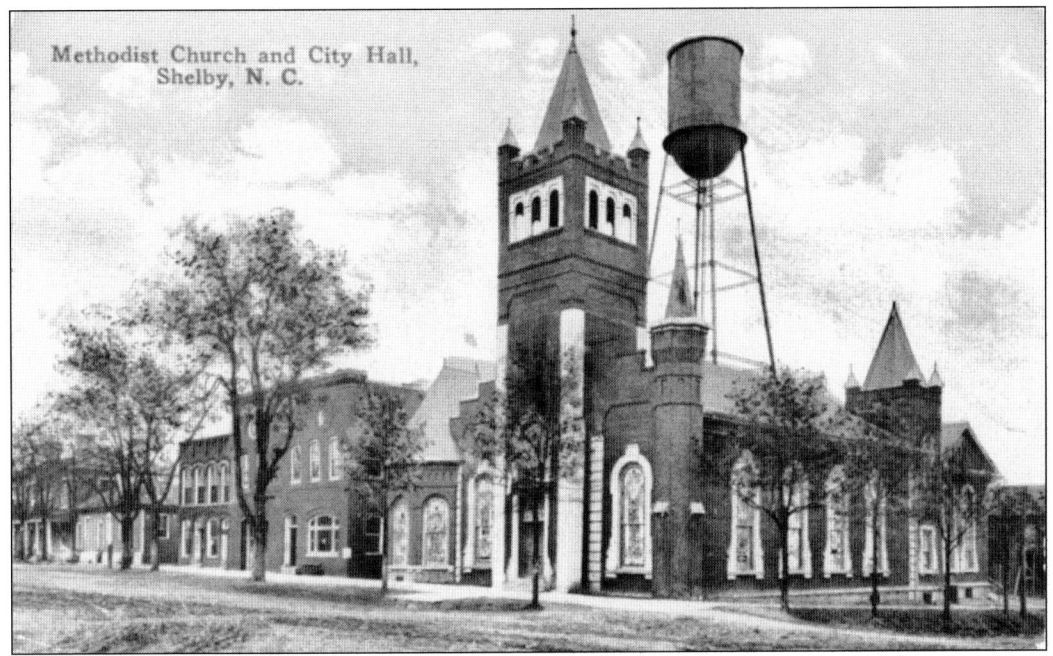

By the beginning of the 20th century, Shelby's uptown was beginning to flourish. The Methodist church was built on the corner of Marion and Washington Streets. The building to the left of the church housed was the first city hall and fire department. Farther down the block were the Cleveland Star building and the Courtview Hotel. (Lloyd Hamrick Collection.)

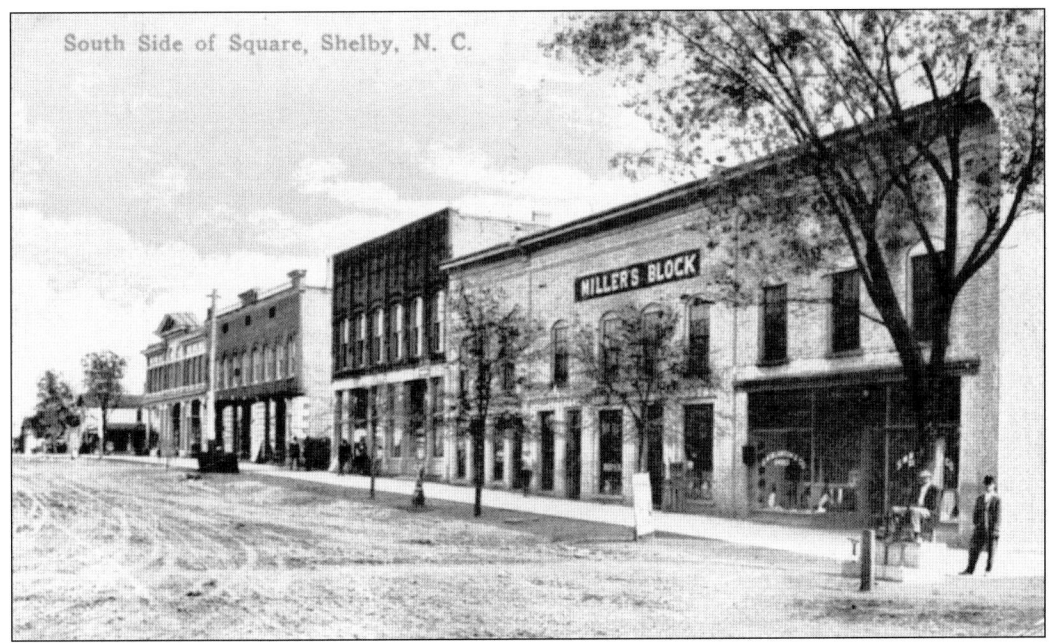

This c. 1910 postcard view shows the businesses along the south side of the courthouse square on Warren Street. Most Shelbians will remember J. C. Penney on the corner. The post office was once housed in the building to the left of the alleyway. Note the city has concrete sidewalks but is yet to have paved streets.

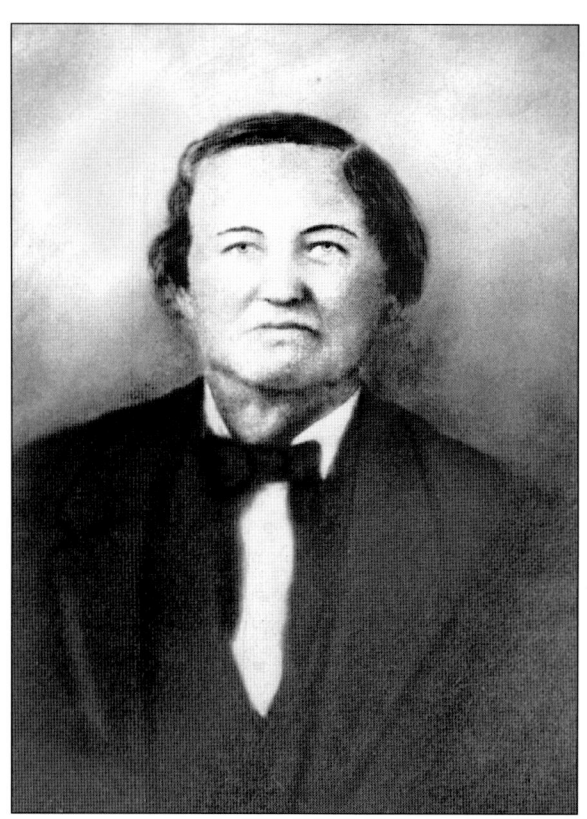

Shortly after Cleveland County was formed in 1841, Charles Blanton was appointed the county's first sheriff. Charles's grandparents were George and Elvira Lee Blanton, who had moved from Virginia in 1769 and settled along First Broad River some 72 years before Cleveland County was formed in what was then Tryon County. Charles married Judith Hamrick, and they were the parents of 12 children, including Burwell Blanton.

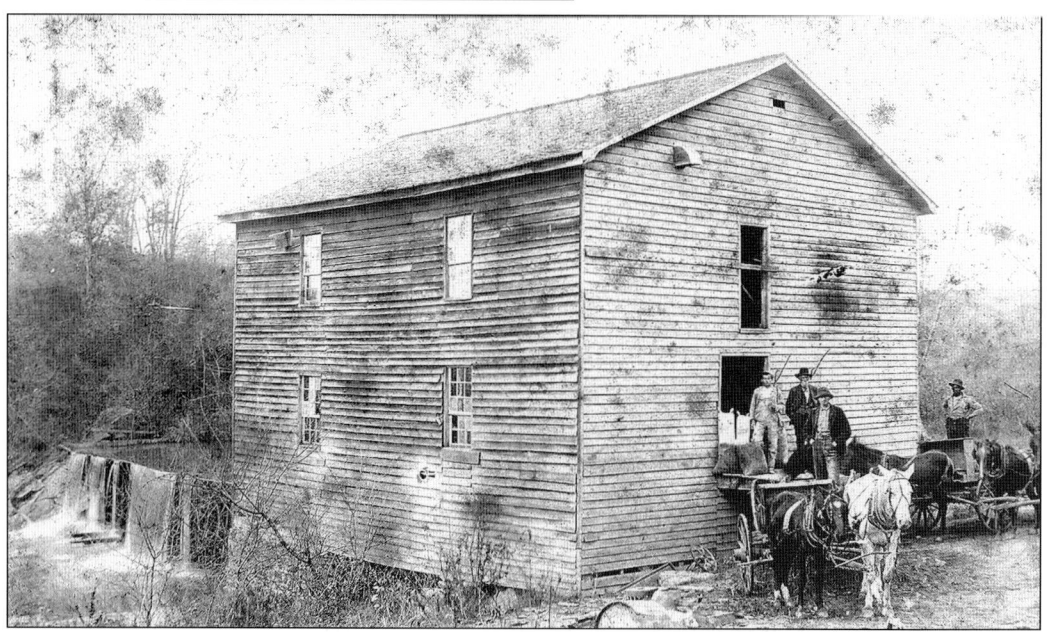

Burwell Blanton is pictured (center) in this c. 1870 photograph of the gristmill he operated on the Brushy Creek, west of Shelby. A successful farmer, miller, and businessman, Burwell is best remembered as a founding member of J. Jenkins and Company, the county's first bank. Formed in 1874, the bank would evolve into First National Bank. (First National Bank.)

Dr. Victor McBrayer graduated with a degree in medicine from the University of New York. "Dr. Vic," as he was known, married Esther Suttle, and they raised five children in their Victorian-style home on North Morgan Street. A civic leader and deacon in his church, Dr. McBrayer was a much-loved member of the community.

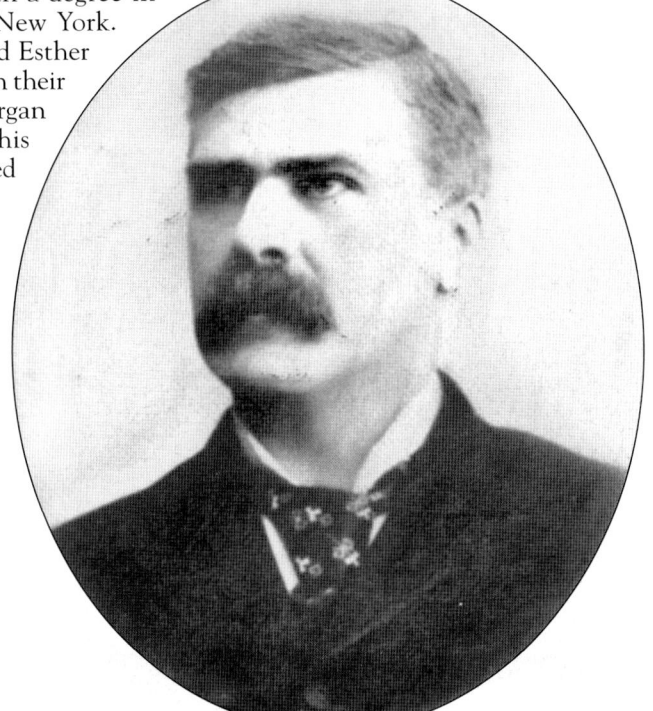

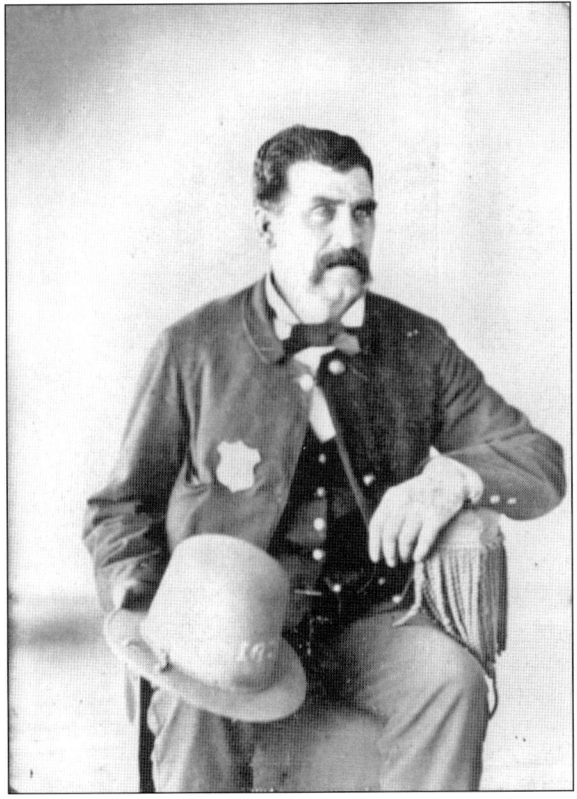

Shelby chief of police Ed Hamrick was killed in the line of duty in 1904. Ben Clark had been arrested for drunkenness. Although Clark had been searched, he produced a gun from his overalls and shot the chief in the chest. Clark was convicted of the crime and hanged, the last public hanging in the county.

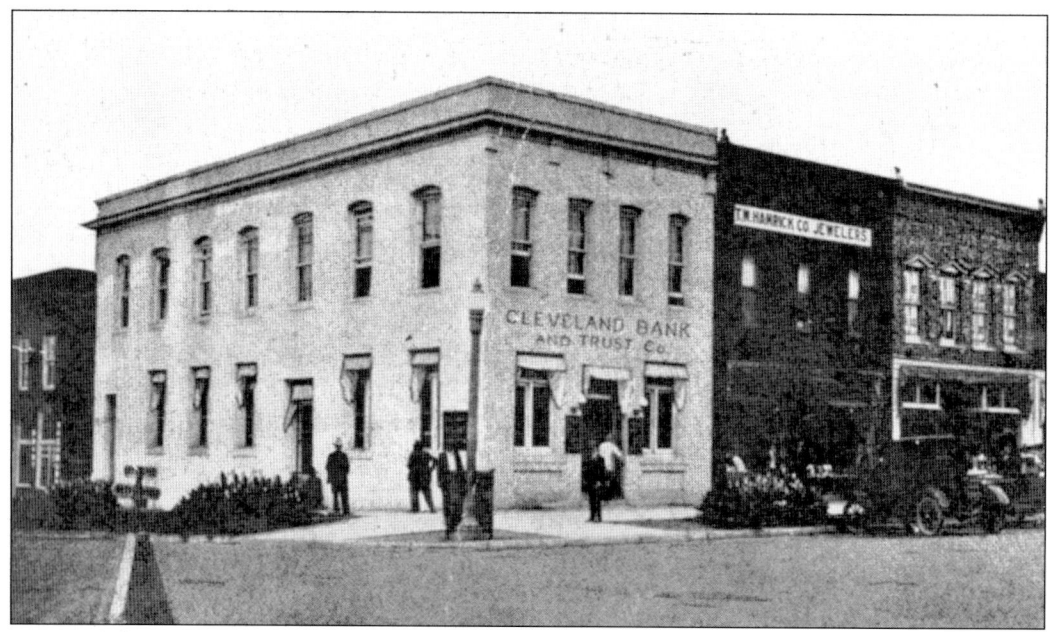

A postcard view shows Cleveland Bank and Trust on the corner of Marion and Lafayette Streets. The Western Union office was on the second floor of the bank building. T. W. Hamrick Company Jewelers and Washburn Hardware can be seen to the right of the bank.

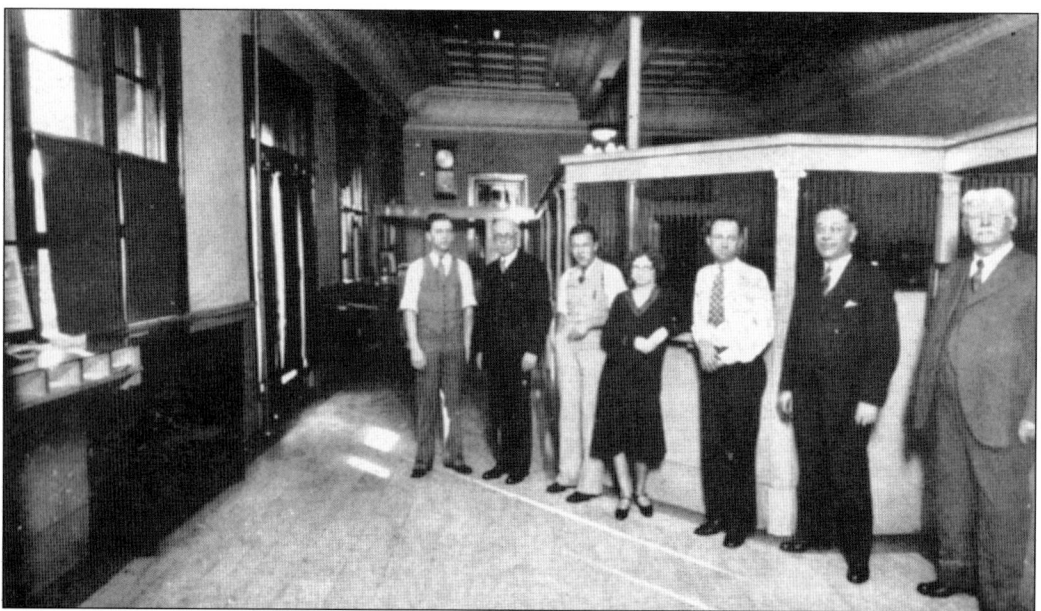

Pictured in this interior view of Cleveland Bank and Trust are, from left to right, Merle (Dick) Green, Joe L. Suttle, James T. Irwin, Effie Propst Wray, Jesse Bridges, William Lineberger, and James T. Bowman.

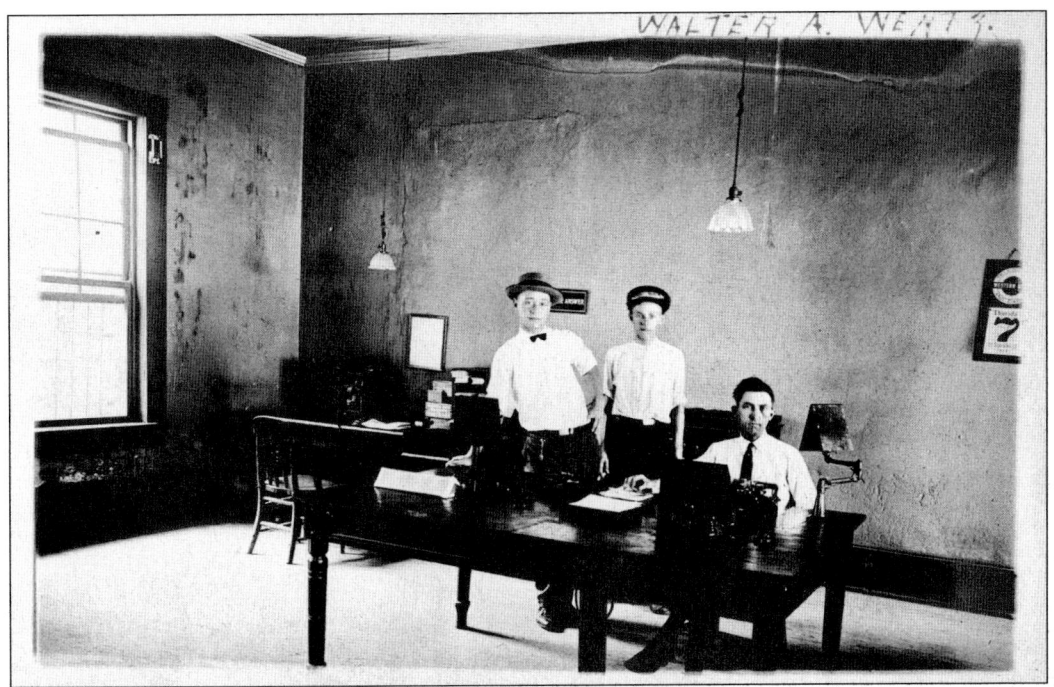

This real-photo postcard shows the interior of the Western Union office above the Cleveland Bank and Trust with, from left to right, M. C. Hamrick, an unidentified messenger boy, and Western Union manager Walter Wentz.

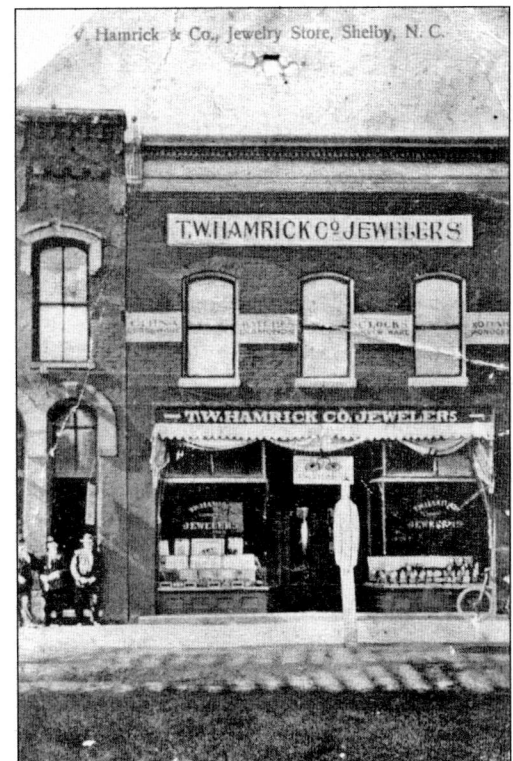

This rare postcard illustrates the front of the T. W. Hamrick Company Jewelers store. Hamrick was instrumental in preserving the history of Shelby, commissioning dozens of local images into postcards. These postcards have become a valuable asset in recording the city's past.

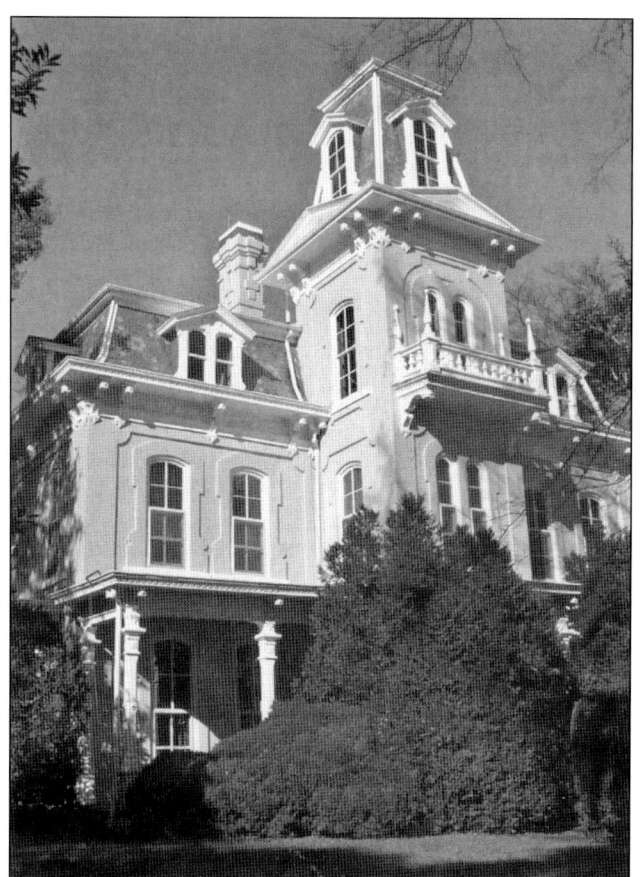

The Bankers House, located at 319 North Lafayette Street, was built by Jesse Jenkins in 1876. This Second Empire–designed house is known as the Bankers House because each of the first six presidents of First National Bank lived in the home. George Blanton Jr. and his wife, Nancy, gifted the home to Preservation North Carolina.

The George Blanton House at 303 West Marion Street was built by Jesse Jenkins prior to 1870. George Blanton Sr. purchased the one-story white cottage with Victorian scalloped trim and tapered columns on the porch in the early 1900s for his new bride, Ida Wood. Over the years, they enlarged and extensively renovated the home into the Colonial Revival style, making it a two-story redbrick with large, white columns. The family later gifted the home to Gardner-Webb University.

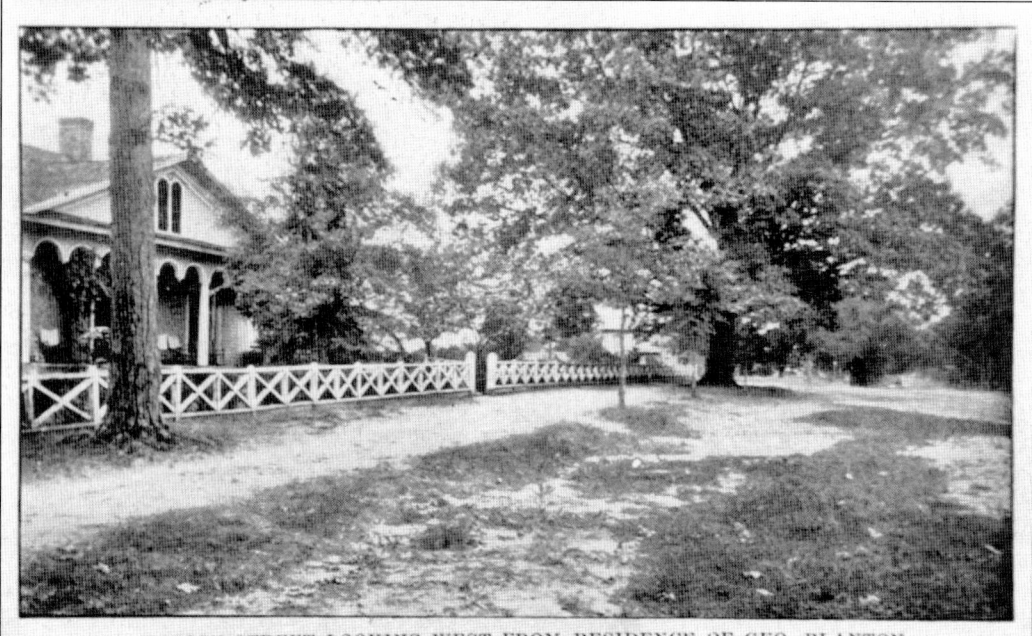

MARION STREET LOOKING WEST FROM RESIDENCE OF GEO. BLANTON.

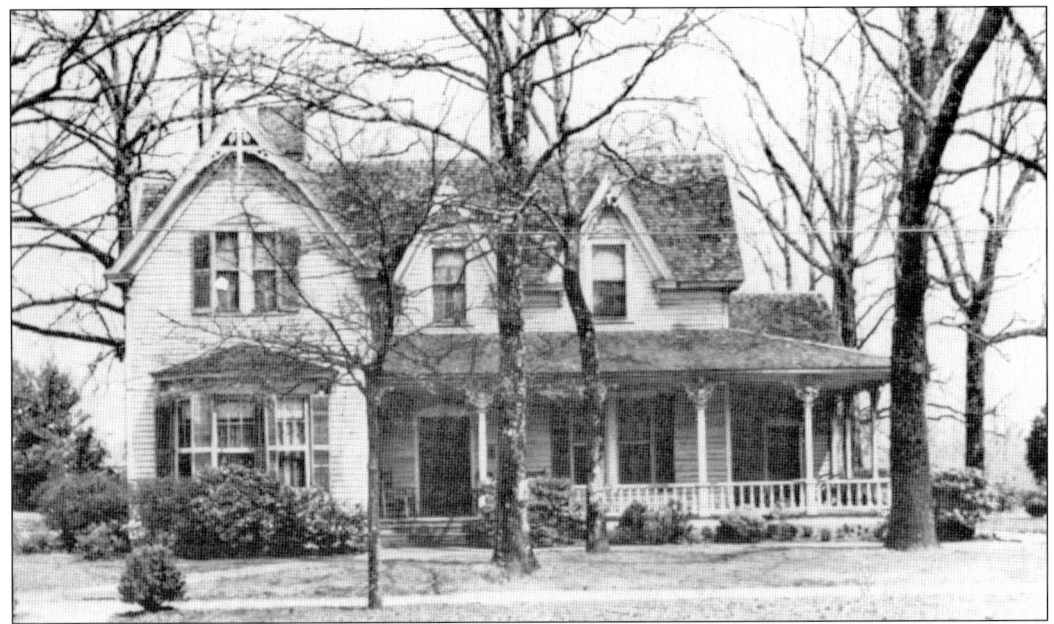

Burwell and Frances Blanton built this house at 533 West Marion Street so they could be closer to town. When the Blantons purchased the Bankers House on North Lafayette Street, they gave the home to their daughter, Mary Judith, and her husband, Richard Eskridge. Their son, Forrest Eskridge, an executive with First National Bank, lived in the home until his death in 1943. The house was later moved to its present location at 515 West Sumter Street. (*The Heritage of Cleveland County*.)

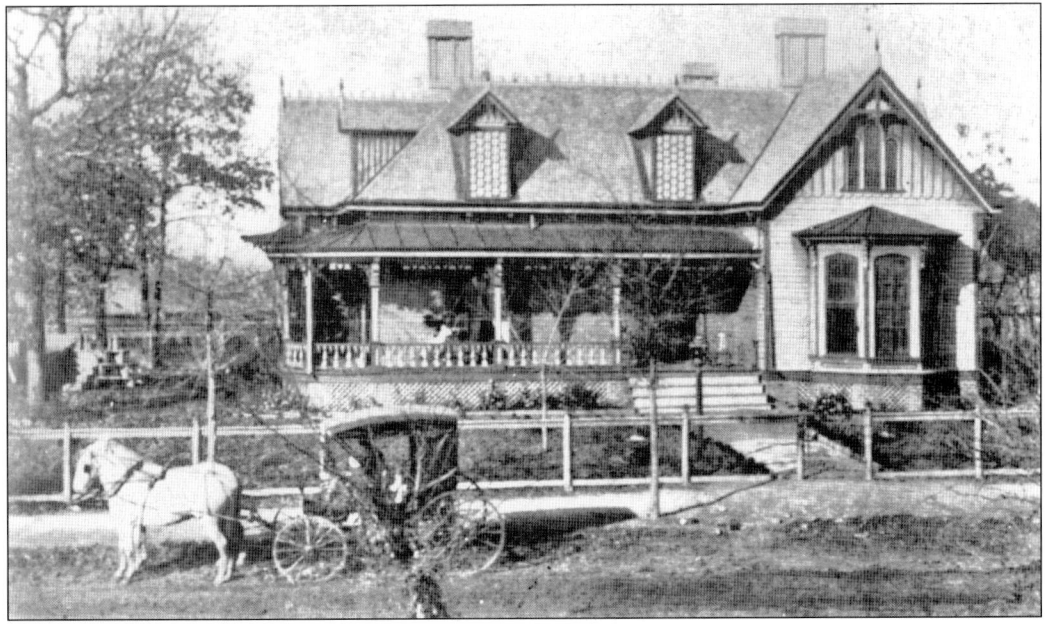

This *c.* 1890 photograph of the Dr. Victor and Esther Suttle McBrayer home at 507 North Morgan Street is regarded as one of the finest early homes built in Shelby with its attention to woodworking detail. The Victorian-style home is on the National Register of Historic Places. (*Architectural Perspectives of Cleveland County, North Carolina*.)

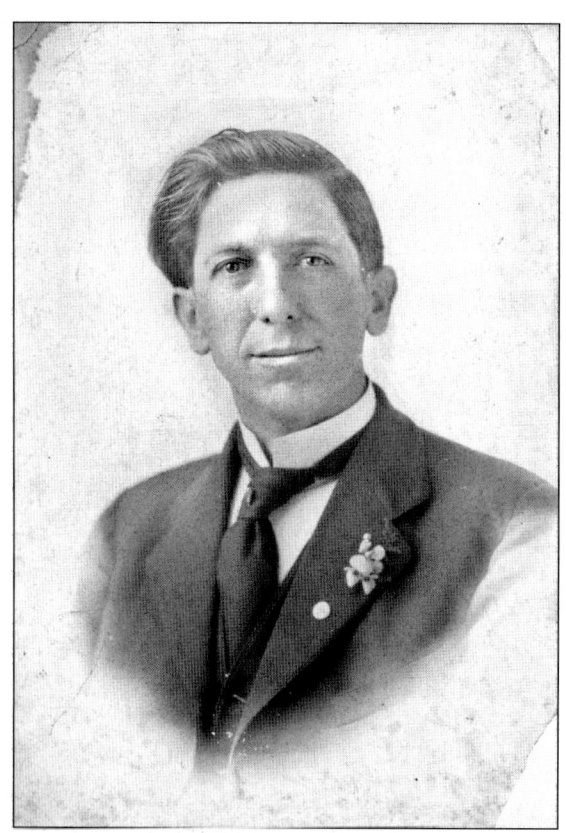

Clyde Roark Hoey (1877–1954) was a prominent Shelby attorney. Hoey purchased the *Shelby Review* in 1894 and served as editor and publisher of the weekly paper for several years. Hoey would later serve as a member of the U.S. House of Representatives from 1919 to 1921, governor of North Carolina from 1937 to 1941, and U.S. senator from 1945 until his death in 1954. (Uptown Shelby Association.)

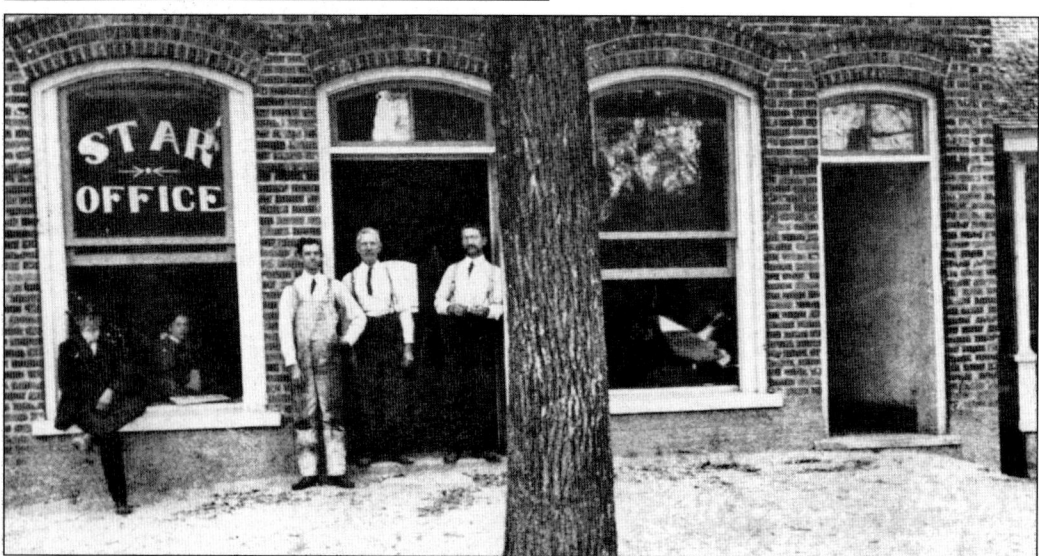

This early-20th-century photograph shows newspaper employees by the entrance of the *Cleveland Star* on East Marion Street. Hoey purchased the *Shelby Review* in 1894 and changed the name to the *Cleveland Star* in 1896. The firm was incorporated as the Star Publishing Company in 1903. Lee B. Weathers took over as editor and publisher in 1911. Weathers purchased the paper and served as editor until his passing in 1958. His son Henry Lee Weathers served as editor from 1958 to 1983. (*Shelby Daily Star 75th Anniversary Special.*)

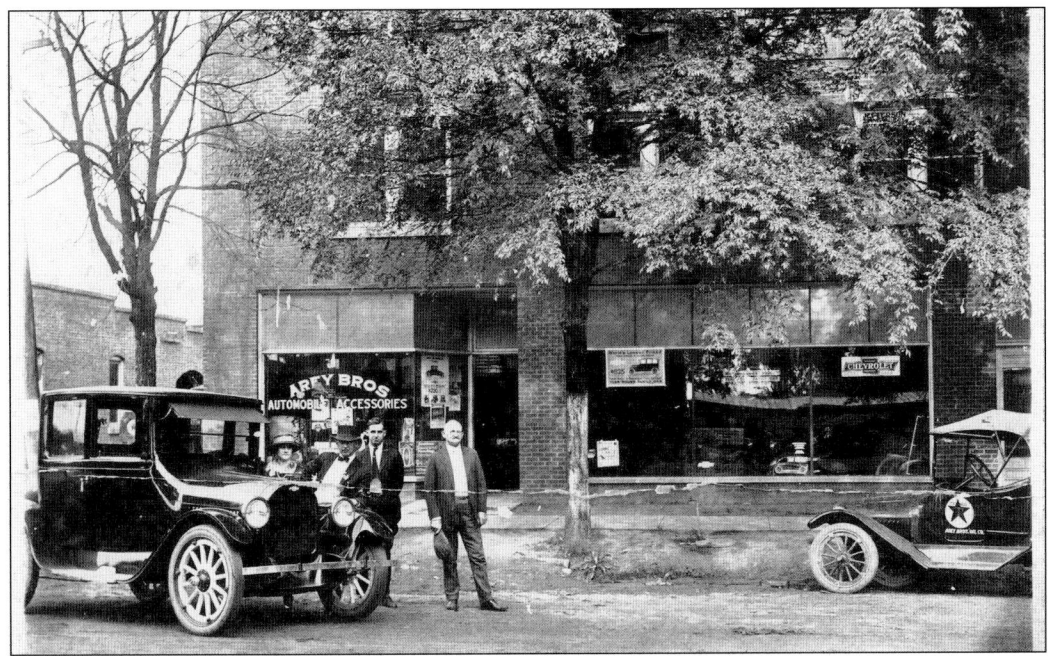

From left to right, Mrs. W. G. (Catherine) Arey, Ward Hunter Arey, William G. Arey, and W. J. Arey stand in front of the Arey Brothers Auto Accessories business on South Washington Street. The Arey family has been in business in Shelby for nearly 100 years. This business sold automobile accessories and Chevrolet and Texaco products. (Robert Arey.)

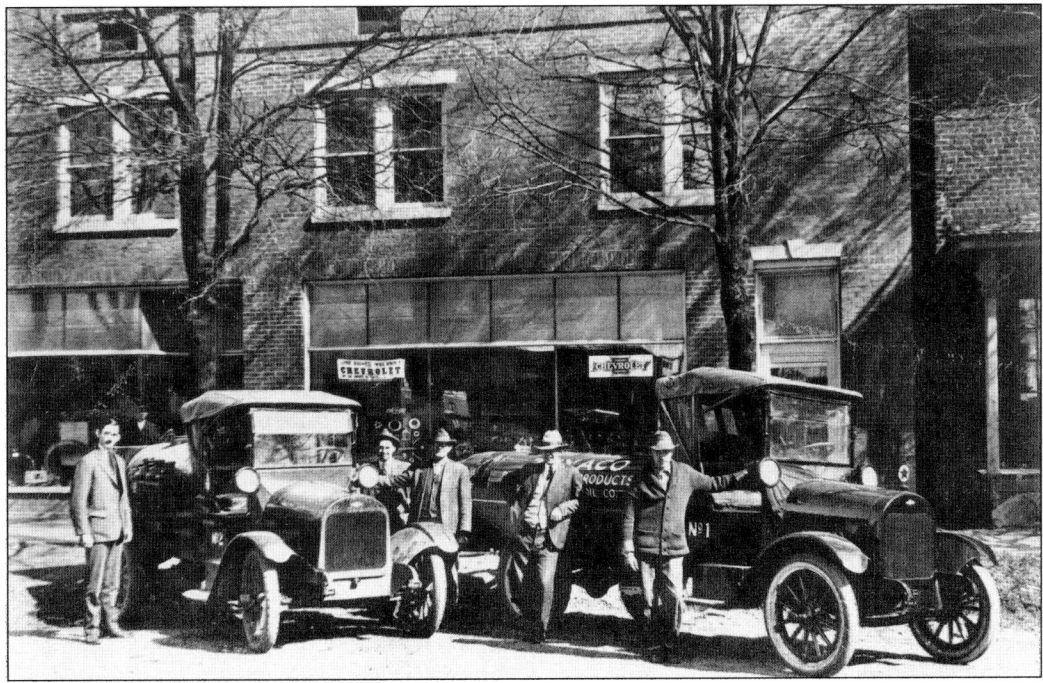

This 1916 photograph including Hugh Arey, Will Arey, Mike Borders, and Ward Arey was made in front of Arey's Garage on North Washington Street. Their early businesses included several auto dealerships and filling stations for gasoline. (Robert Arey.)

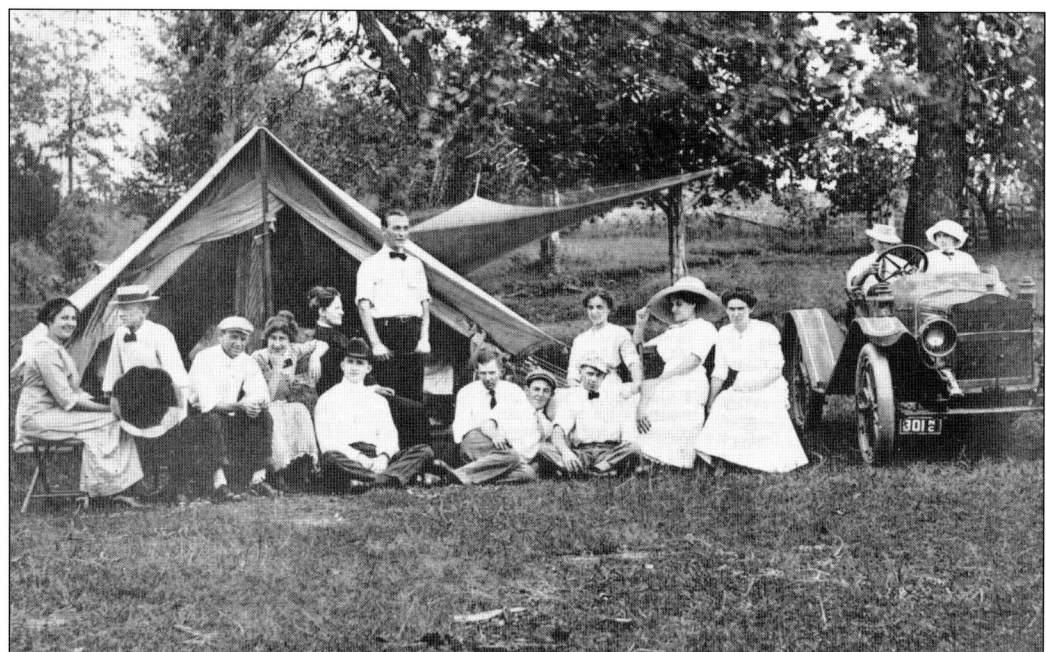

Even after the second Cleveland Springs Hotel burned in 1909, the springs were a favorite destination for socializing. Local citizens gathered to camp out by the springs. This was a prosperous time for Shelbians; cotton was king, and the local economy flourished with the growing and ginning of cotton and the operation of cotton mills. (*The Heritage of Cleveland County.*)

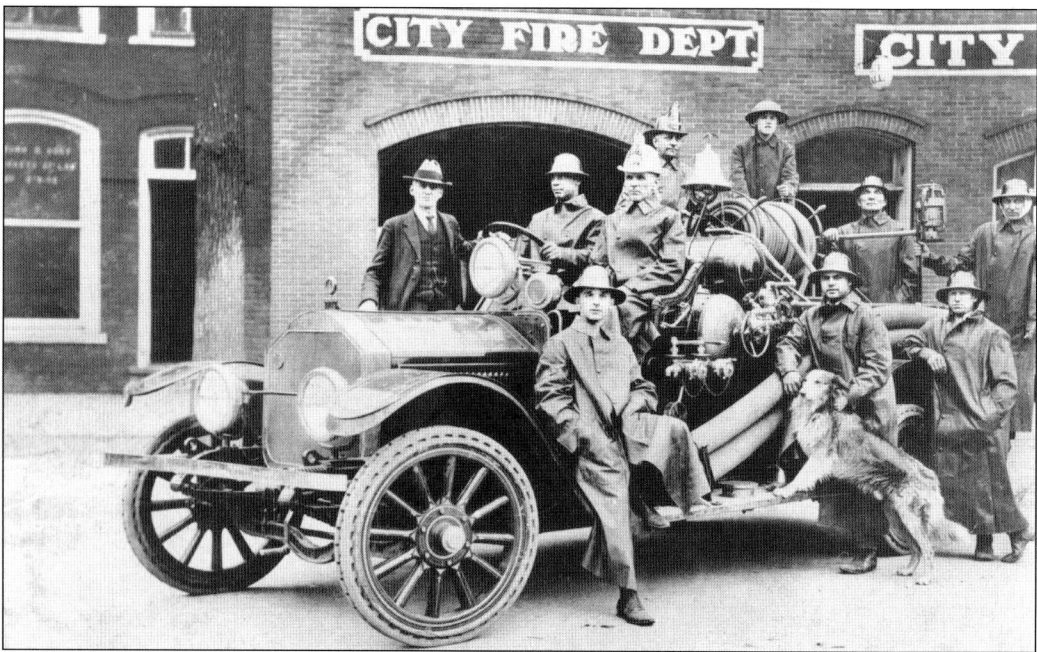

Shelby mayor W. D. Lackey poses with members of the fire department in this 1919 photograph. The Cleveland Star building is just to the left of city hall. The East Marion Street site of the city's first fire department and city hall has been restored, and today its architecture captures the era from 100 years before.

Two
People and Places
1921–1970

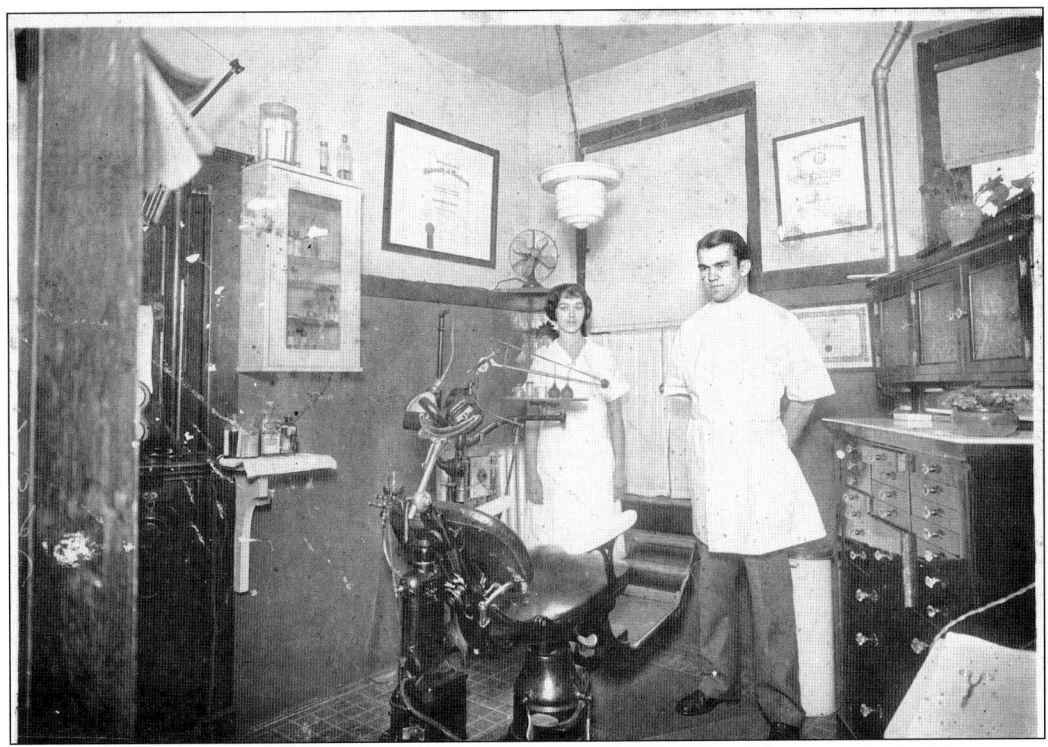

Dr. Hubert Plaster is seen in his early dentist office in the Royster Building in 1927. Ina Watterson was the receptionist. Dr. Plaster was a leading figure in Shelby for decades as a dentist, Boy Scout leader, Red Cross worker, and later as mayor of Shelby. He also sang bass in the choir at First Baptist Church.

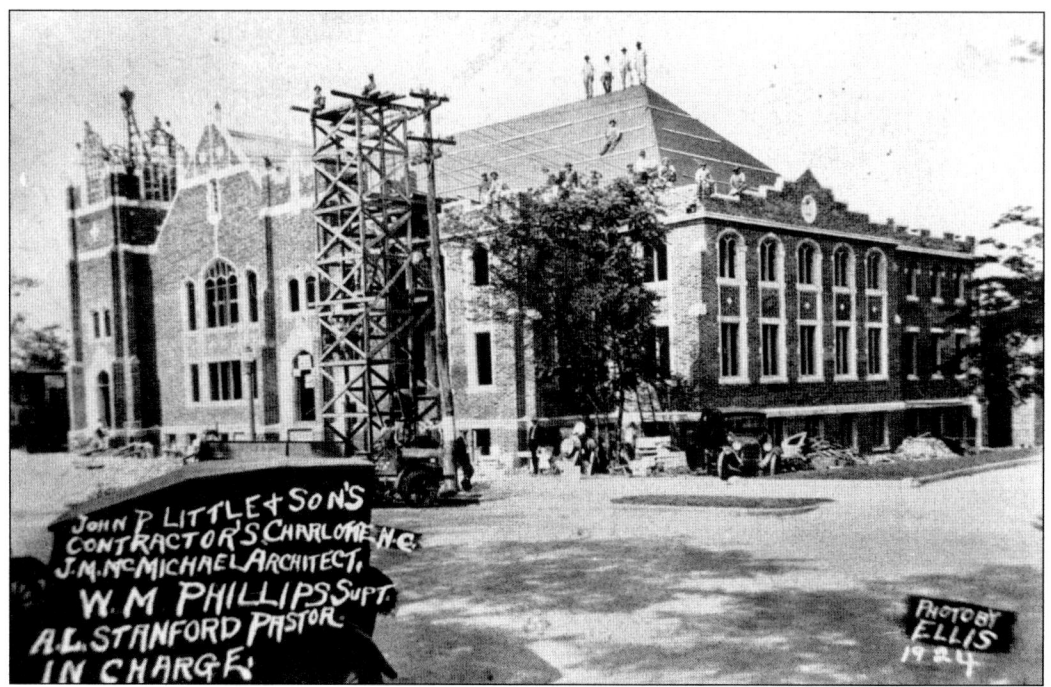

The 1920s brought a major change on the courthouse square. The Central Methodist Church relocated from its old home on Marion Street and built a new structure across the corner on Washington Street. The building seen under construction in this photograph is still in use in 2007. The date on the cornerstone is 1924. (Lloyd Hamrick Collection.)

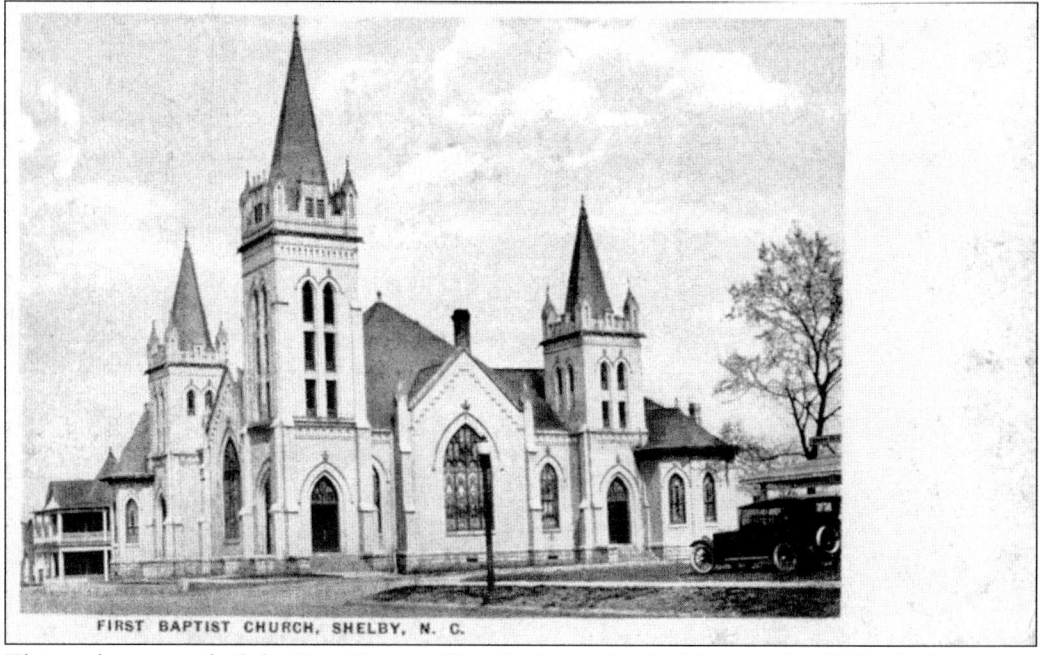

This early postcard of the First Baptist Church shows the building in the 1920s, before it was enlarged. The parsonage can be seen at the left. It was moved when a four-story educational structure was built. The church celebrated its 160th anniversary in 2007 with 1,137 resident members.

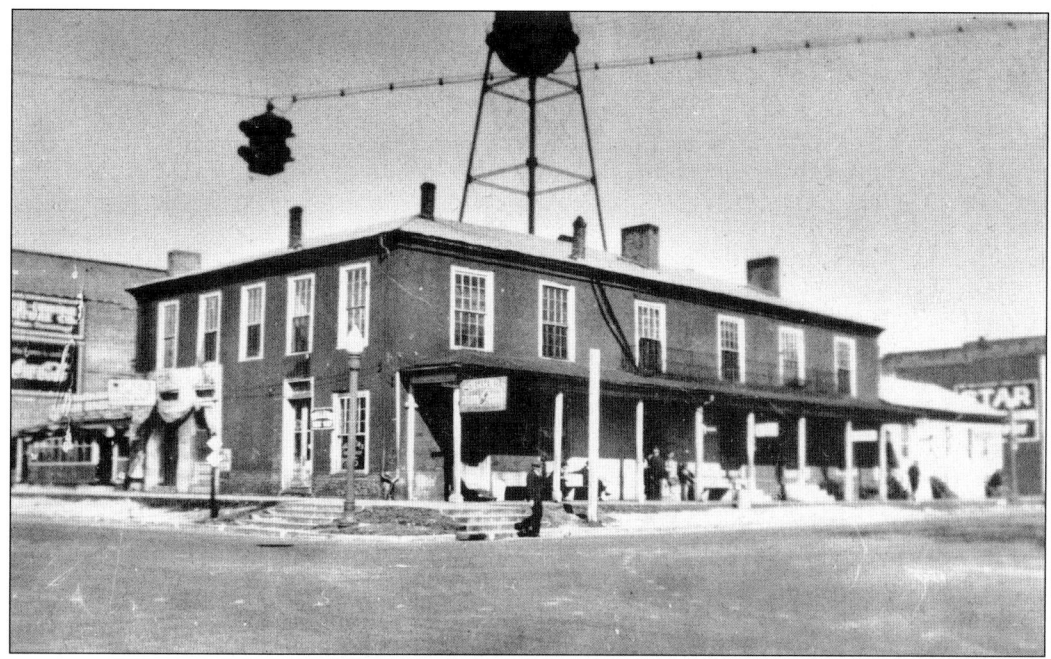

This c. 1925 photograph shows an historic landmark on the corner of Marion and Lafayette Streets. The Courtview Hotel was on the north side of the courthouse. It was torn down in the late 1930s for the building of Sterchi's Furniture Store. The Dixie Diner and Campbell's Department Store are at the left, and the soon-to-be-removed city water tank is behind the hotel.

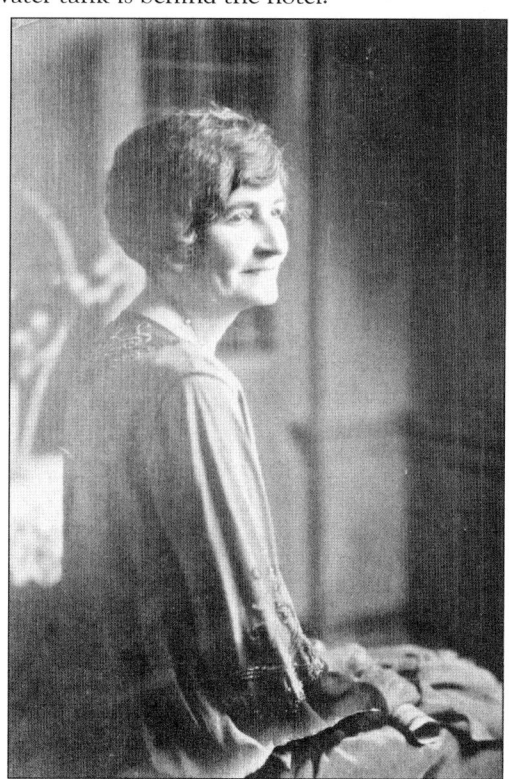

After her husband passed away, Katie Bridges North ran the boarding house at the Courtview. Two of North's daughters met their husbands at the boardinghouse. (Alison Gilbert.)

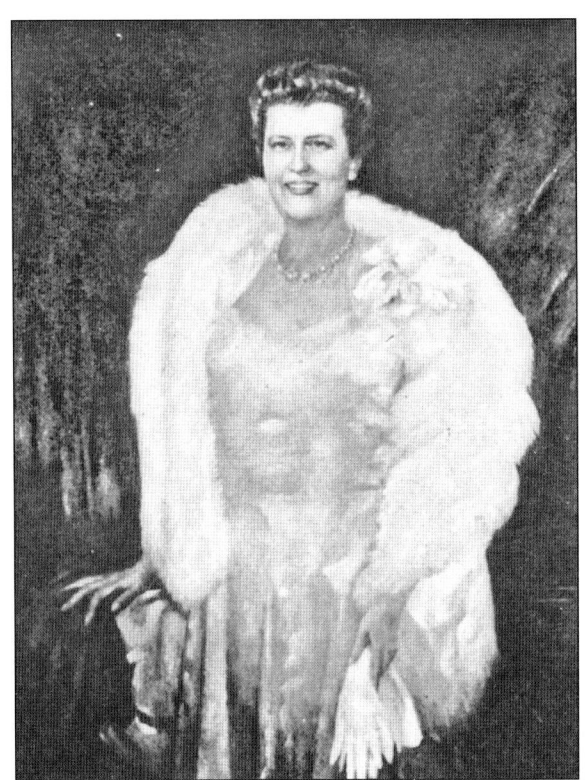

The "Shelby Dynasty" produced its first governor in 1928, when native son O. Max Gardner was elected. His wife, Fay Webb Gardner, served as North Carolina's first lady from 1929 to 1933 and remained a regal lady for over three decades thereafter. This portrait hangs in Webb Hall, named for Fay, at Gardner-Webb University.

In 1936, Governor Gardner's brother-in-law, Clyde R. Hoey, was elected governor of North Carolina. Bess Gardner Hoey served as first lady from 1937 to 1941. She had been a Shelby social leader and was a leader of the Shelby Woman's Club. She died a year after she left Raleigh.

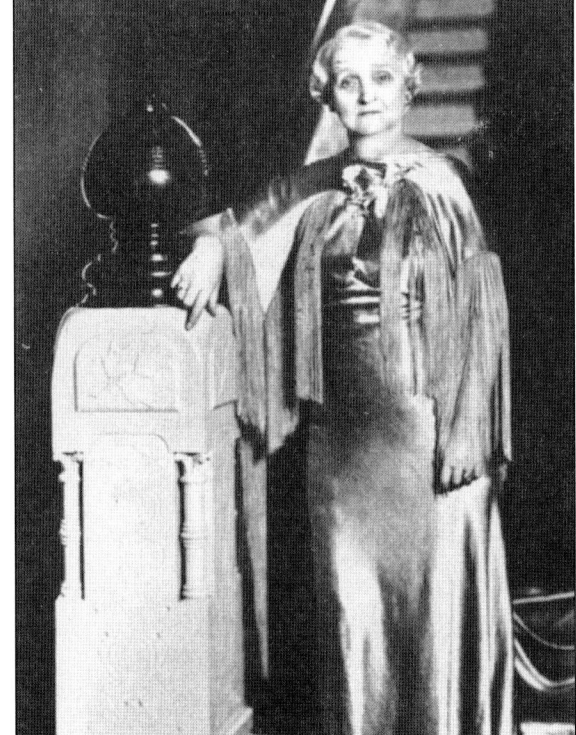

In some ways, a major social leader was Erma Johnston Drum, who is pictured in a 1925 shot. She worked for the *Shelby Daily Star* for 34 years and was the editor of the society women's page. She won numerous awards and served as president of the North Carolina Press Women in 1960–1961. She also typed the manuscript for W. J. Cash's classic work *The Mind of the South*. (Cleveland County Heritage.)

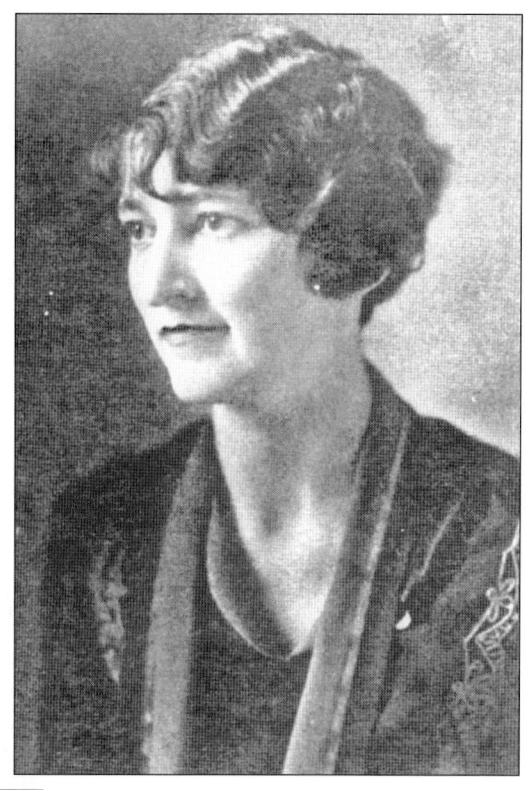

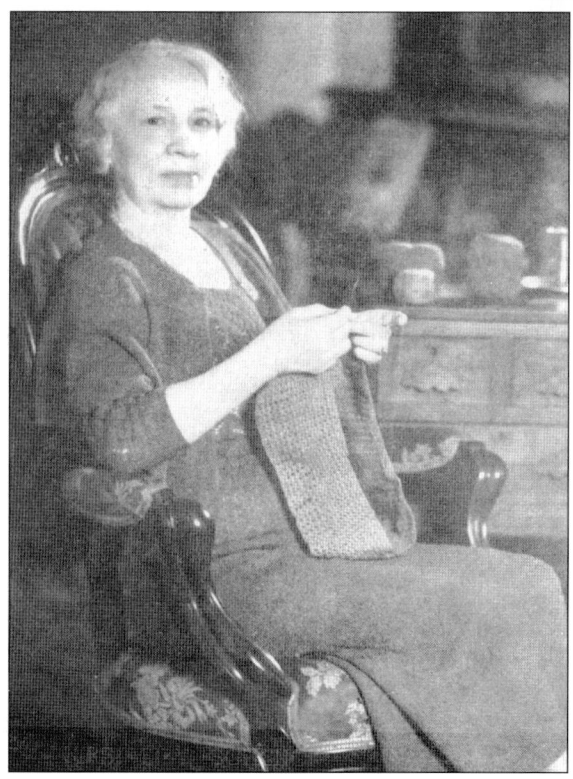

Textile mills in the county were often named for wives and daughters of the mill owners. Lily Schenck was honored in that way. Lily Mills produced sewing thread and became a leader in the field. (Tommy Forney.)

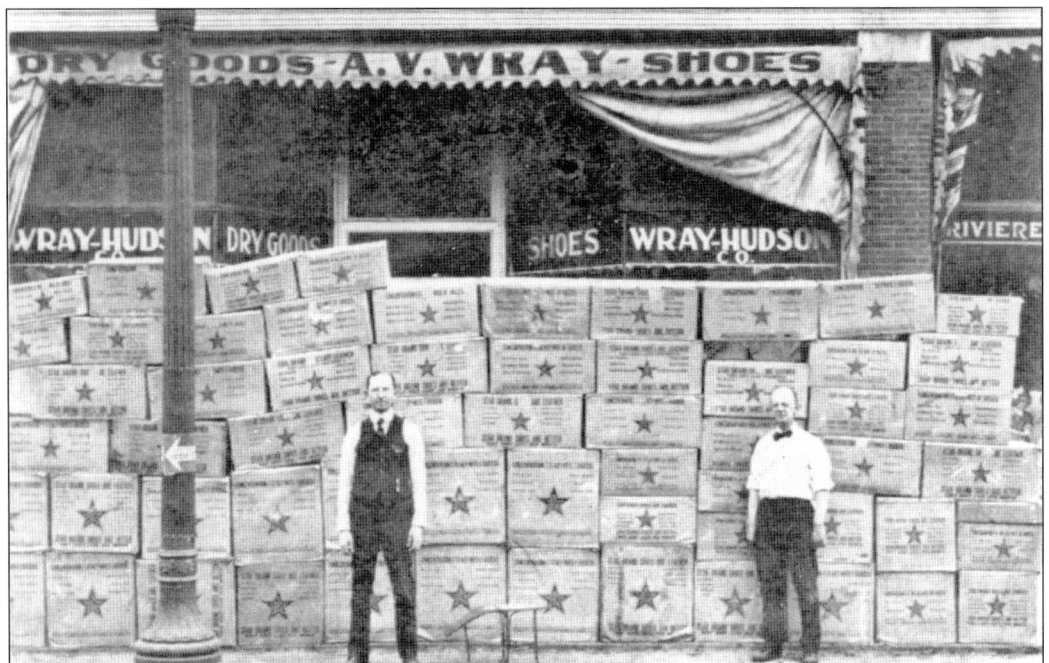

For decades, part of the Lafayette block on the west side of the courthouse was occupied by A. V. Wray Department Store, which ultimately was known as Shelby's predominating department store. A. V. Wray (left) started the business in 1911. In this 1920s photograph, A. V. Wray and F. Stough Wray stand in front of a large shipment of shoes. At this time, W. H. Hudson Sr. was a partner in the business. (Stough Wray Jr.)

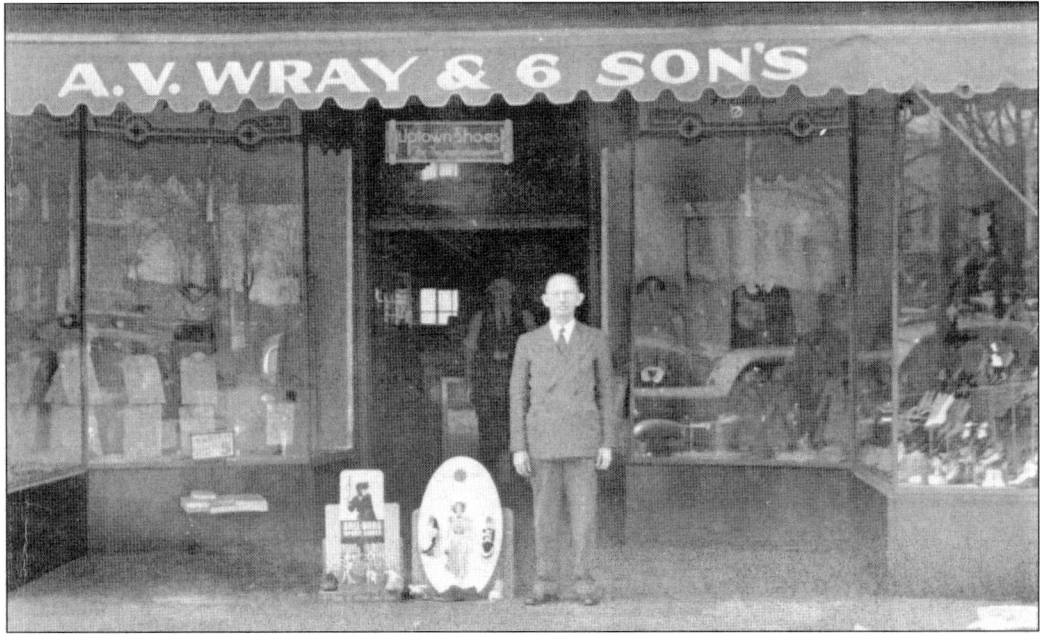

In the late 1930s, the store had acquired the name of A. V. Wray and 6 Son's. A. V. Wray Sr. stands in front of the store in this photograph. The store occupied the building that is the northern part of First National Bank in 2007. (Stough Wray Jr.)

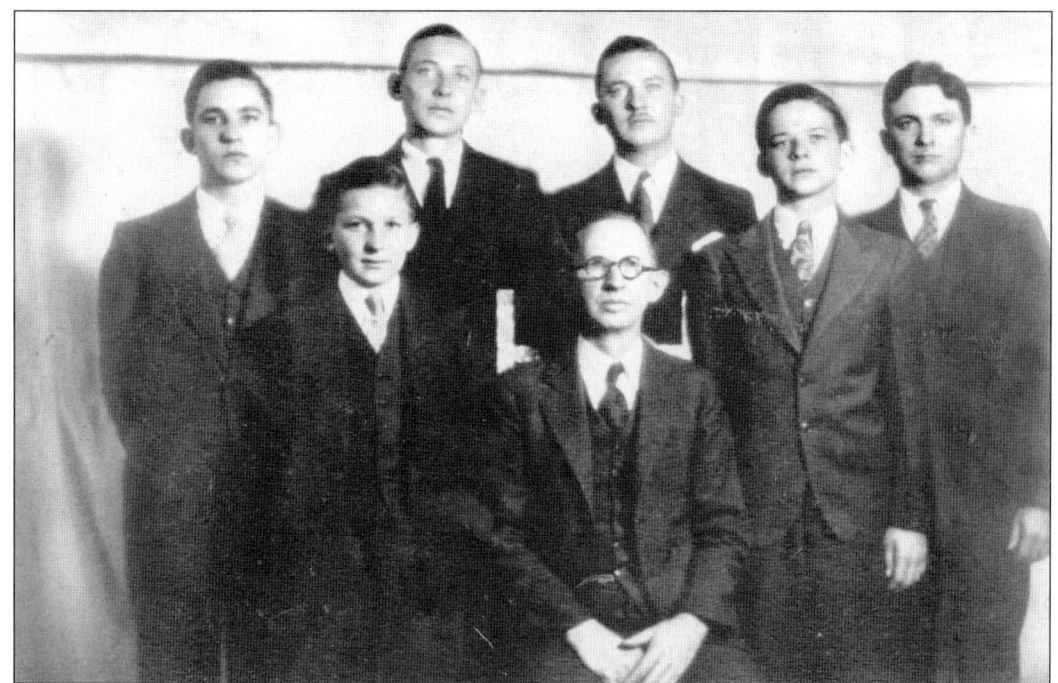

The Wray family is seen in this c. 1933 picture. From left to right are (first row) Stough A. Wray, A. V. Wray Sr. (seated), and Charles W. Wray; (second row) sons Harvey L. Wray, A. V. Wray Jr., George W. Wray, and Robert L. Wray. (Stough Wray Jr.)

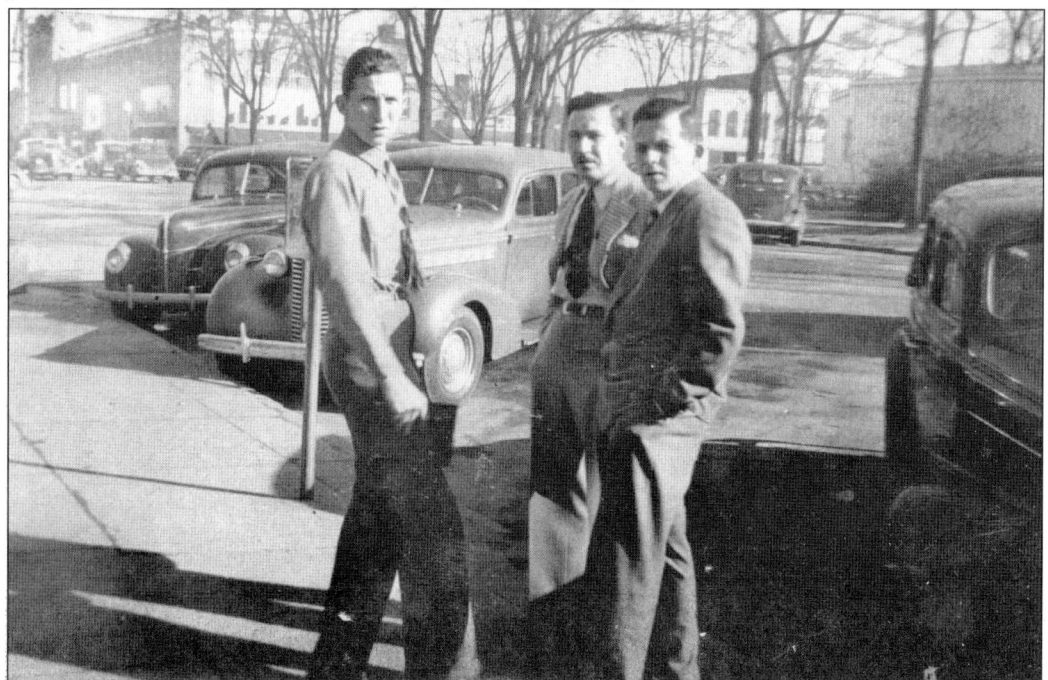

A. V. Wray Sr. retired in 1939. In 1940, the store was remodeled and expanded to 5,000 square feet. In January 1946, brothers Stough, Harvey, and Charles Wray (pictured from left to right) returned from service in World War II to run A. V. Wray and 6 Son's. (Stough Wray Jr.)

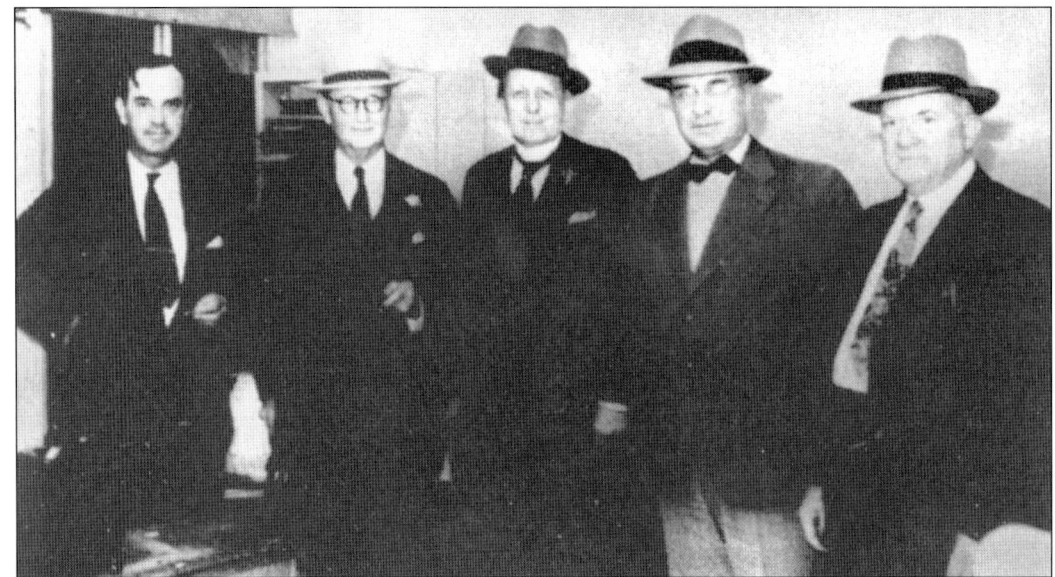

In 1936, when Clyde R. Hoey was elected governor of North Carolina, election returns were received by members of the Shelby Dynasty in the offices of the *Shelby Daily Star*. Pictured with the *Star*'s publisher, Lee B. Weathers (far left), are, from left to right, Judge E. Y. Webb, Clyde R. Hoey, O. Max Gardner, and Odus M. Mull. (*A Living History of Cleveland County*.)

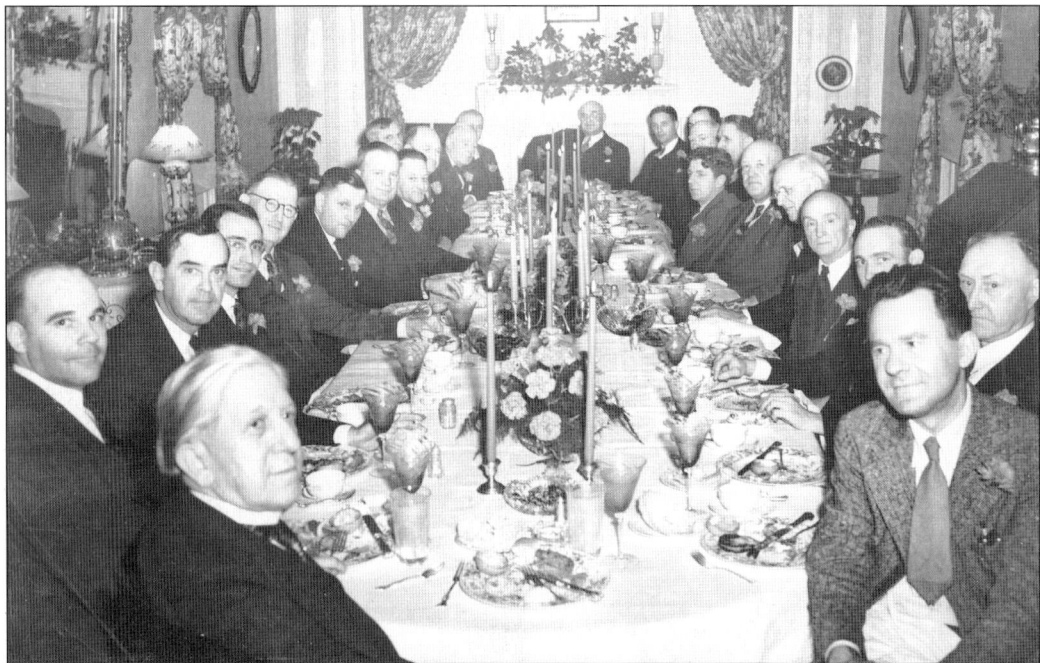

Pictured at a dinner at the home of John F. Schenck Sr. in December 1942 are a number of Shelby's attorneys and many political figures of the day. From left to right are Clyde R. Hoey, Joseph M. Wright, Lee B. Weathers, L. T. Hamrick Jr., E. Y. Webb, J. W. Osborne, C. C. Horn, James S. Cline, W. L. Angel, D. Z. Newton, C. B. McBrayer, unidentified, O. Max Gardner, Henry B. Edwards, Horace G. Kennedy, O. M. Mull, A. A. Powell, John Cannon, John F. Schenck Sr., D. A. Tedder, Gerald B. Goforth, B. T. Falls Sr., and Bynum E. Weathers.

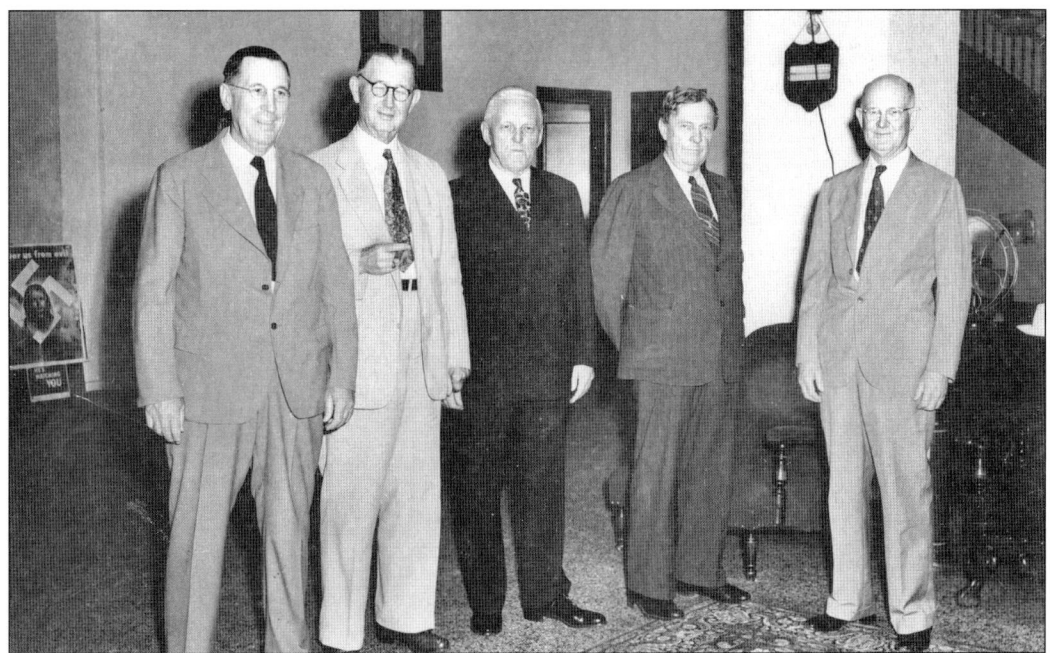

Shelby's leaders covered various fields of work. Dr. Zeno Wall (left) served over 20 years as pastor of Shelby's largest church, First Baptist. With him are, from left to right, federal district judge Edwin Yates Webb, businessman Charles Durham, Dr. E. B. Lattimore, and First National Bank president George Blanton Sr.

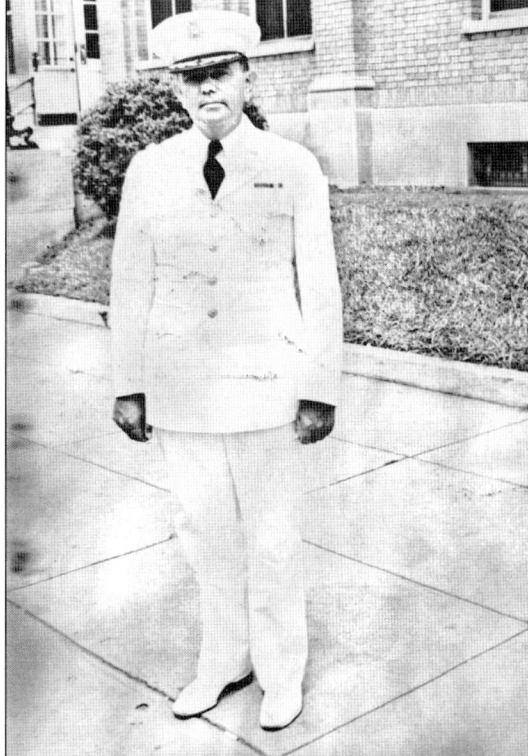

A leading figure in Shelby in the 1920s and 1930s was Peyton McSwain. He served in the military in World War I and World War II and reached the rank of colonel. He graduated from University of North Carolina and practiced law. He also served in the North Carolina Legislature and was elected to the position of superior court judge. (Alison Gilbert.)

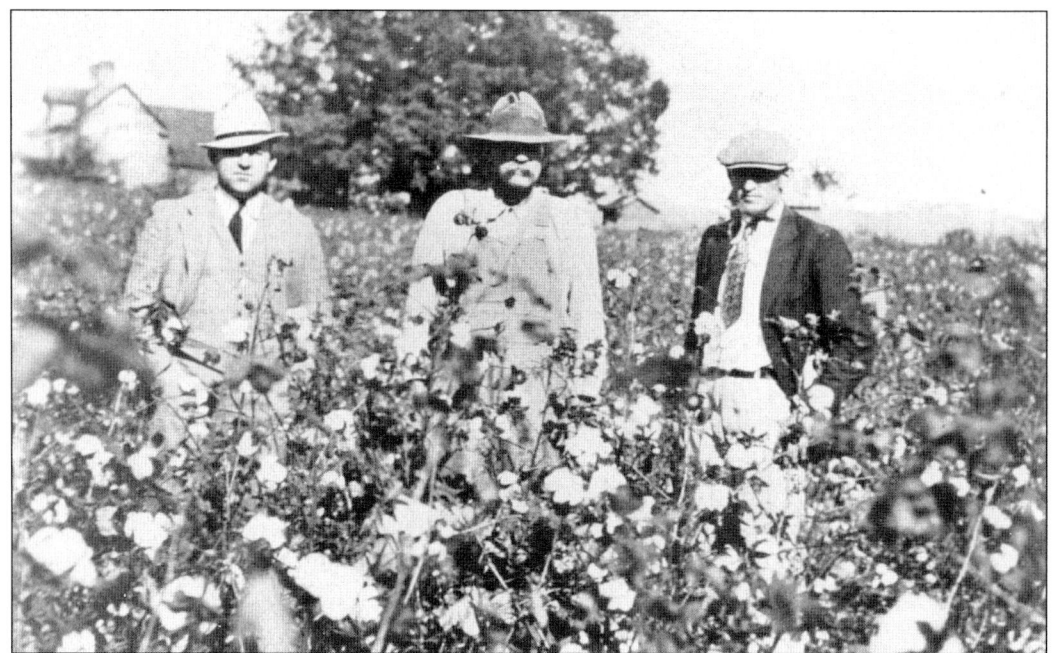

Shelby had become the center of a cotton-growing county by the 1930s. It also was in reality a mill town. Cotton was at that time vital to the county's economy. From left to right, O. Z. Morgan, John D. Honeycutt, and R. P. Weathers can be seen standing in high cotton. (Jack Morgan family.)

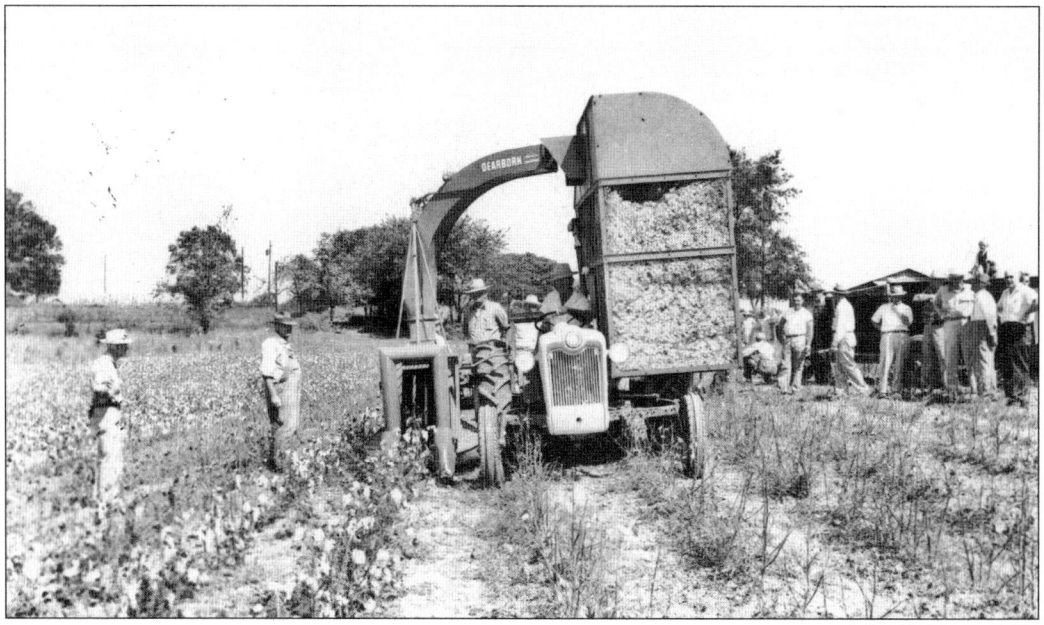

For decades, men, women, and children picked cotton by hand. Adults boasted about picking 300 pounds per day, and children looked forward to the day that they could pick 100 pounds. Loafing did not pay, since pickers were paid daily or weekly by how many pounds that they picked. However, with progress came the cotton picker; though less effective in getting all the cotton, it was more cost-effective than the old method.

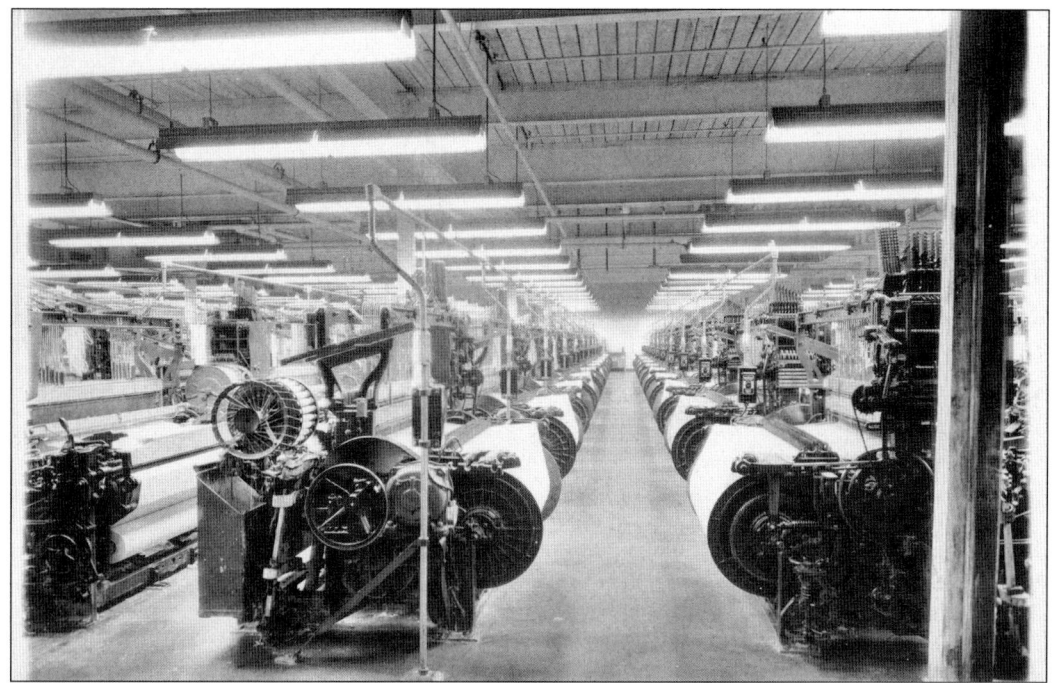

Mills sprang up in towns such as Shelby, and people left the farms to get jobs in the city. Mill villages were created for the new residents. Over time, conditions in mills improved, and manufacturing reached the cleaner and more efficient style seen in this photograph.

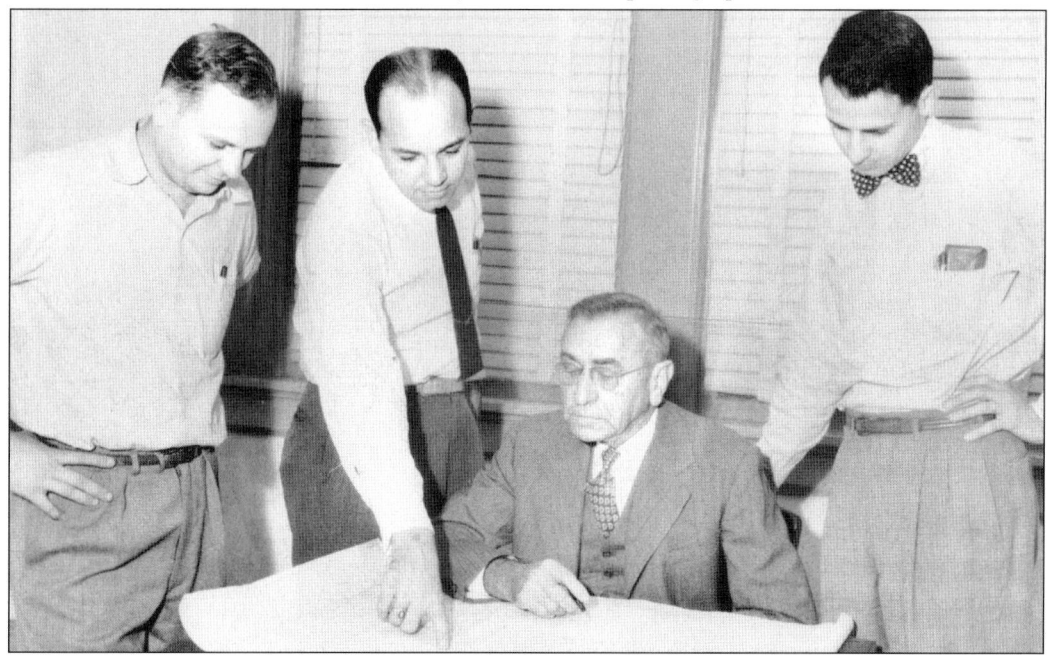

Mill owners not only built plants and provided jobs but also became civic and religious leaders. One such example in Shelby was the LeGrand family, which owned the Shelby Cotton Mill. R. T. LeGrand Sr. (seated) is flanked by his sons, from left to right, Gene, Dick, and Bill. (Gene and Bill LeGrand.)

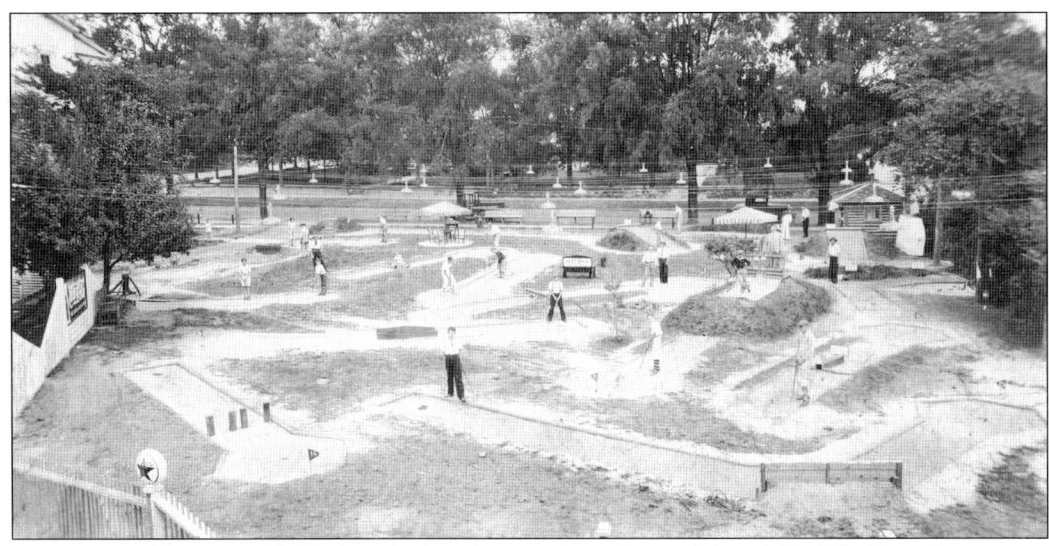

Miniature golf came to Shelby long before the Putt-Putt chain of the 1960s. The Peter Pan course was uptown just below the College Hotel on South Washington Street.

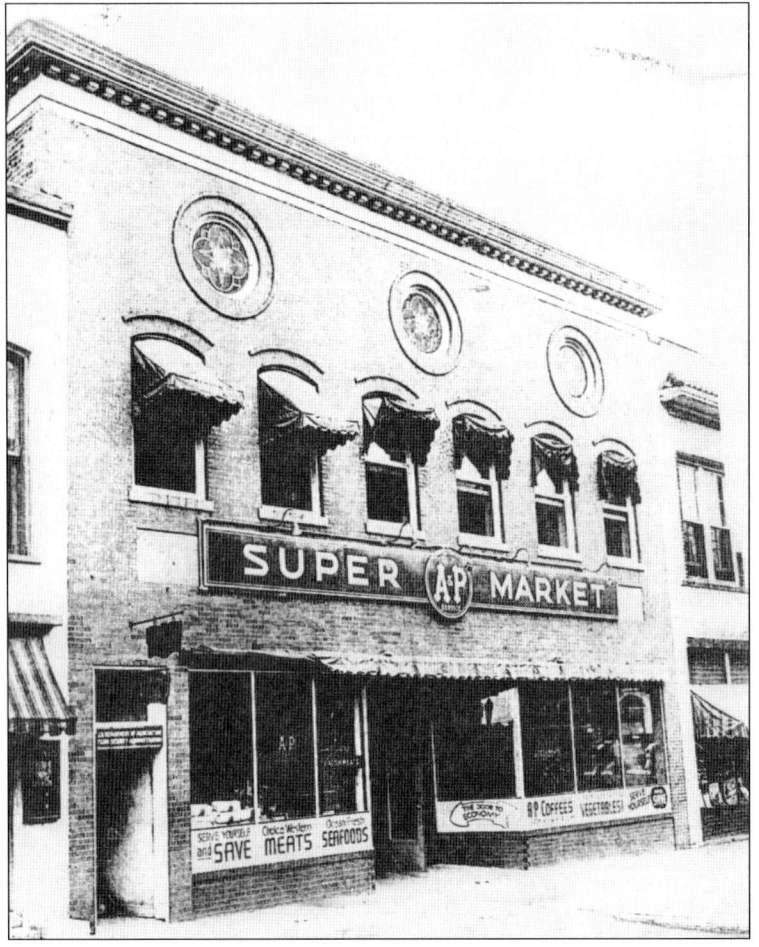

Down the block from the Courtview Hotel in the old city hall (now 5 East restaurant) was a "modern" supermarket, the A&P. The Great Atlantic and Pacific Tea Company operated one of the largest chains of grocery stores in the nation. A careful look at the building shows the three round windows still visible at 5 East.

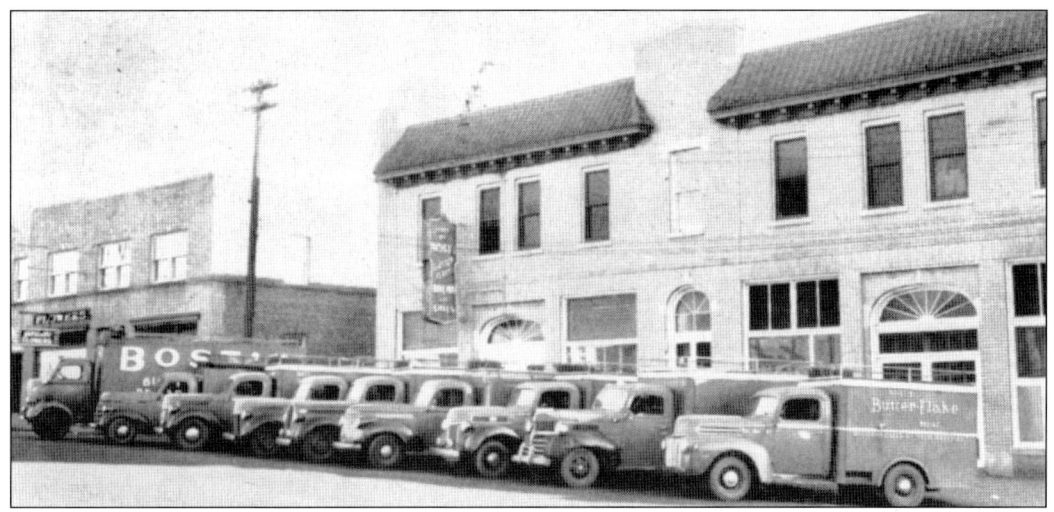

West Marion Street was the original home of a local industry that became a leading producer of bread in the area. L. C. Bost Sr. founded the Bost Bakery, which was later run by his sons Lloyd, Floyd, Ned, and Bennett. WBTV commercials said, "If it is fresher than Bosts, it is still in the oven."

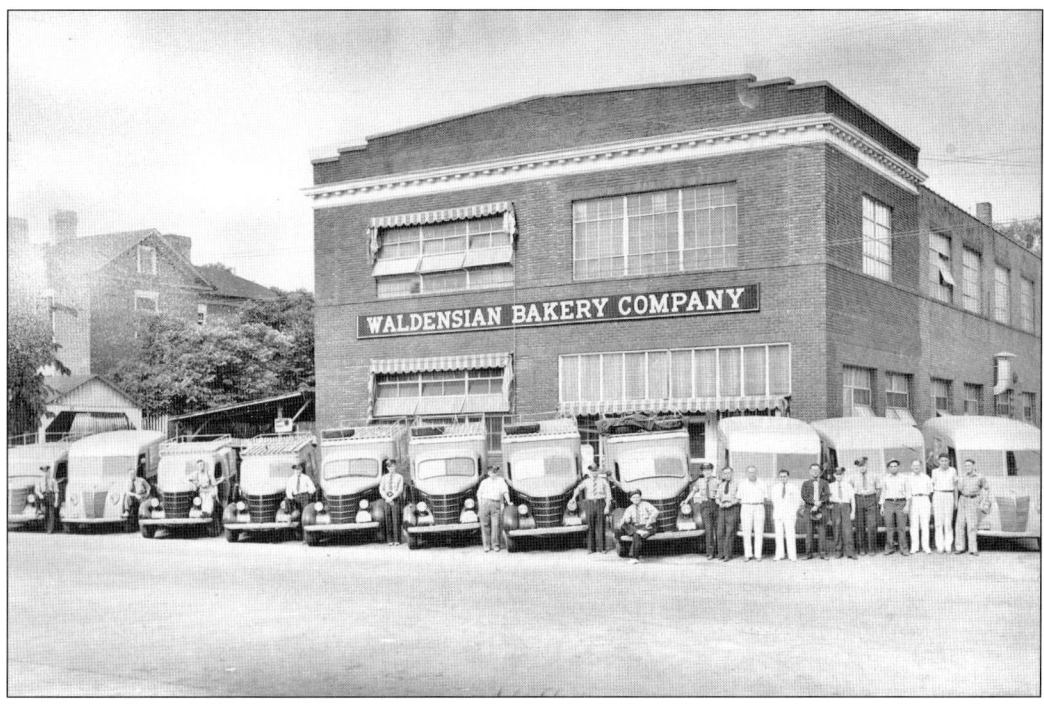

Located on South Lafayette Street, where the Shelby Police Department currently stands, the Waldensian Bakery was Shelby's other major bakery. The name was linked to the town of Valdese, which was settled by the Waldensian religious group from Southern France. Athos Roston ran the company, which sold Sunbeam bread.

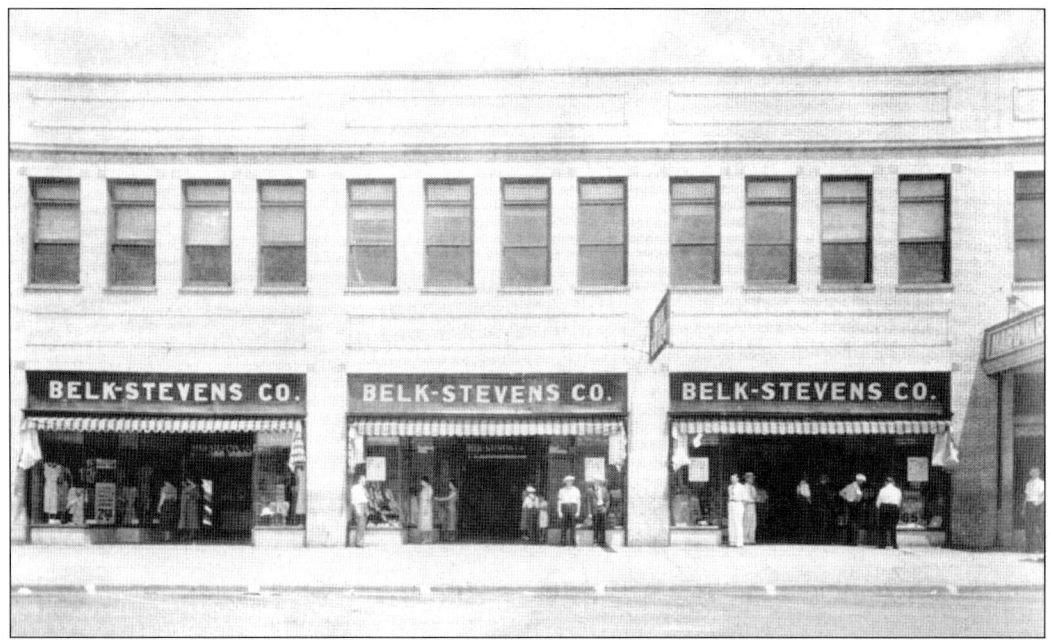

Long before the arrival of the Cleveland Mall, Belk-Stevens Company was located on South Lafayette Street in uptown Shelby. W. P. Ellis was the longtime manager of the store. (Lloyd Hamrick Collection.)

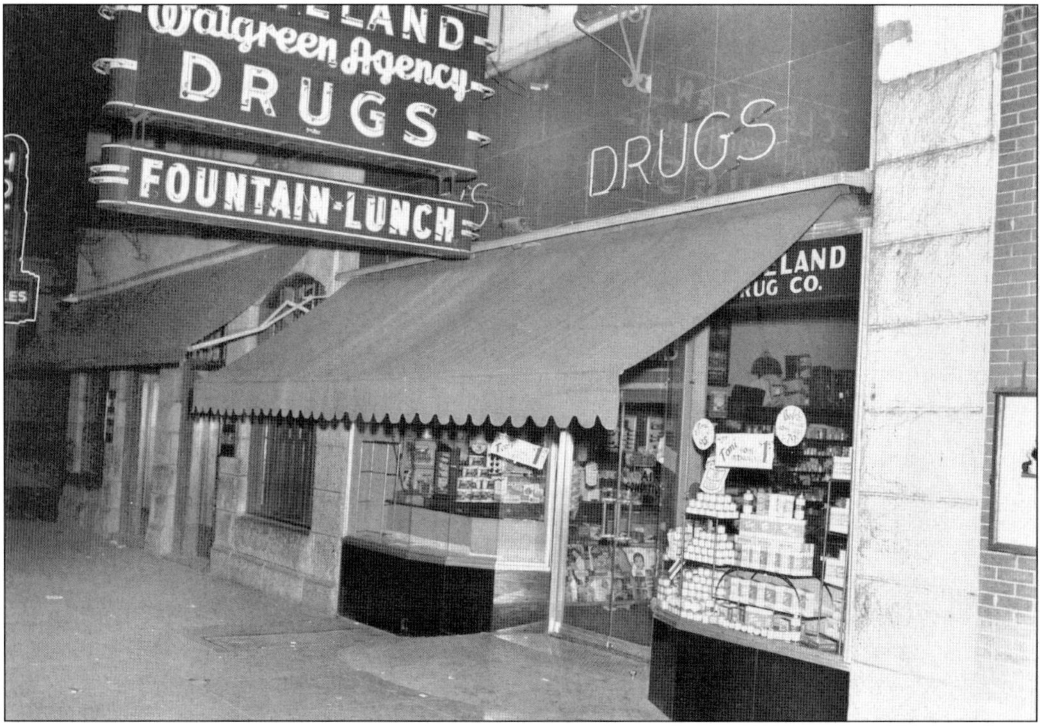

The Cleveland Drug Company was located next to the First National Bank on Lafayette Street. In the years after World War II, men gathered on the benches in front of the store to discuss politics and solve the problems of the day. (Lloyd Hamrick Collection.)

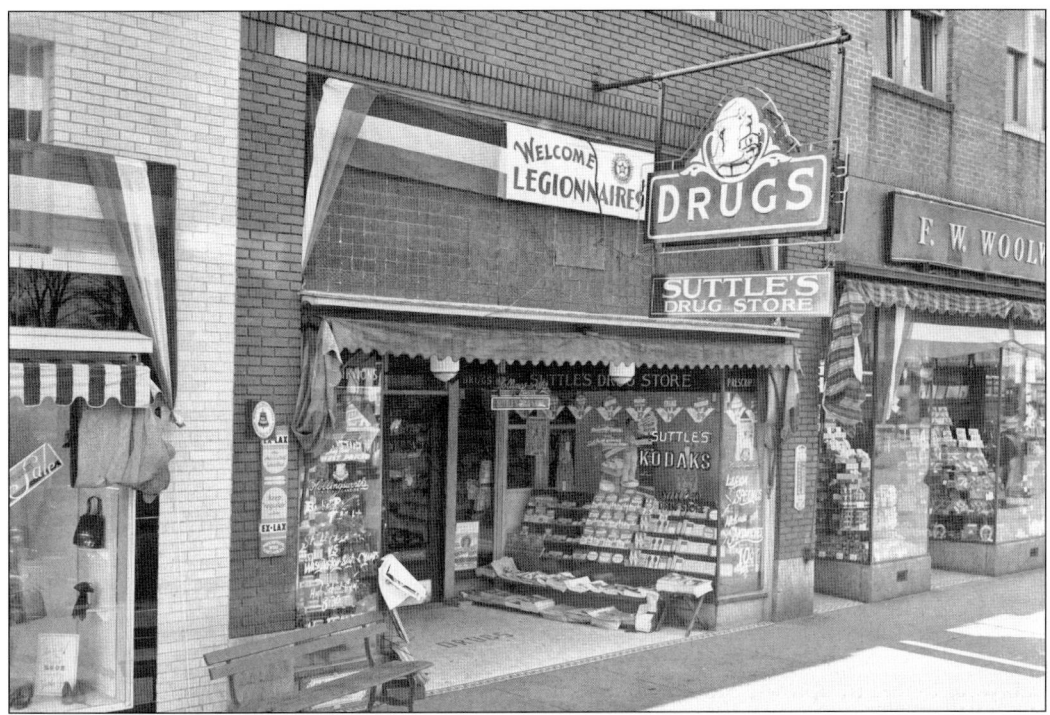

In the 1950s, located between Cohen's Department Store and F. W. Woolworth was Suttle's Drug Store. Albert Suttle's store served sandwiches and filled prescriptions. New prescriptions earned one a coupon for a free fountain coke. (Lloyd Hamrick Collection.)

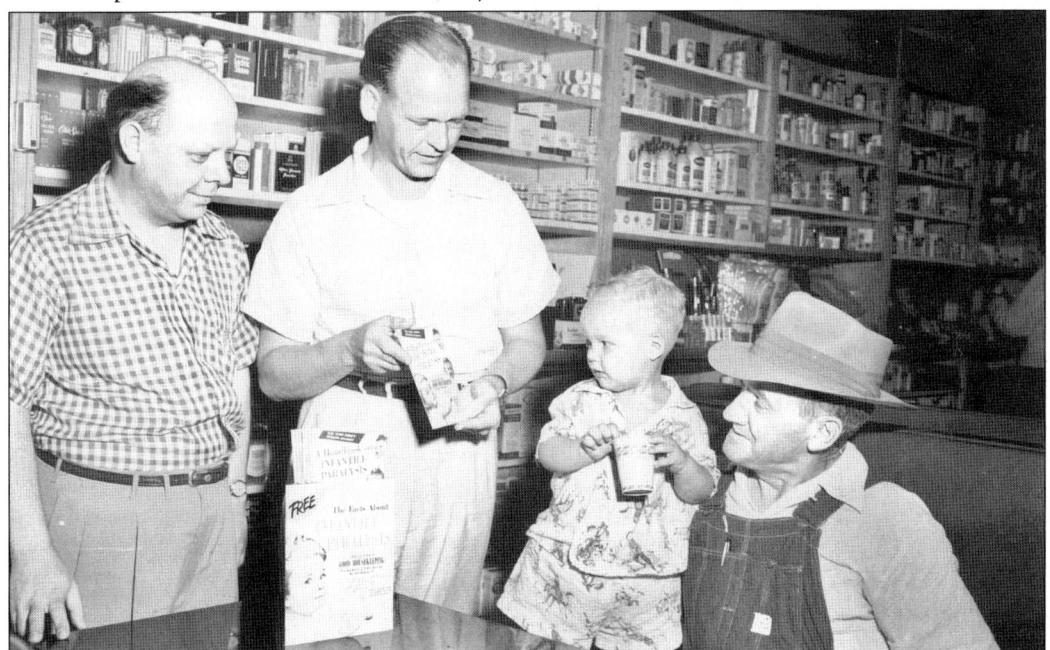

This view is of the inside of Suttle's. Owner Albert Suttle (left) stands next to local businessman Jack Palmer of Palmer's Mortuary. Palmer later served as a county commissioner, and in 2007, is in his 80s and serves on the Uptown Shelby Revitalization Committee. (Lloyd Hamrick Collection.)

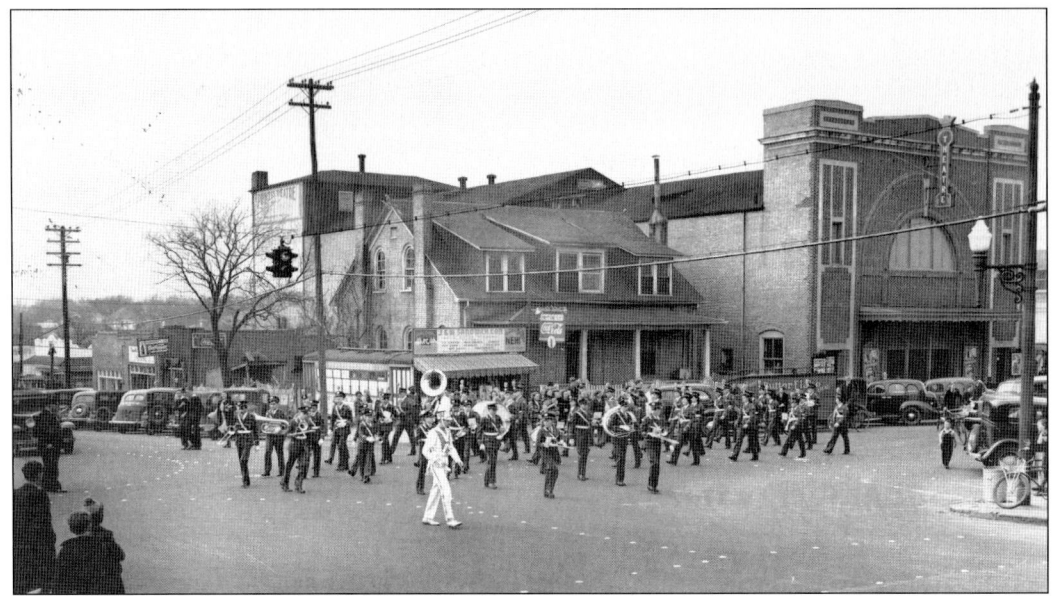

In the era before and after World War II, Shelby had four uptown theaters. This c. 1940 photograph shows the theater built by Zeb and Enos Beam during World War I. It was originally the Princess and later the Carolina. The theater closed around 1960, when the building was remodeled to become an F. W. Woolworth store. The house on the Graham Street corner, or South Lafayette Street, would soon be torn down. In the 1940s and 1950s, this was the location of the Wigwam Pool Hall.

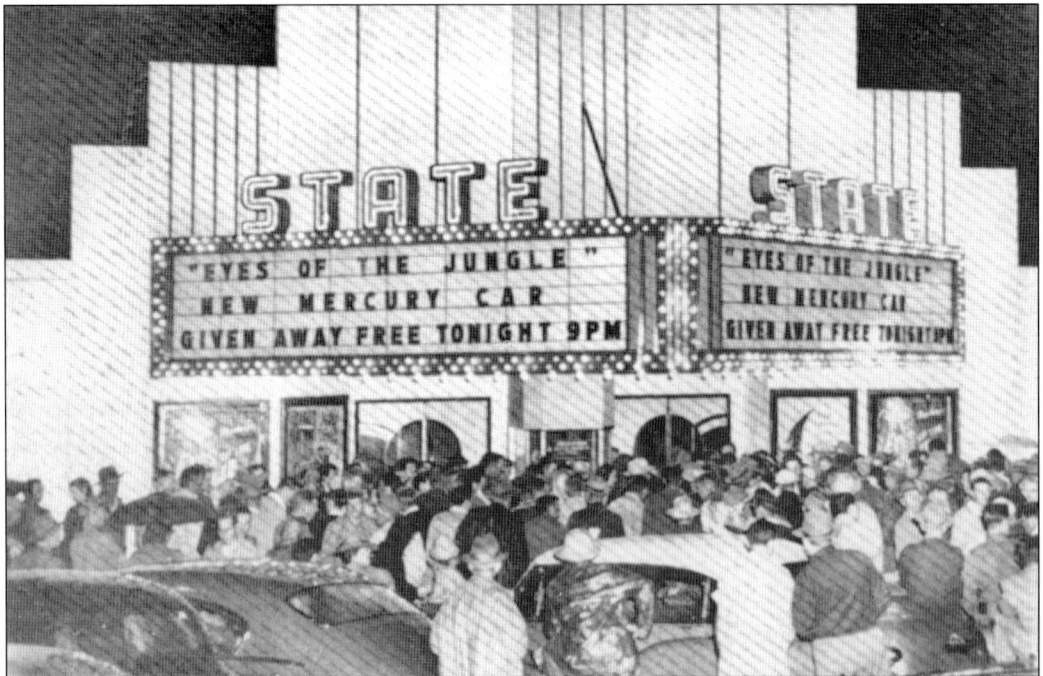

Just two blocks from the Carolina Theater, the State Theater was opened in 1939. Winning a car in 1953 was a big event, as the crowd in this picture suggests. The car was won by local taxi driver Coyt "Black Cat" Self. (Uptown Shelby Association.)

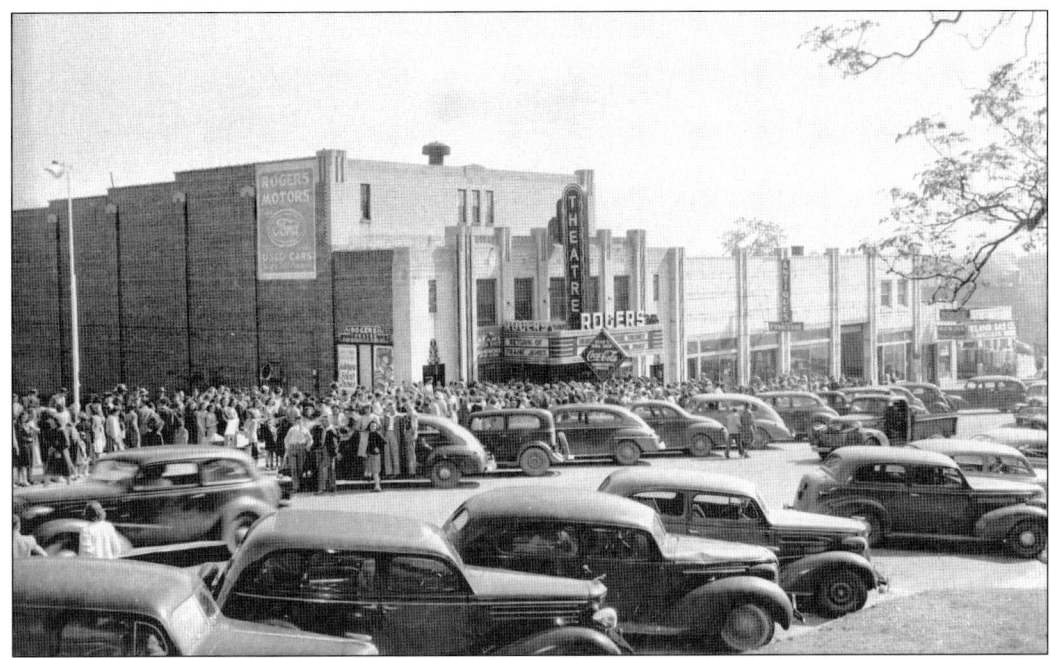

The Rogers, just east of the courthouse square on East Marion Street, became the leading local theater and was open into the 1970s. This picture shows a major motion picture event, as *Gone with the Wind* came to Shelby. Note the dress style for going to the movies before World War II. (Lloyd Hamrick Collection.)

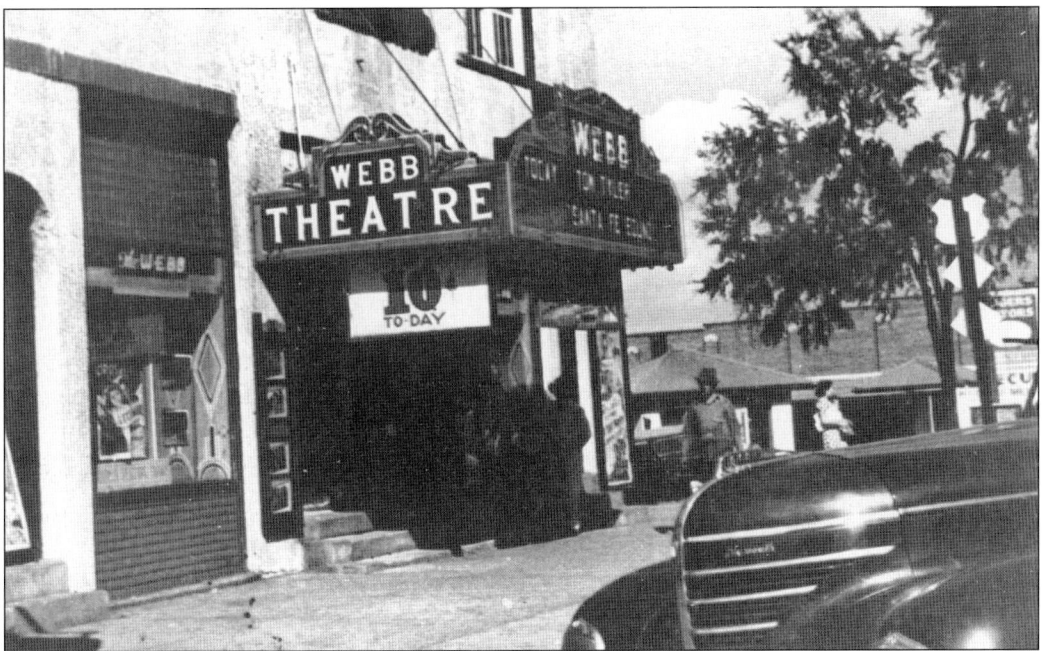

The Webb Theatre was on the corner of Marion and Washington Streets, which would become the home of the Union Trust Company in the 1960s. The Webb was well known in the 1940s and 1950s for its adventure serials, which took several weeks to complete, requiring that fans go back to the theater every week.

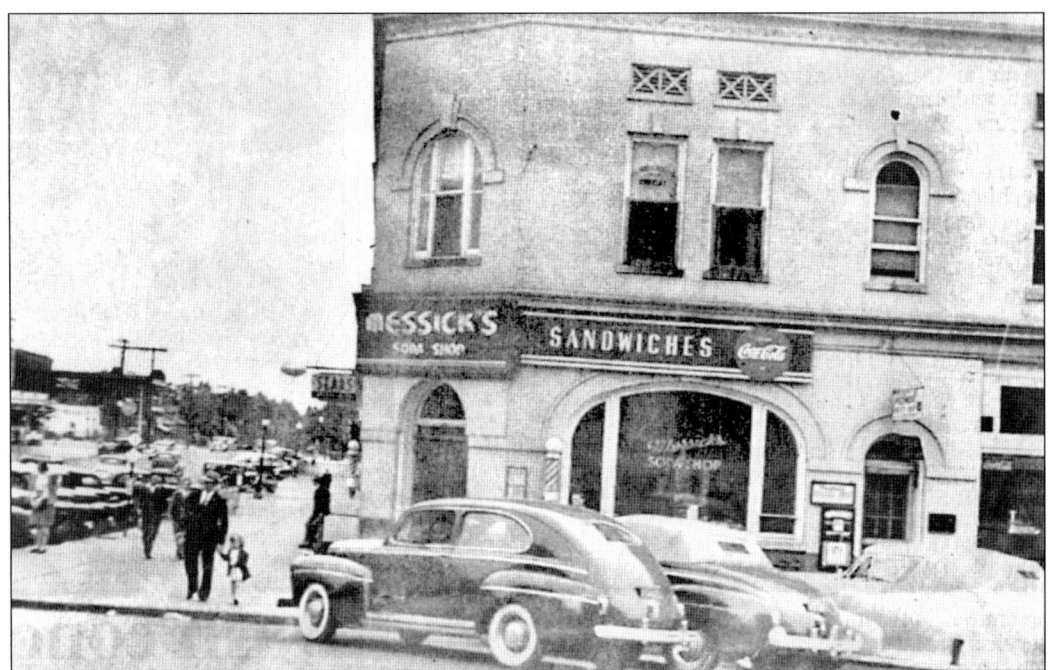

A block south of Suttle's was the Messick Soda Shop, which in the time of World War II was an uptown institution. Upstairs were offices, such as dentist and law offices. The building had housed a bank earlier and later was home for the Shelby Jewelry and Loan. It was destroyed in the 1979 fire and explosion in uptown Shelby. (Uptown Shelby Association.)

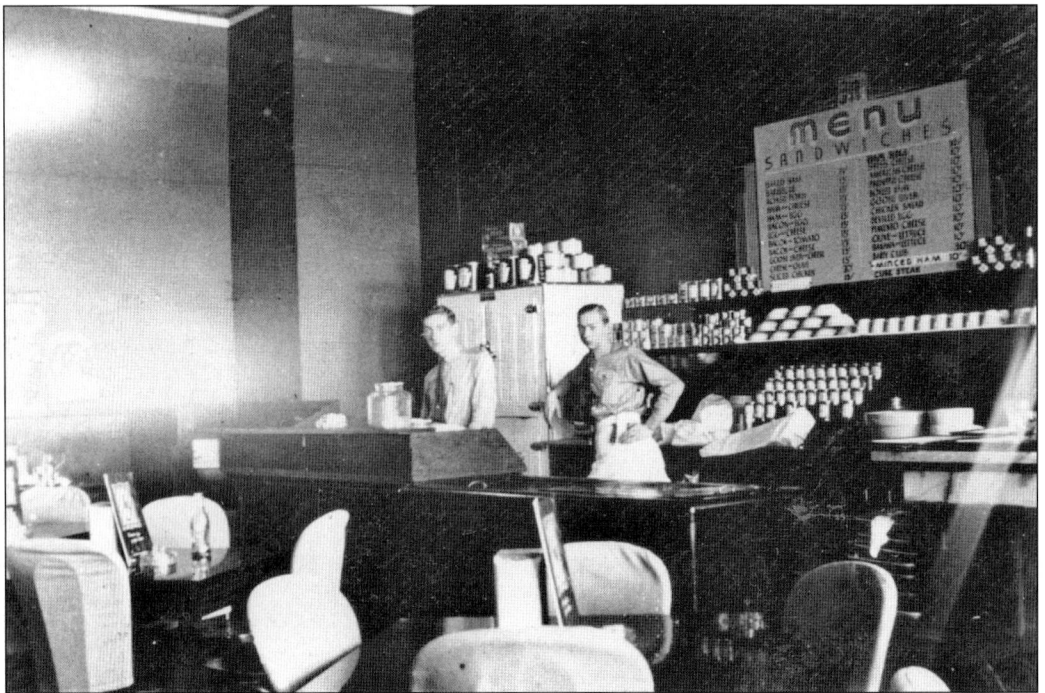

This view shows the interior of Messick's Soda Shop around 1940. Harry Robinson is seen behind the counter. (Uptown Shelby Association.)

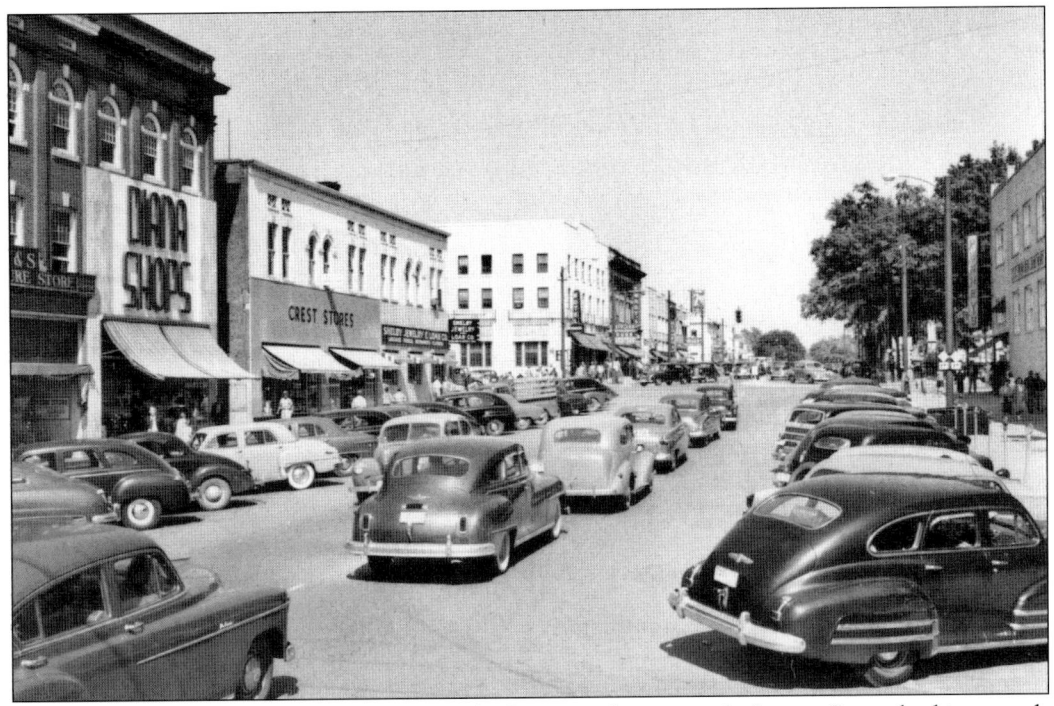

This photograph of uptown Shelby shows the business district on Lafayette Street looking north toward First National Bank. This photograph was used to produce a popular postcard image of the uptown. (Lloyd Hamrick Collection.)

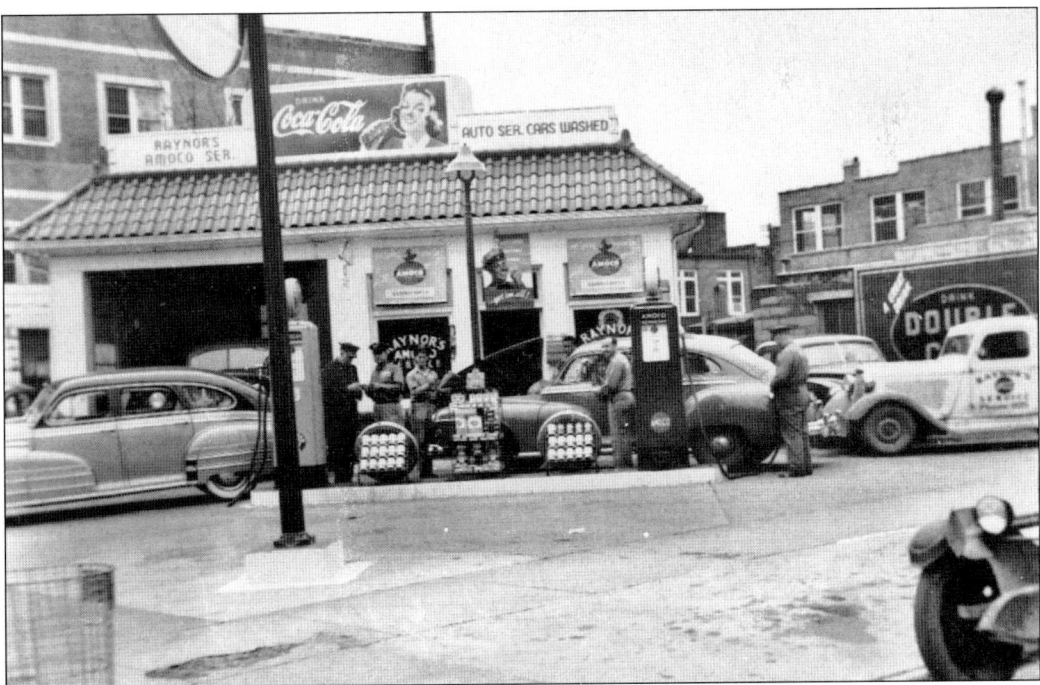

Across from city hall was Raynor's Amoco Service, in the day when service meant service. Note the number of attendants servicing the customer.

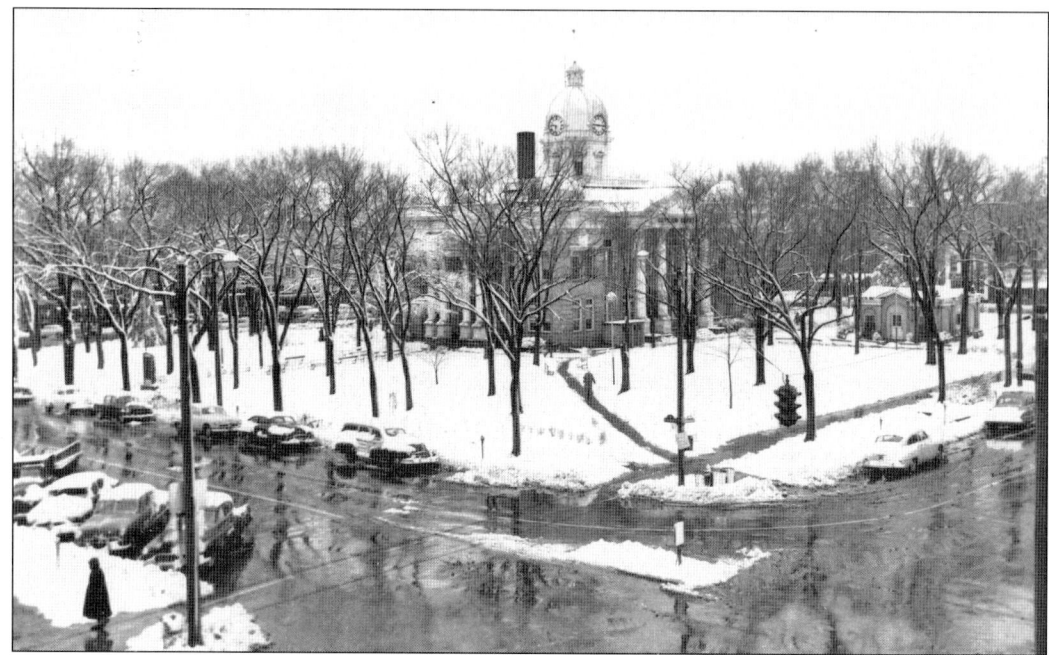

The Cleveland County Courthouse was the center of Shelby in location and activity. This is a snowy view from around 1950. A close look shows the traffic pattern, which had one-way traffic around the square, with parallel parking on the inside and angle parking on the outside. (Lloyd Hamrick Collection.)

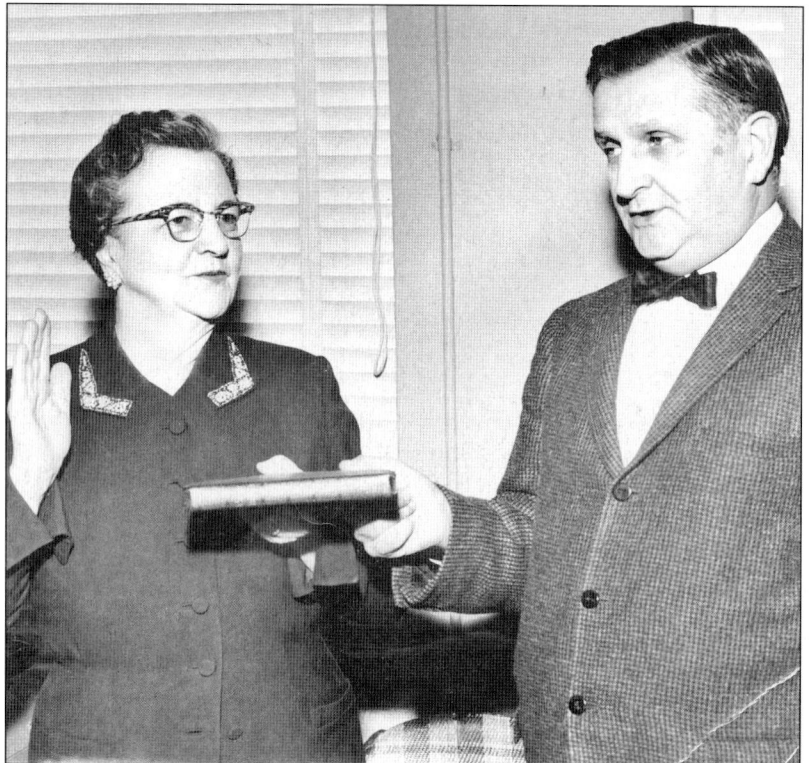

A leading figure in the courthouse was Lillian Eaker Newton, who served as Cleveland County treasurer from 1932 to 1966. In this picture, Bill Osborne administers the oath of office to Newton around 1950. (Alison Gilbert.)

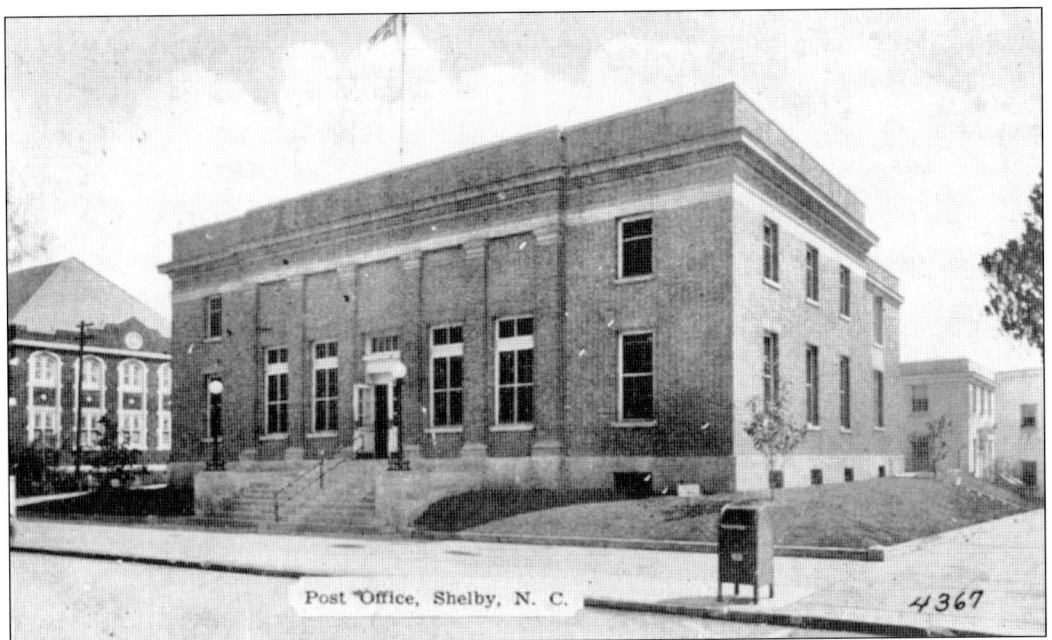

For over three decades, the U.S. Post Office in Shelby was located in this building next to the Central Methodist Church. Note the classic mailbox on the sidewalk. Today this building houses the Cleveland County Arts Council.

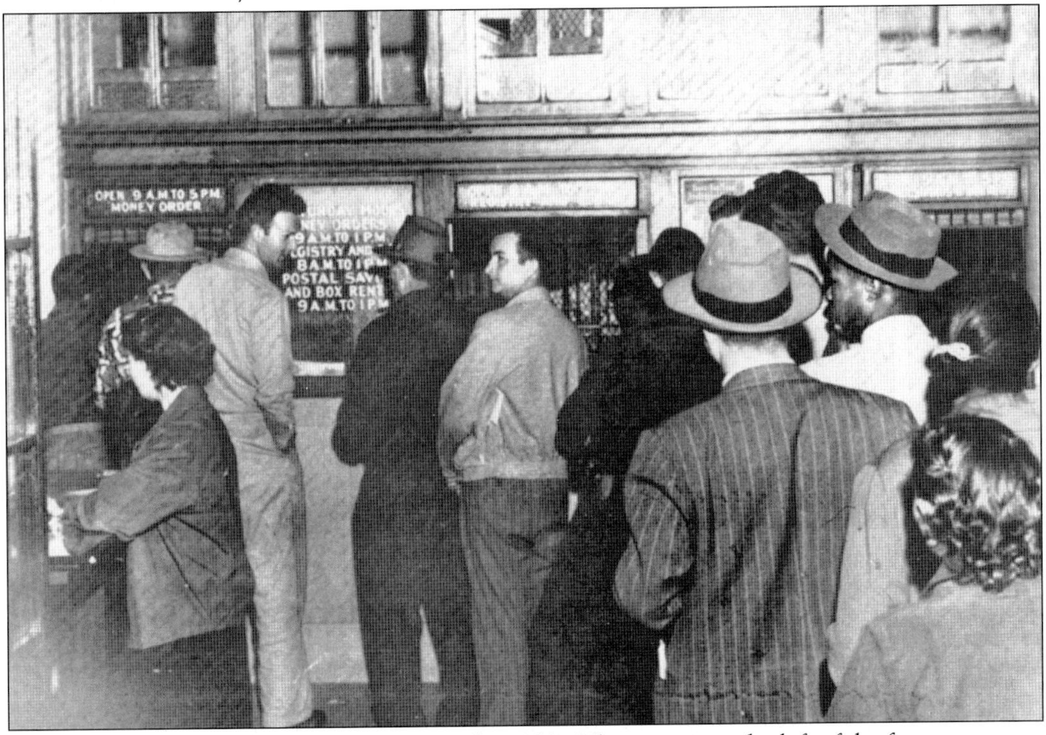

This scene shows the post office interior in the 1950s. This view is to the left of the front entrance, where one could buy money orders, which were filled out by pens with black ink rather than processed by computers and printed by machines. (Uptown Shelby Association.)

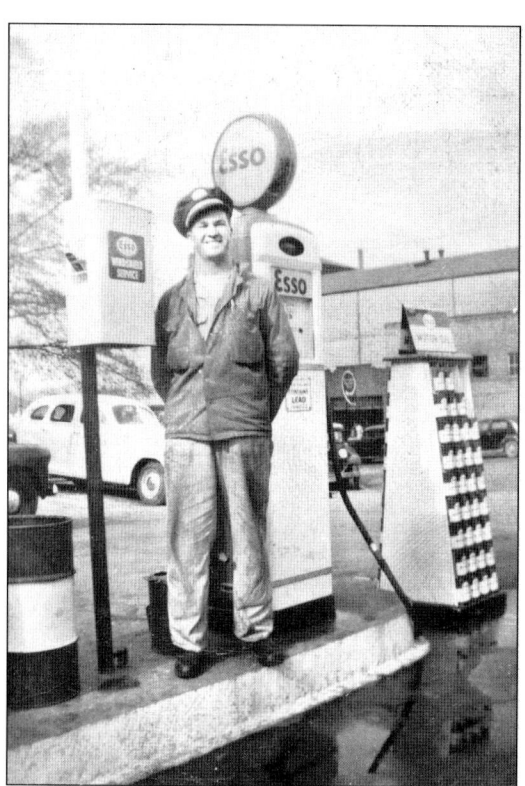

In the days when service stations lived up to their name, many men established long-term businesses. Jasper Warren "Bill" Gamble was an Esso dealer in uptown Shelby for years. (Bill Gamble.)

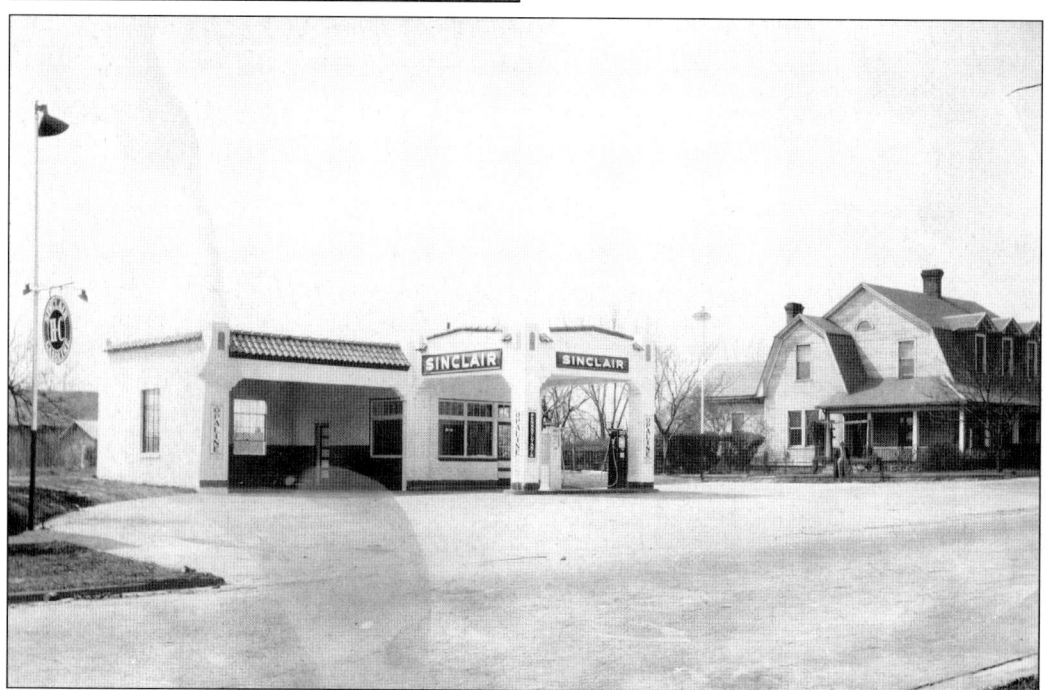

This early station on West Warren Street at Clyde Street was a Sinclair station—another long gone brand of gasoline. The house in the picture was the home of Jim Austell, who was the father of Mrs. Lee (Sara) Nolan, Mrs. Roscoe (Mary) Lutz, and Charles Austell.

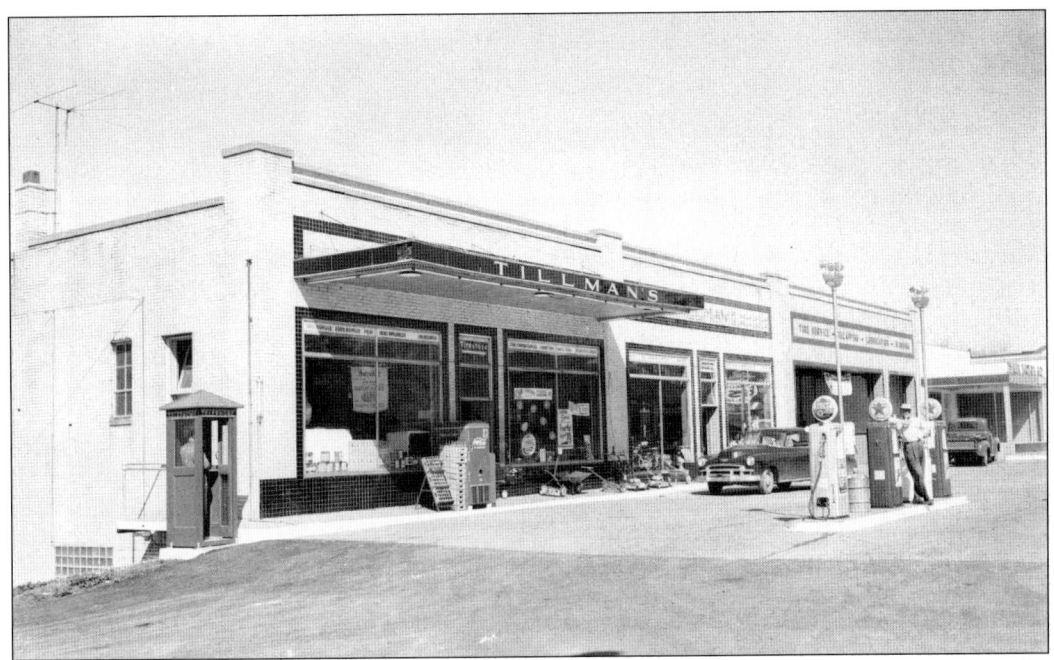

A well-known 1950s business located on East Marion Street at Dekalb Street was Tillman's Firestone. The business dealt in a variety of products from gasoline and automobile items to sporting goods. (Lloyd Hamrick Collection.)

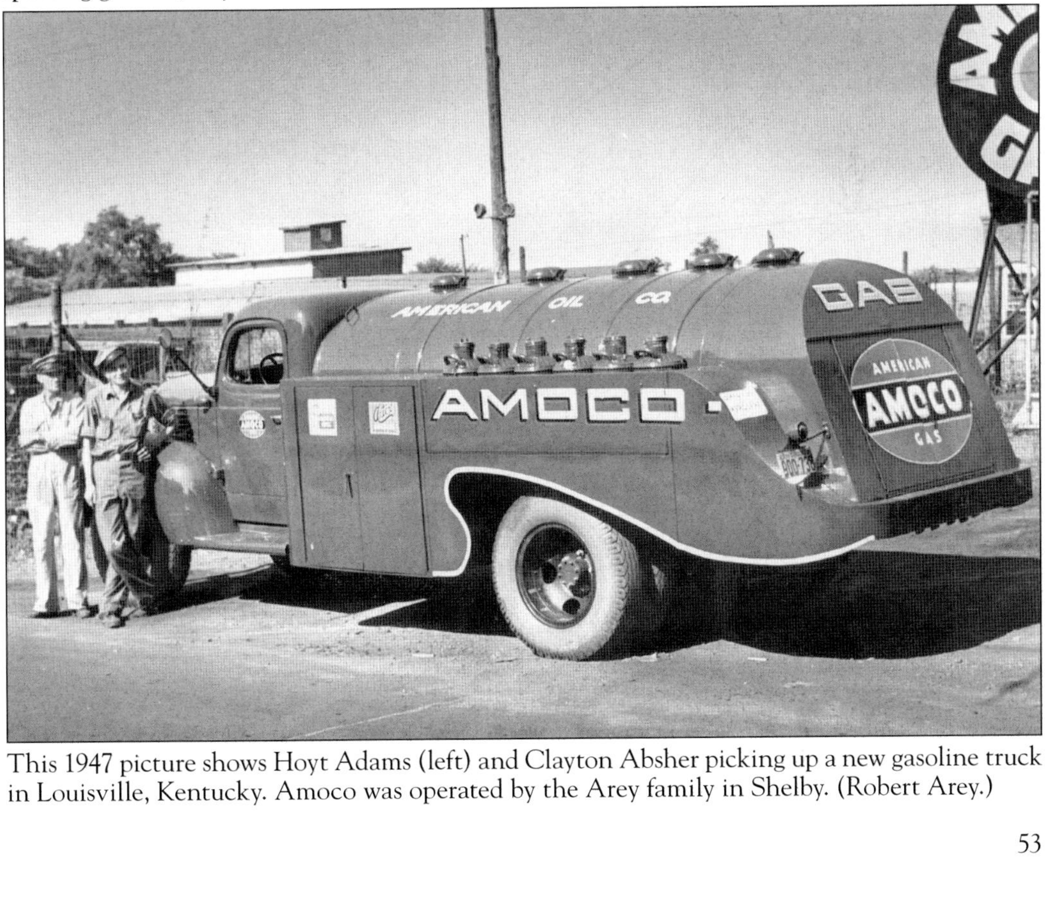

This 1947 picture shows Hoyt Adams (left) and Clayton Absher picking up a new gasoline truck in Louisville, Kentucky. Amoco was operated by the Arey family in Shelby. (Robert Arey.)

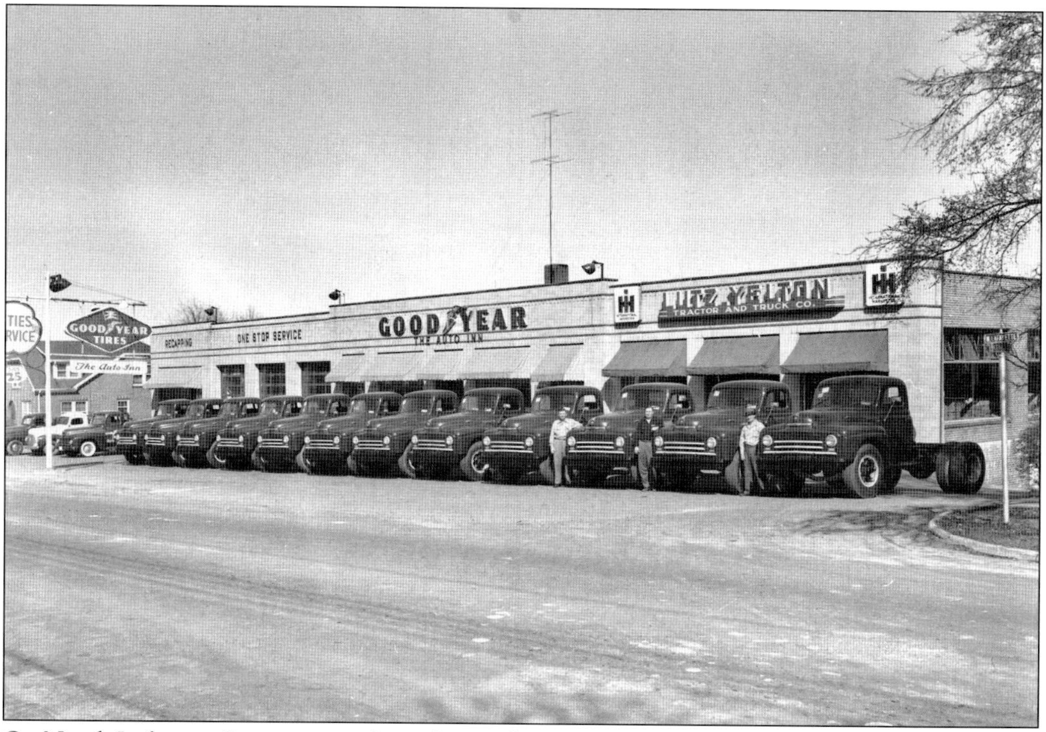

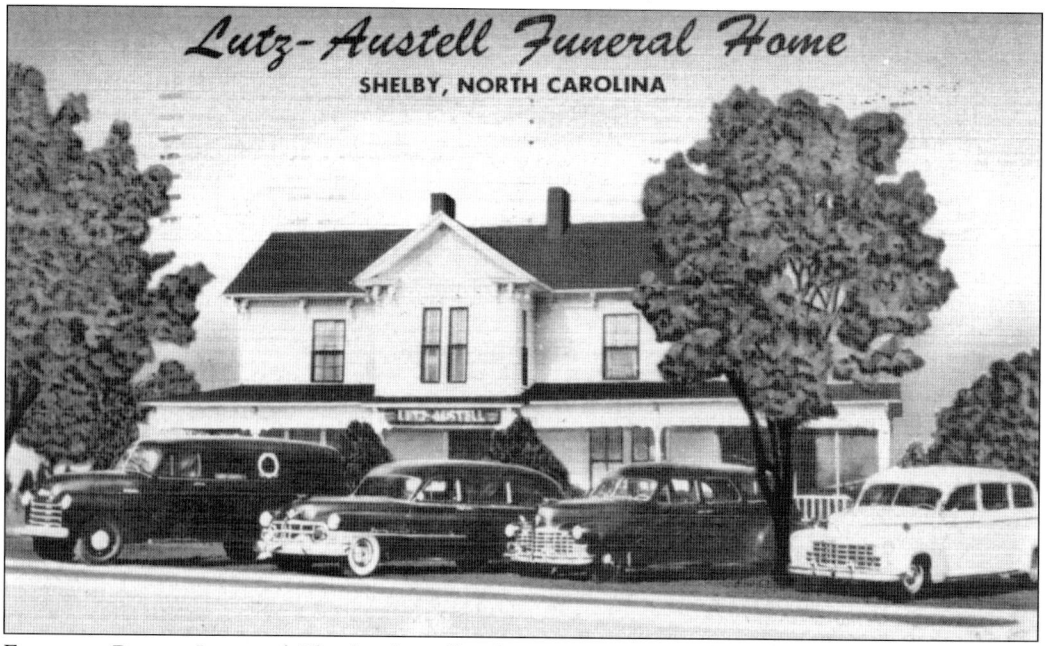

On North Lafayette Street, across from the Bankers House, was the Auto Inn or Lutz-Yelton. The signs show the variety of products carried by the company: Cities Services gasoline, Goodyear tires, and International trucks. (Lloyd Hamrick Collection.)

For years, Roscoe Lutz and Charles Austell, who were brothers-in-law, operated Shelby's leading funeral home. The 1950s location on West Sumter Street was on the corner of Martin Street, at the entrance to Sunset Cemetery.

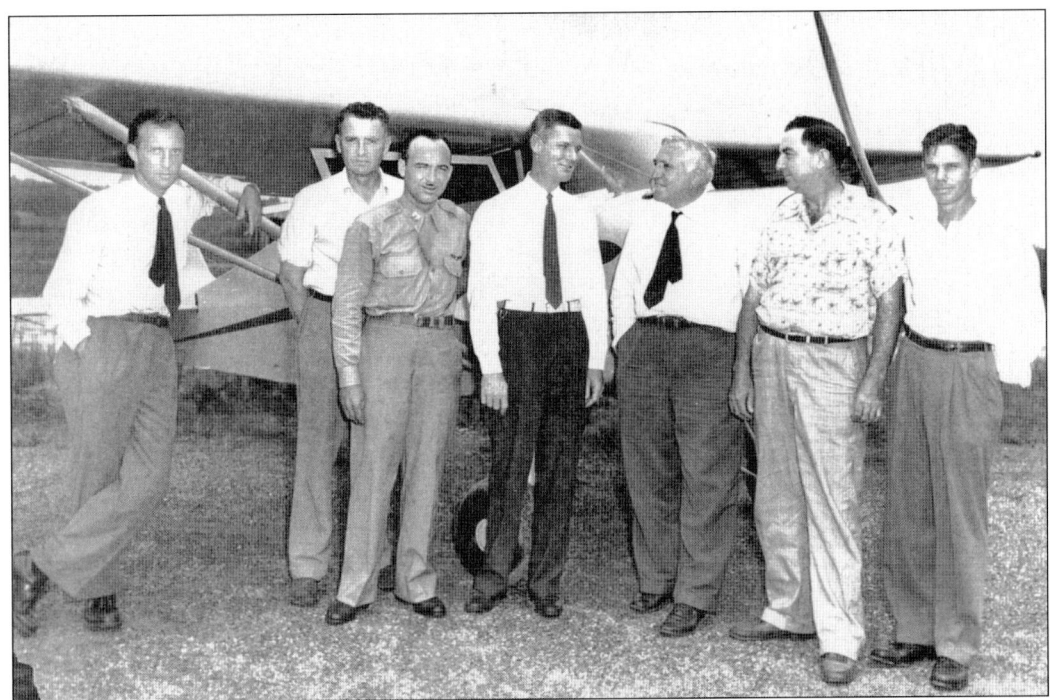

This 1950s photograph was made at Bridges Airport with, from left to right, William Piper Jr., Evan Wilson, D. L. Willis, George Blanton Jr., William Piper Sr., William Paul Bridges (owner and manager of the airport), and Max Freeman. The plane in the background is a Piper Pacer. (Tom Bridges.)

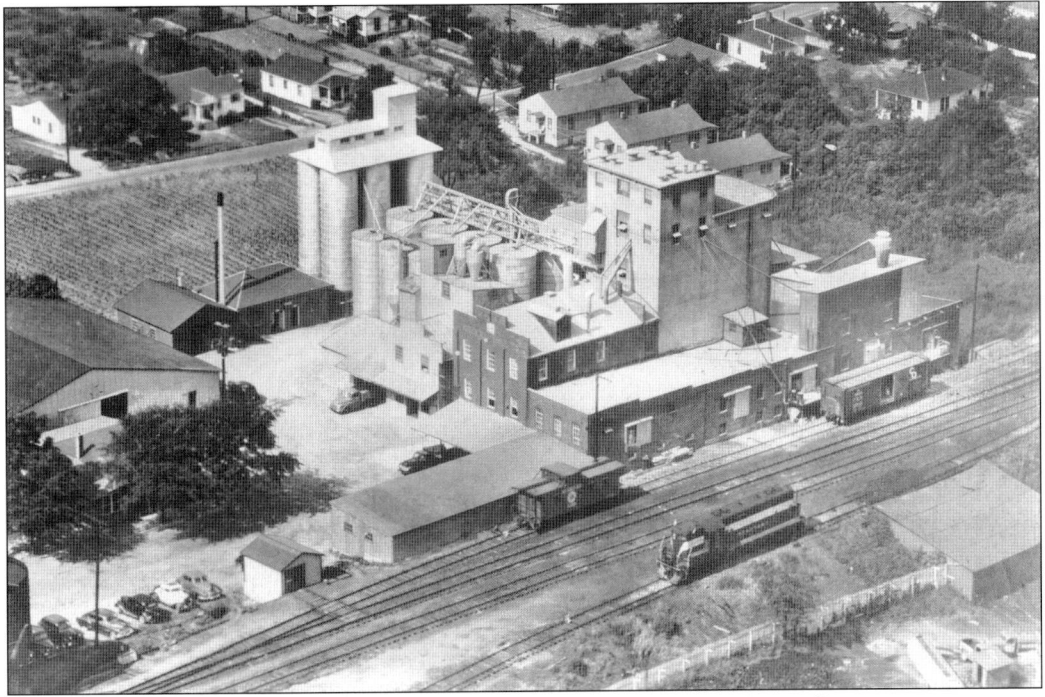

Among George Blanton's many business ventures was the Eagle Roller Mill.

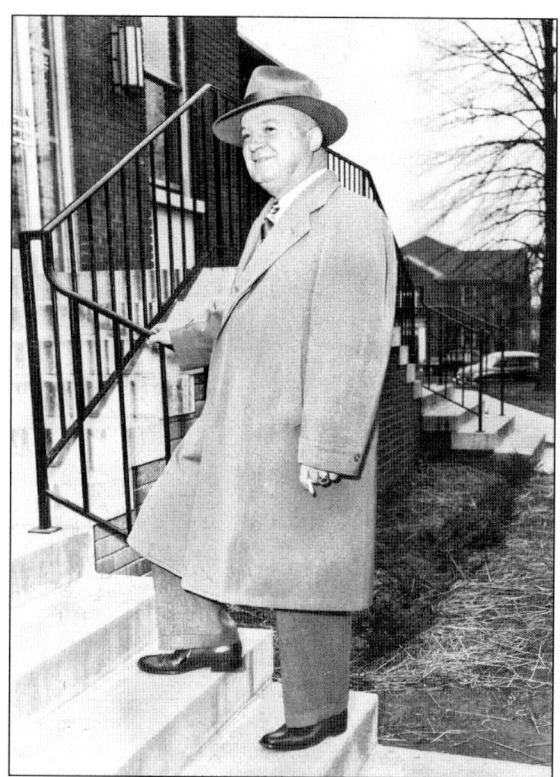

This man was a leading figure in uptown Shelby for decades. C. C. "Cobby" Horn was one of the leading attorneys in Shelby. He was also a leading Democrat and leader at First Baptist Church of Shelby. He practiced law with W. L. Angel in the early days and later with J. A. West and his son Charley Horn. His other son, Jim, served as a North Carolina legislator. (Jim Horn.)

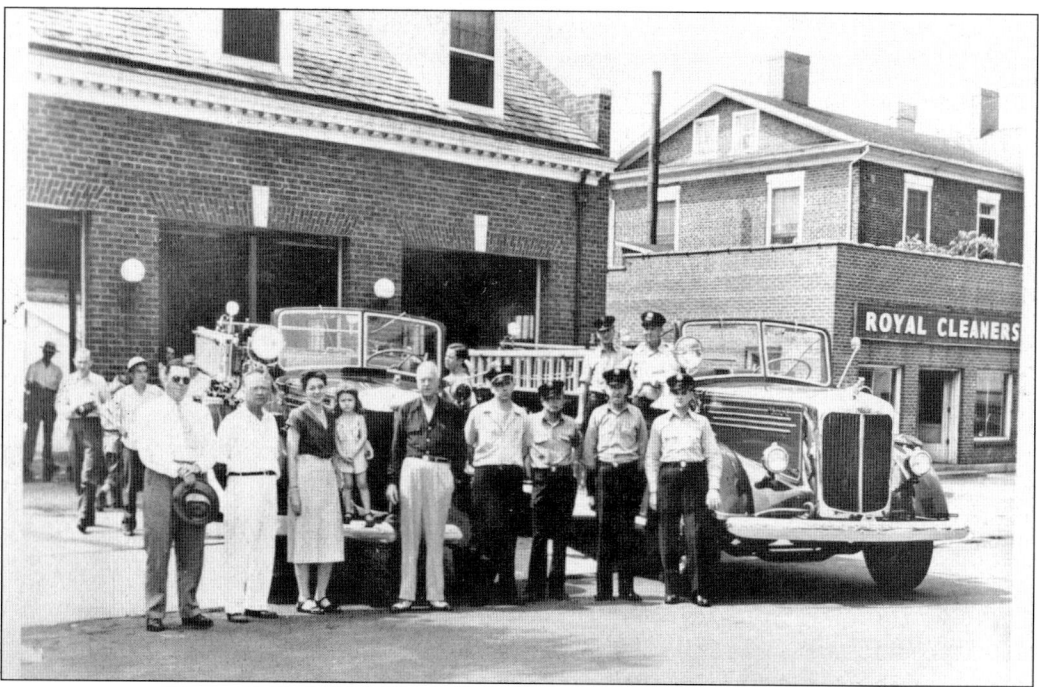

Shelby City Hall was built in the 1930s on East Graham Street. For years, the Shelby Fire Department was a part of this structure. The Royal Cleaners can be seen in this 1950s photograph. The house in the background was beside the Waldensian Bakery on Lafayette Street.

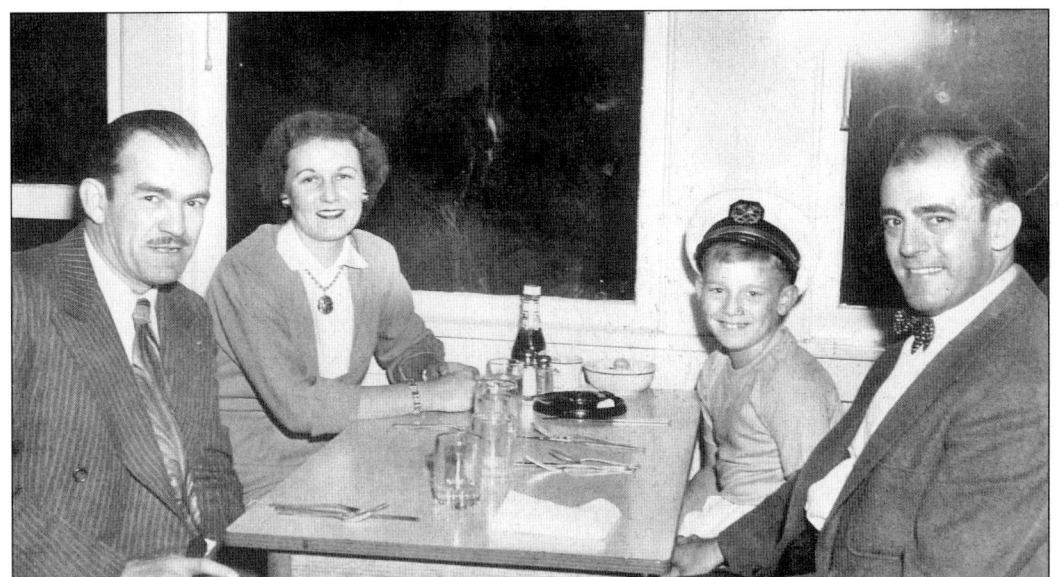

These four individuals are all well-known Shelbians. From left to right are Dr. Hubert Plaster, Mrs. Harold (Helen) Plaster Sr., Harold "Bubba" Plaster Jr., and Dr. Harold Plaster Sr. Young Bubba would follow in his father's footsteps and become a dentist as well. (Dr. Will Plaster.)

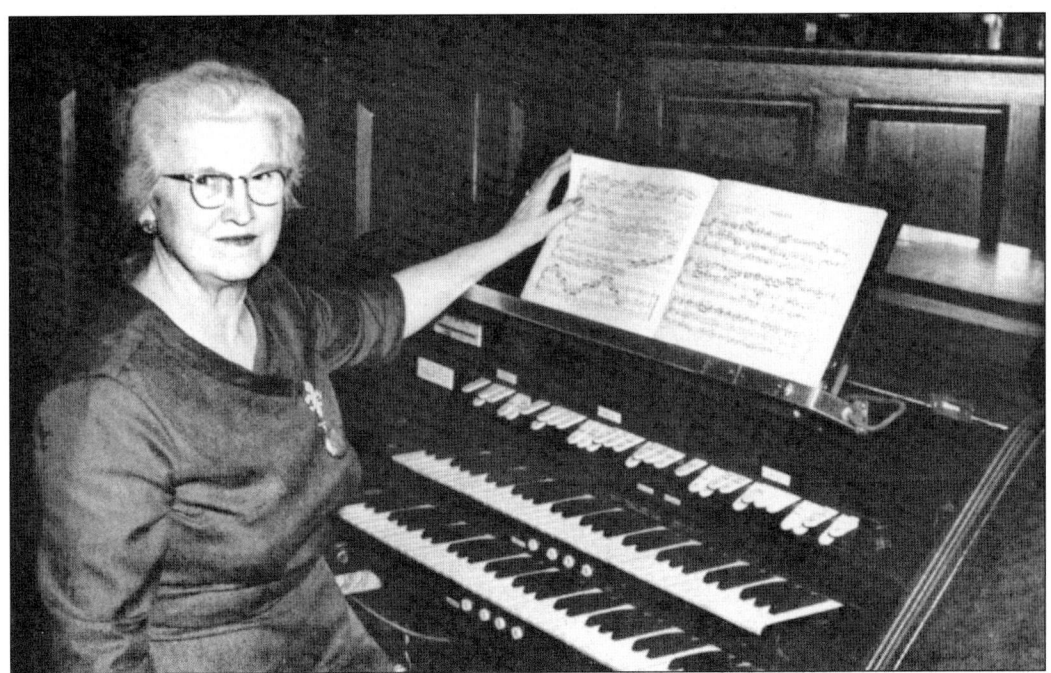

Ruth Howie Plaster had a long tenure as organist at First Baptist Church, serving for over 40 years. During those years, she married Dr. Hubert Plaster and also taught organ at Gardner-Webb College (which became Gardner-Webb University in the early 1990s). (*A History of First Baptist Church.*)

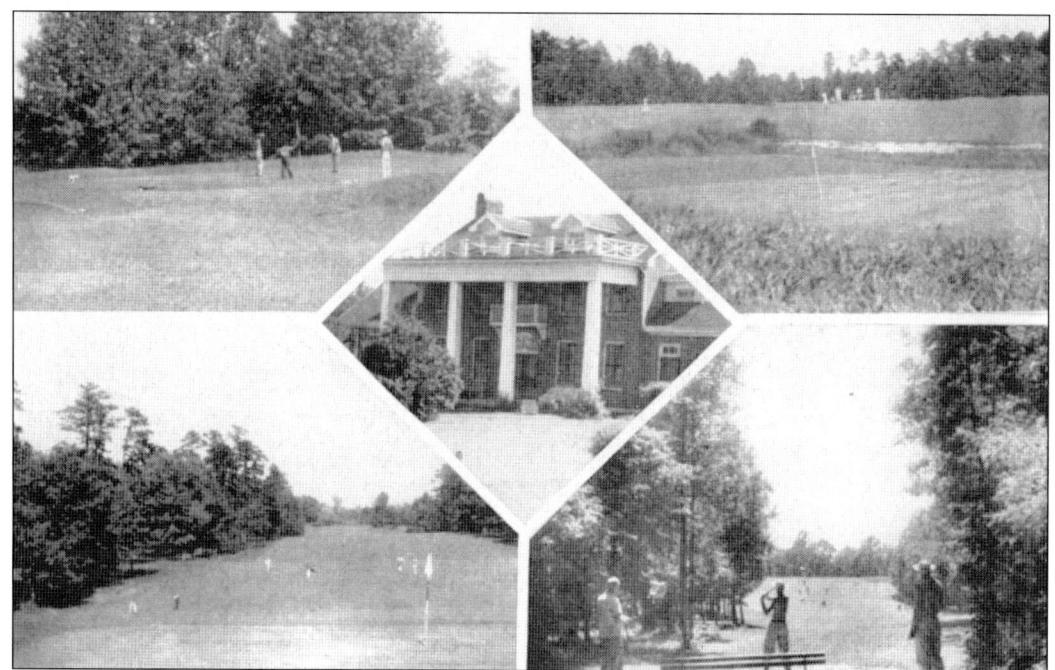

In the 1930s, golf was not as popular as it would become after World War II. Pictured are scenes from the early days of the Cleveland Country Club, just east of Shelby.

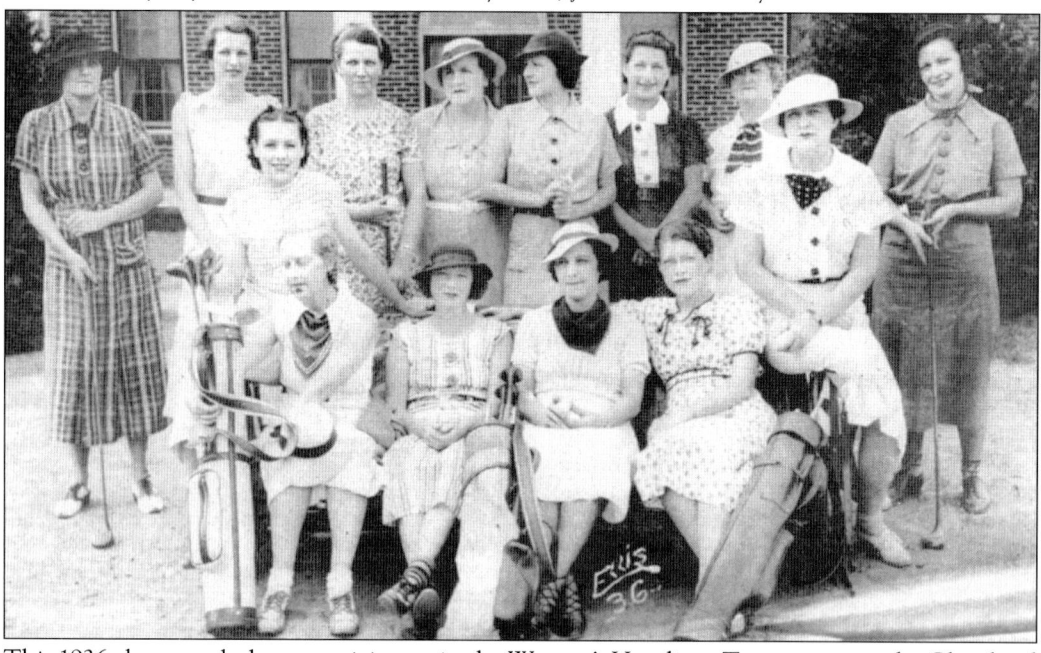

This 1936 photograph shows participants in the Women's Handicap Tournament at the Cleveland Springs County Club. Note the golf attire of 70 years ago. The ladies are, from left to right, (first row) Mrs. Spurgeon Hewitt (sitting on the left arm), Mrs. Clyde Short, Mrs. Sam Schenck, Mrs. J. J. Owens, Mrs. B. B. Matthews, and Mrs. Dick Brabble (sitting on the right arm); (second row) Mrs. Claude Mabry, Mrs. Whitelaw Kendall, Mrs. M. E. Olsby, Mrs. Frank Hoey, Mrs. Jean Schenck, Mrs. Harry Cohen, Mrs. Ward Arey, and Mrs. Hal Schenck.

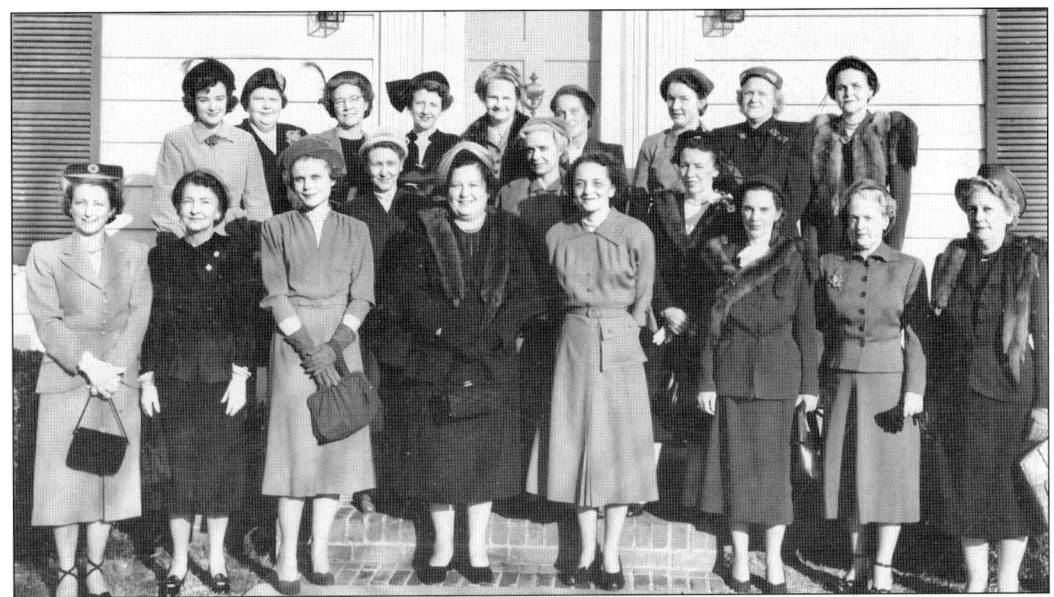

A leading women's book club around 1950 includes many women seen in the top photograph. The group includes Mary Adelaide Austell, Minnie Eddins Carpenter, Rosalind Gilliatt, Bea Suttle, and Graham School principal Ruby T. Hudson (dark dress front row right). (Uptown Shelby Association.)

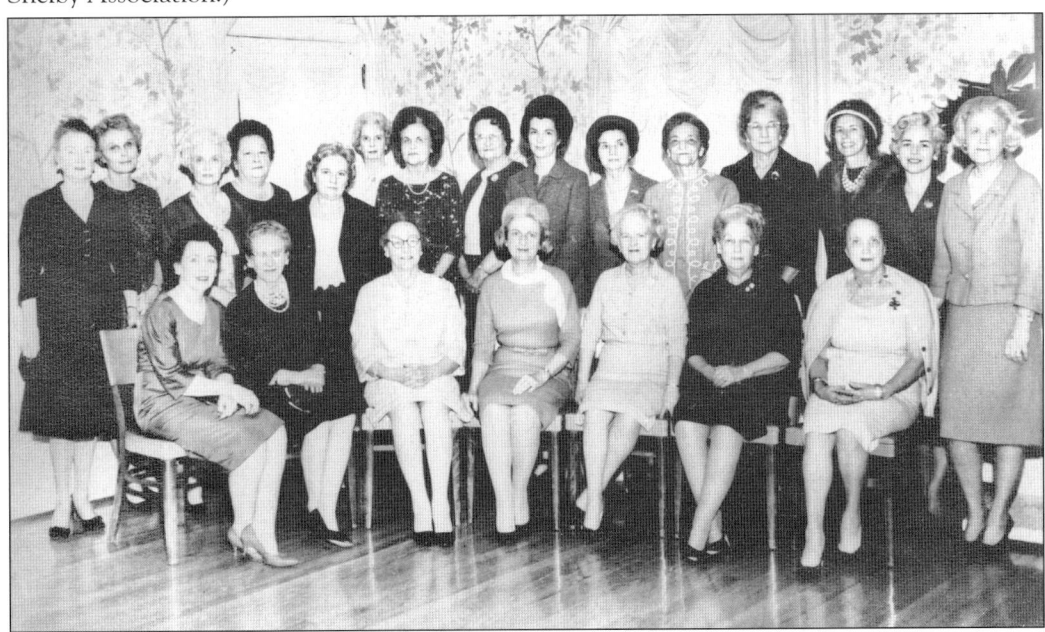

This 1966 photograph shows many of the social leaders in Shelby attending the 40th anniversary tea of the Contemporary Book Club. From left to right are (seated) Harriet Anthony, unidentified, Mrs. Walter Abernathy, Mrs. Hugh Wall, Mrs. Larry Moore, Mrs. Harry Hudson, and Mrs. Harry Woodson; (standing) Mrs. Everett Houser, Mrs. George Blanton Jr., Mrs. Casey Morris, Mrs. Shem Blackley, Mrs. Dwight Bridges, unidentified, Mrs. Charles Austell, Mrs. Cecil Gilliatt, Mrs. Edgar Hamilton, Mrs. Clyde Hoey, Mrs. Charles Hoey, Mrs. Mildred Hord, Mrs. Nita Burns, Mrs. Dick Ferchaud, and Mrs. George Carpenter. (Uptown Shelby Association.)

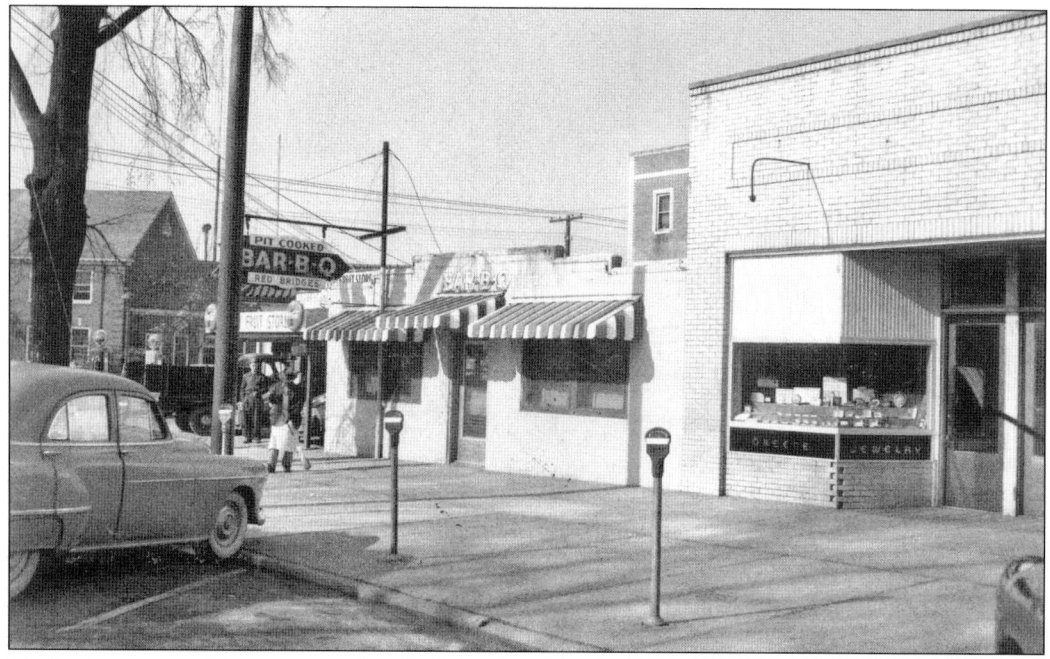
Only those over 50 can remember Red Bridges Bar-B-Q on South Washington Street. Red Bridges started in business on Highway 18 North and ultimately built Bridges Barbecue Lodge on Highway 74 East, but in the early 1950s, he had this small restaurant in uptown Shelby. (Lloyd Hamrick Collection.)

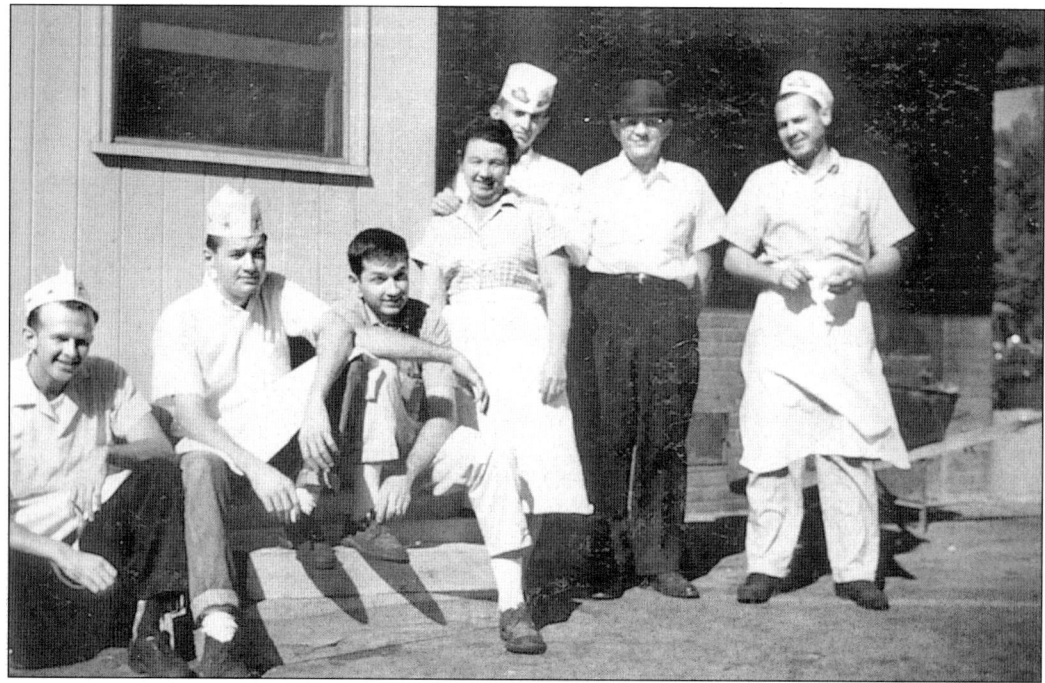
Across town on Grover Street is the cooking crew of Alston Bridges Barbecue. From left to right are Howard Granger, Don Bridges, Milton Bridges, Mabel Bridges, Kent Bridges, Alston Bridges, and Bob Bridges in this c. 1960 image. (Reid Bridges.)

Across from the Shelby Fire Department on East Graham Street was the Shelby Hotel. This three-story hotel was for decades one of Shelby's two uptown hotels. A restaurant was open in the hotel.

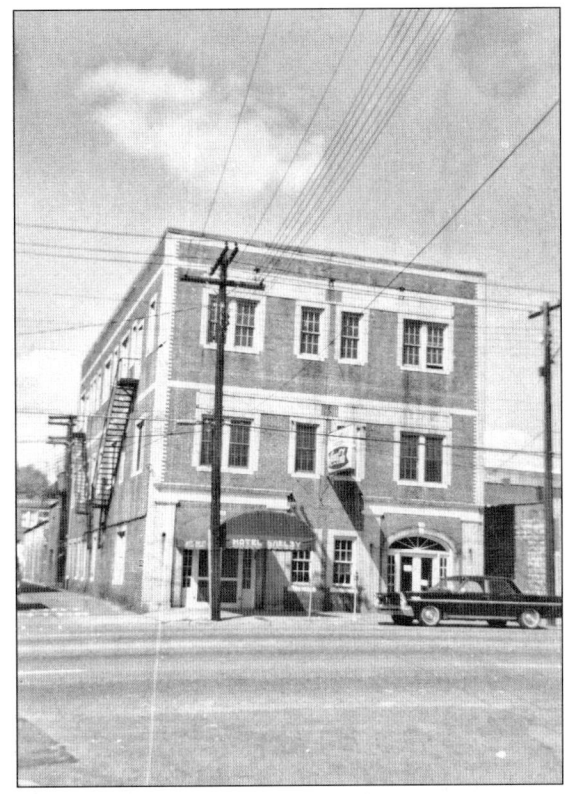

The Weathers family owned the *Star* 1911. Lee B. Weathers purchased it and owned it until it was sold in the 1980s. This building on East Warren Street was the home of the newspaper for years. In the 1950s, the *Shelby Daily Star* was published six afternoons each week. (*Shelby Daily Star 75th Anniversary Special*.)

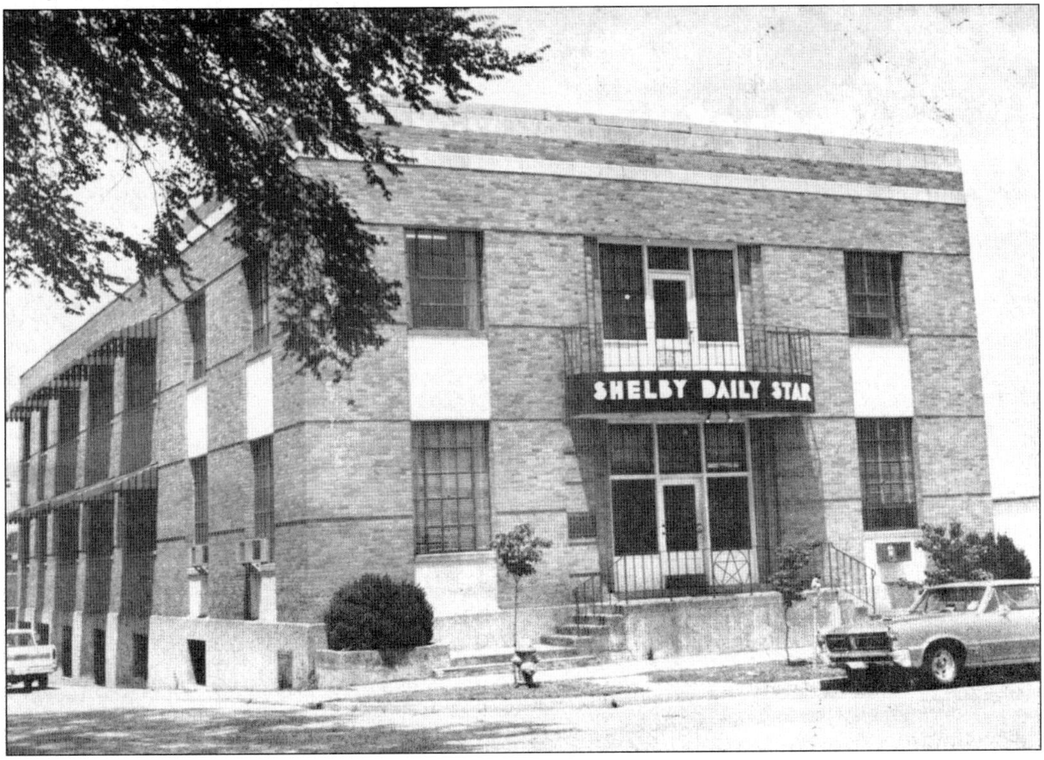

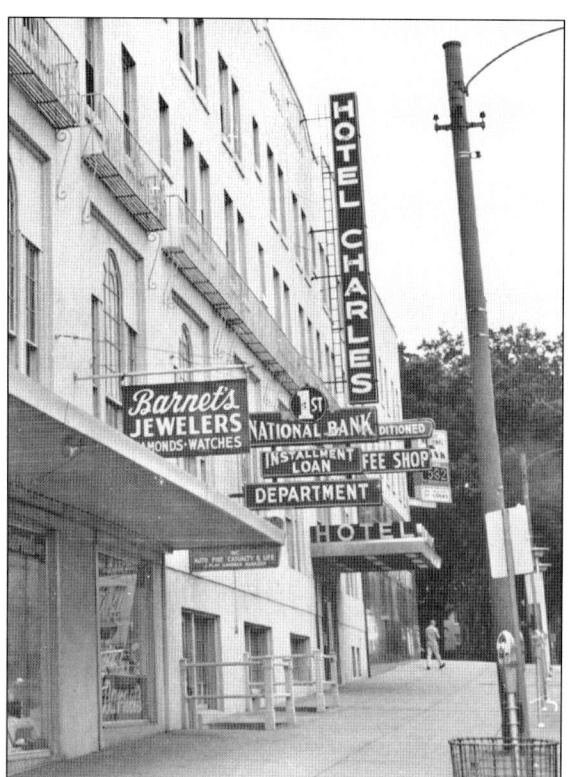

Looking from West Warren Street to the courthouse square, one can see the various businesses located in the First National Bank Building. The Hotel Charles was still open at this point.

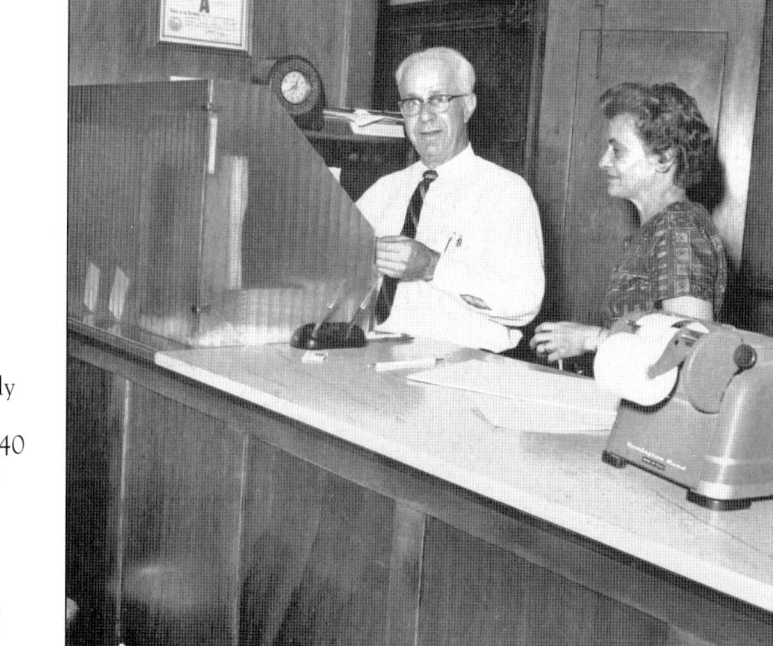

The desk of the Hotel Charles provided friendly service to guests. The hotel was open for over 40 years. After the Central Hotel was damaged by fire in 1928, it was remodeled and named the Charles for banker Charles Blanton. (Lloyd Hamrick Collection.)

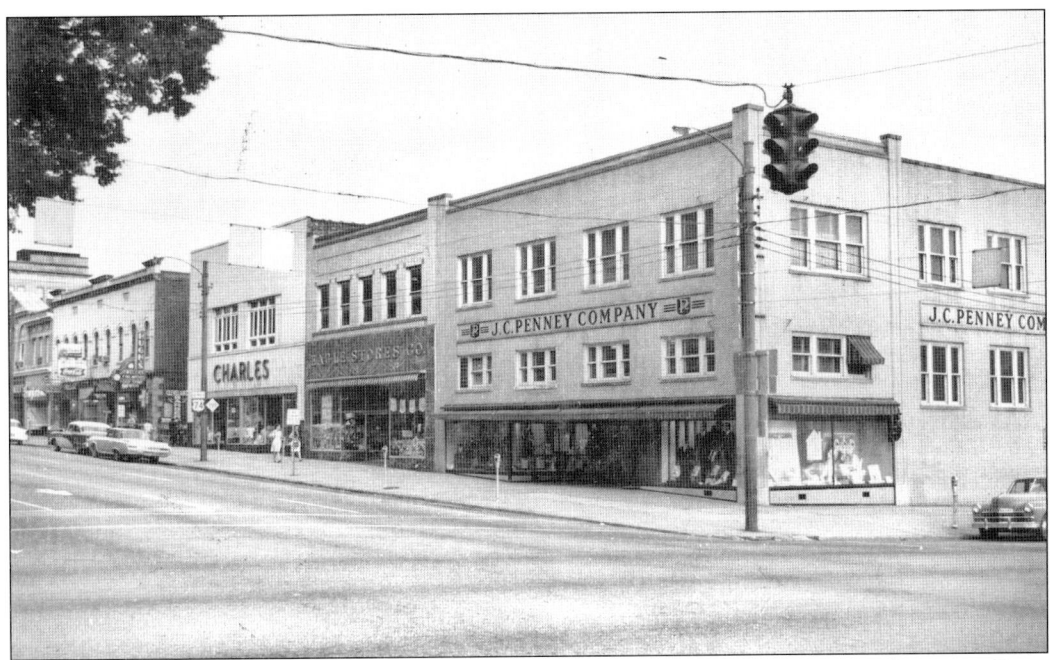

The Warren Street block south of the courthouse square is seen with the stores that were there in the post–World War II era. On the Lafayette Street corner was J. C. Penney and Company, which was a three-story department store. In the middle was Eagles 5-10-and-25¢ store. Beside Eagles was the Charles Department Store.

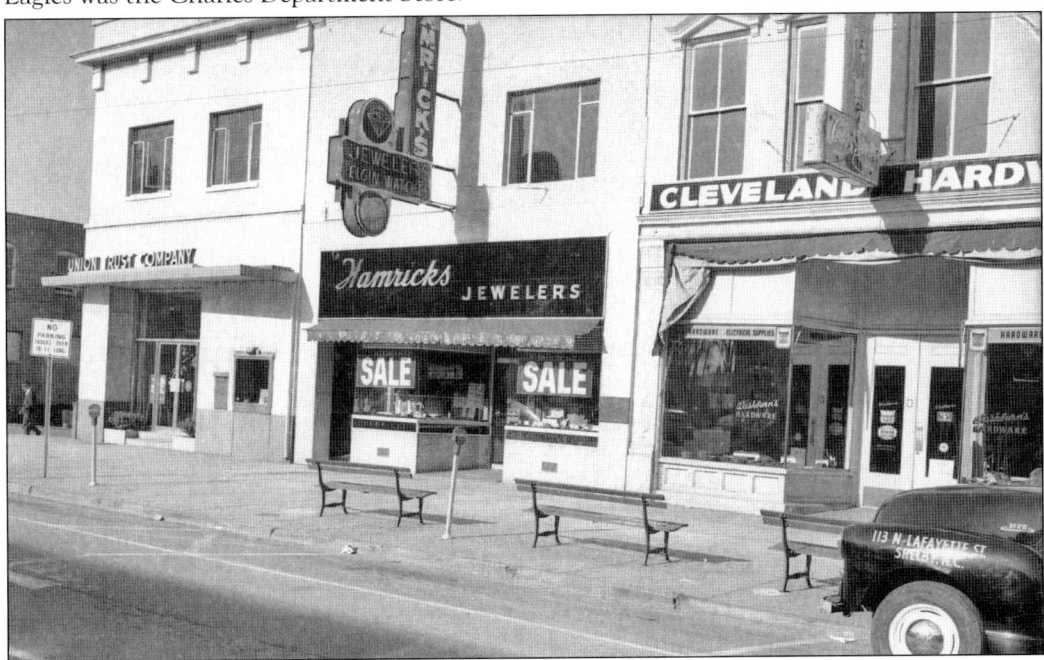

Three longtime businesses can be seen in this picture of North Lafayette Street. On the corner was the Union Trust Company, which was one of Shelby's two banks. Hamricks Jewelers' history went back to pre–World War I. Finally, Washburn's Cleveland Hardware provided hardware, paint, and sporting equipment. (Lloyd Hamrick Collection.)

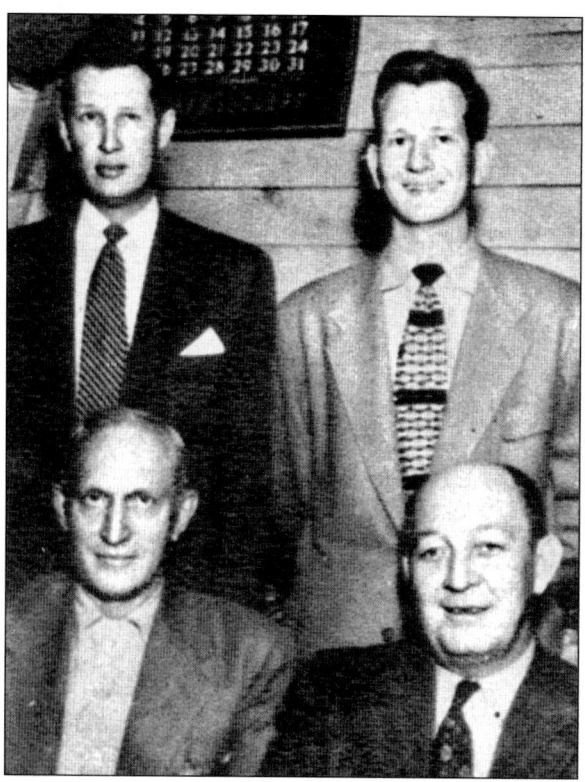

Morgan and Company, Inc., was a well-known local business. It advertised itself as a dealer in wholesale and retail feed seeds, insecticides, and fertilizers, as well as being ginners and buyers of cottonseed. The company was organized by O. Z. Morgan in 1935. Pictured are, from left to right, (seated) O. Z. Morgan and Oscar Evans; (standing) Robert and Jack Morgan.

In a 1950s parade on West Marion Street, the Morgan and Company truck carries a large group of children. The building next to Washburn's Hardware was the Union Trust Company. The large sign on top of the building was an advertisement for 7-Up.

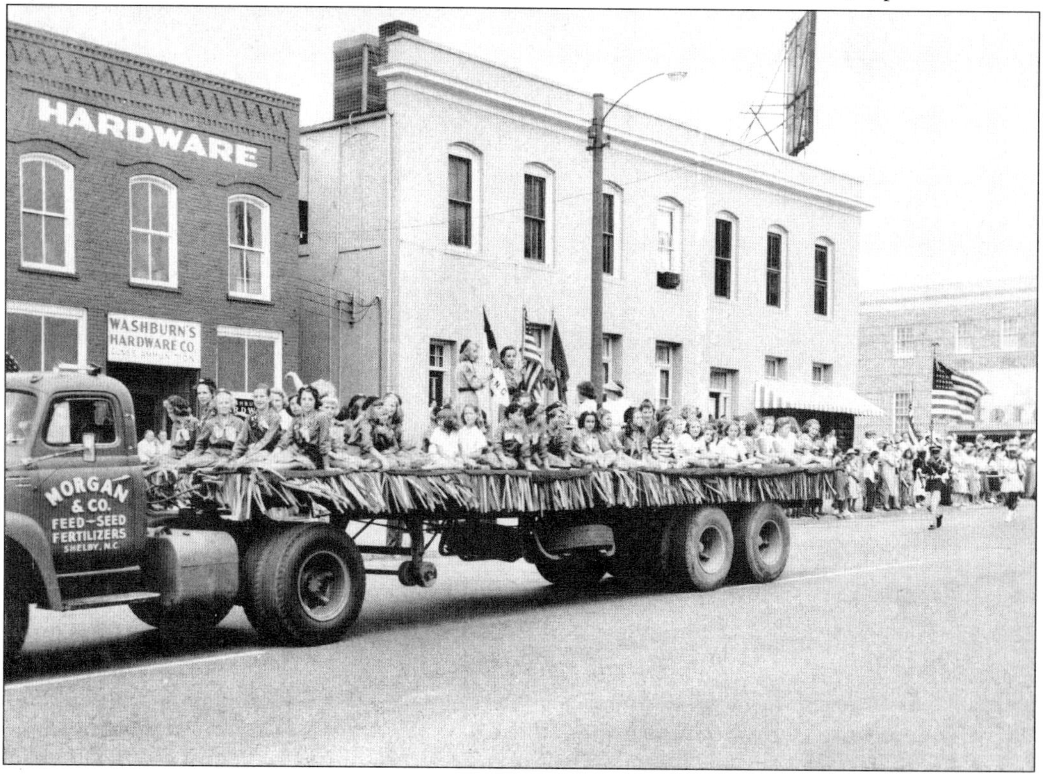

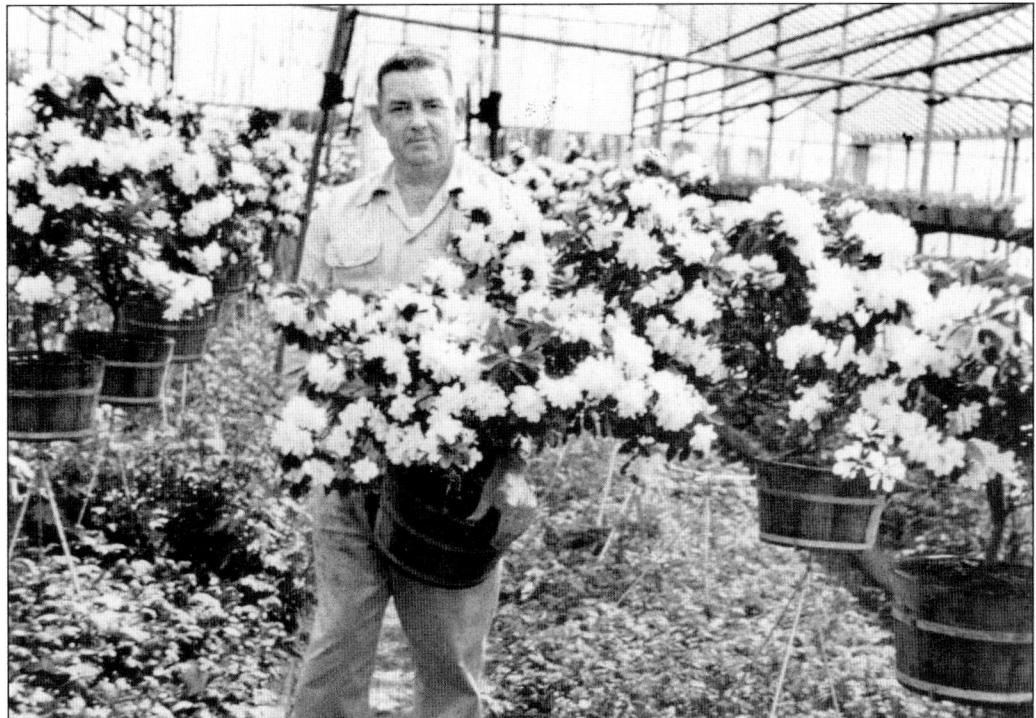

U. L. and Edna Patterson opened Patterson's Flowers in 1929. The business grew to become the largest commercial flower-growing operation in the Southeast, supplying over 500 florists in five states in the South with flowering plants and cut flowers. U. L. is seen in a greenhouse filled with azaleas ready for sale.

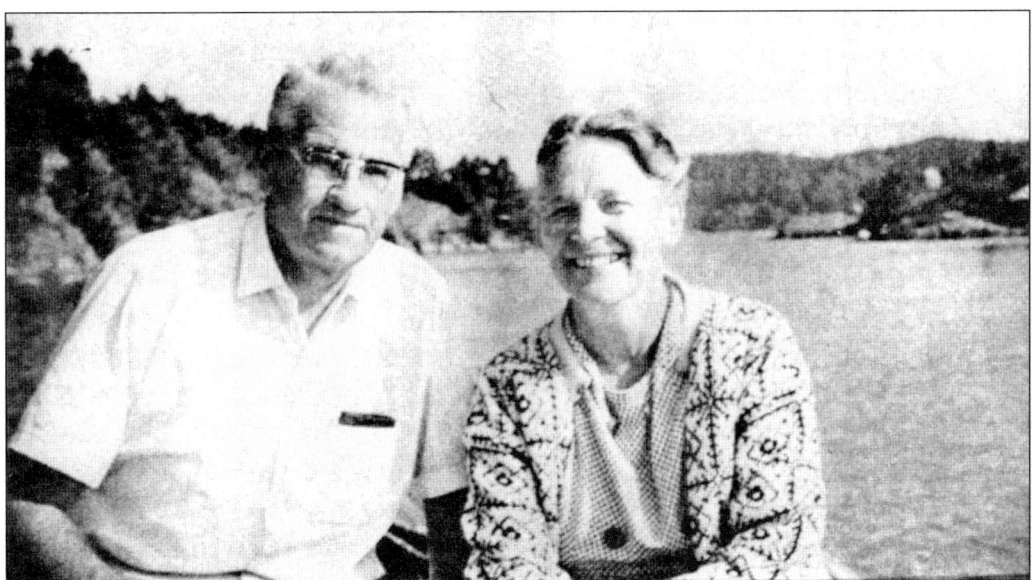

Sigvart and Solveig Jorgensen moved to the United States from Norway during the Second World War. Sigvart was head grower at Patterson's Flowers for over 40 years. Speaking five languages, Sigvart was recognized internationally as a leading horticulturist.

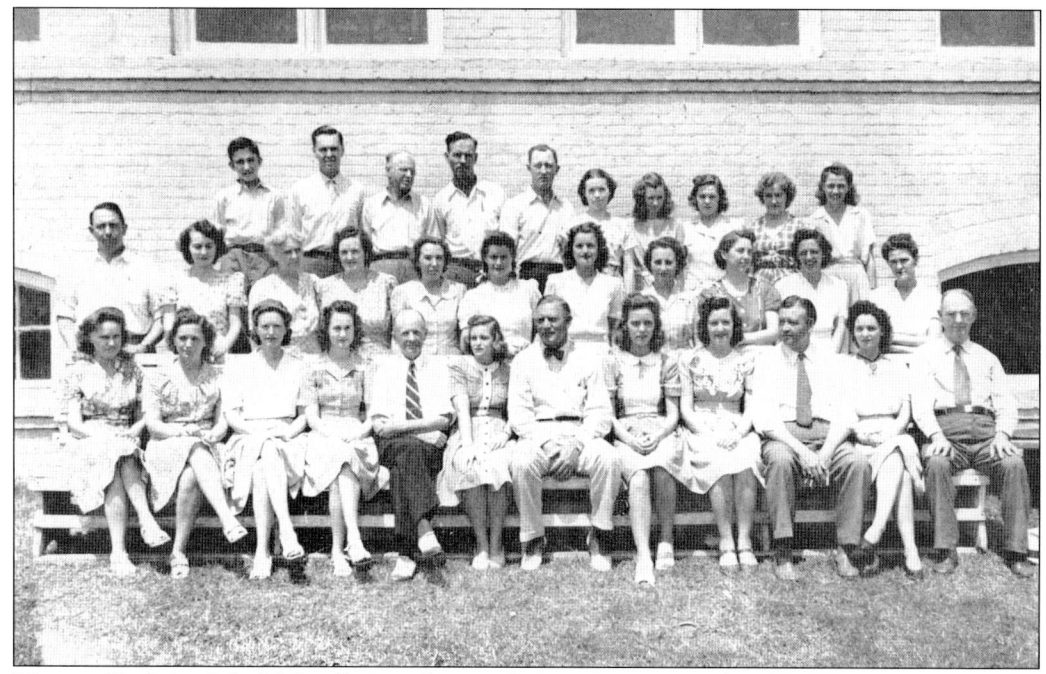
The staff of the Lily Mill office and store department poses for this c. 1940 photograph. (Tommy Forney.)

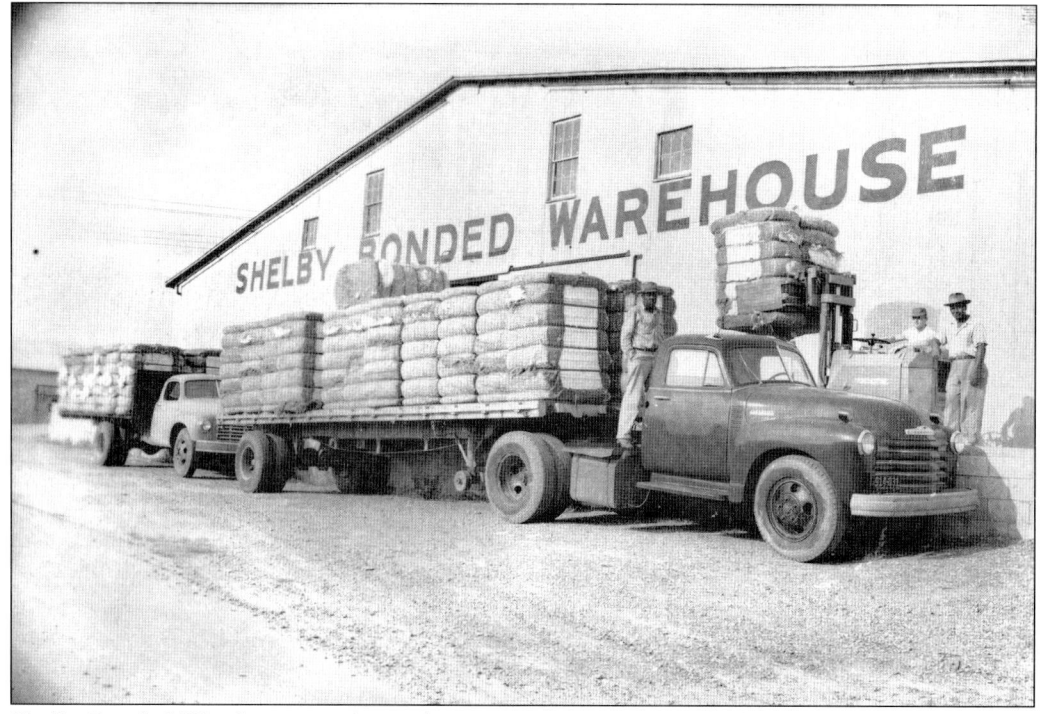
Shelby Bonded Warehouse was located on East Marion Street. The business was run by Johnny and Virginia Bridges and later by their son, Charles.

The late 1950s brought economic change to Cleveland County. Pittsburgh Plate Glass built a fiberglass plant west of Shelby. Local school students were able to ride "The Fiberglass Flyer," a special Southern Railway train, to visit the new plant. (Judith Parker-Procter.)

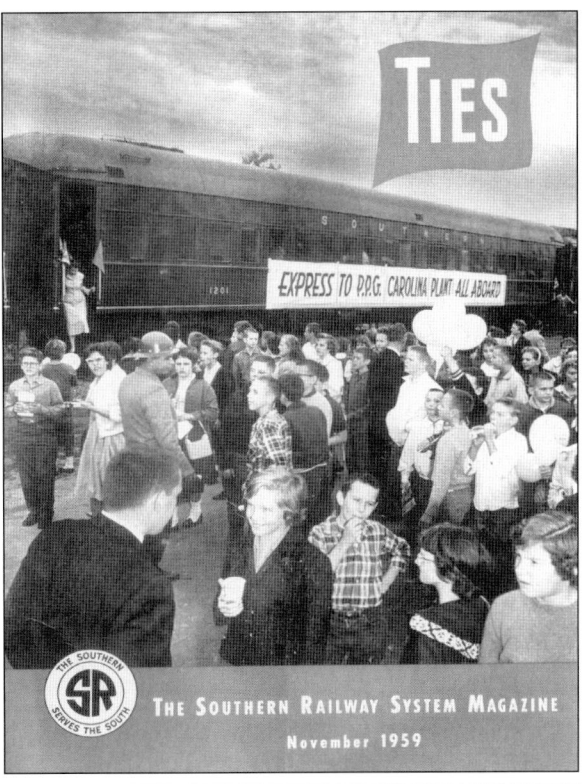

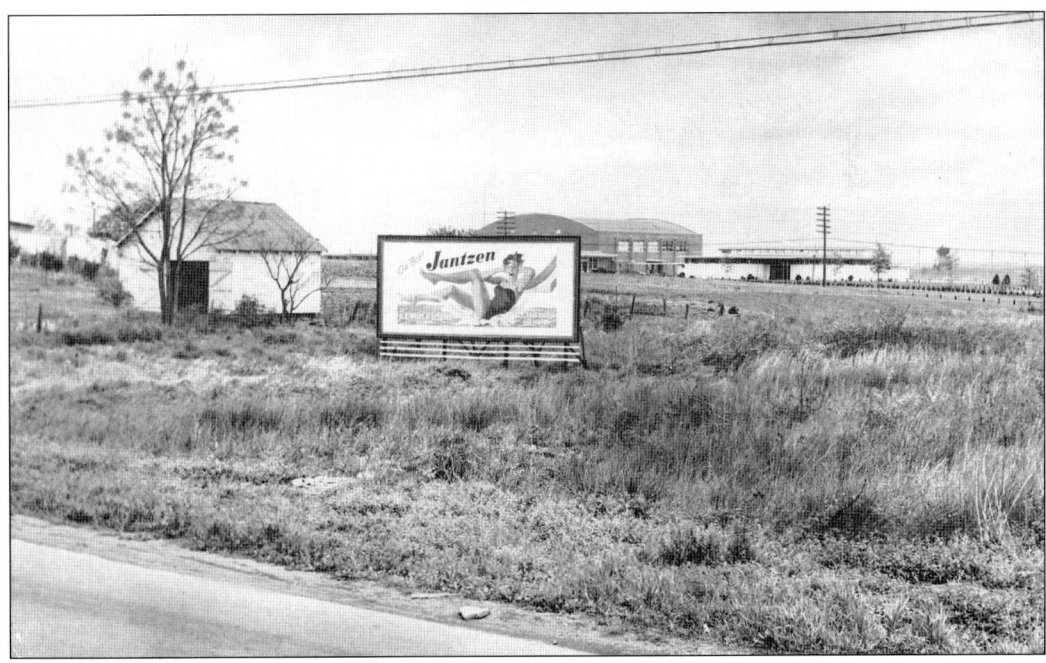

The 1950s brought recreation on a large scale with the Shelby Community Center (usually called the city park). Citizens were offered golf, bowling, basketball, tennis, swimming, baseball fields, a train, and a merry-go-round. The new park is seen from West Marion Street with part of the buildings blocked by an A. V. Wray billboard. (Stough Wray Jr.)

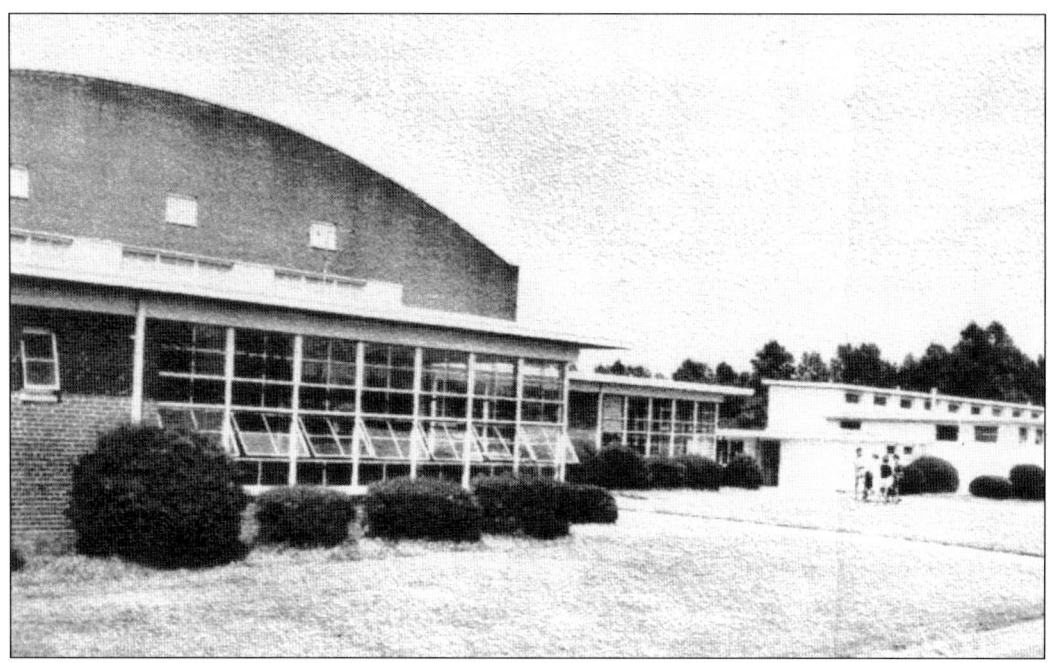
The main building of the new community center had no air conditioning when it opened. Teens in Shelby in the 1950s and 1960s will remember attending dances at the center and sitting by the open windows for a cool breeze. The white building was the office and dressing rooms for the new pool.

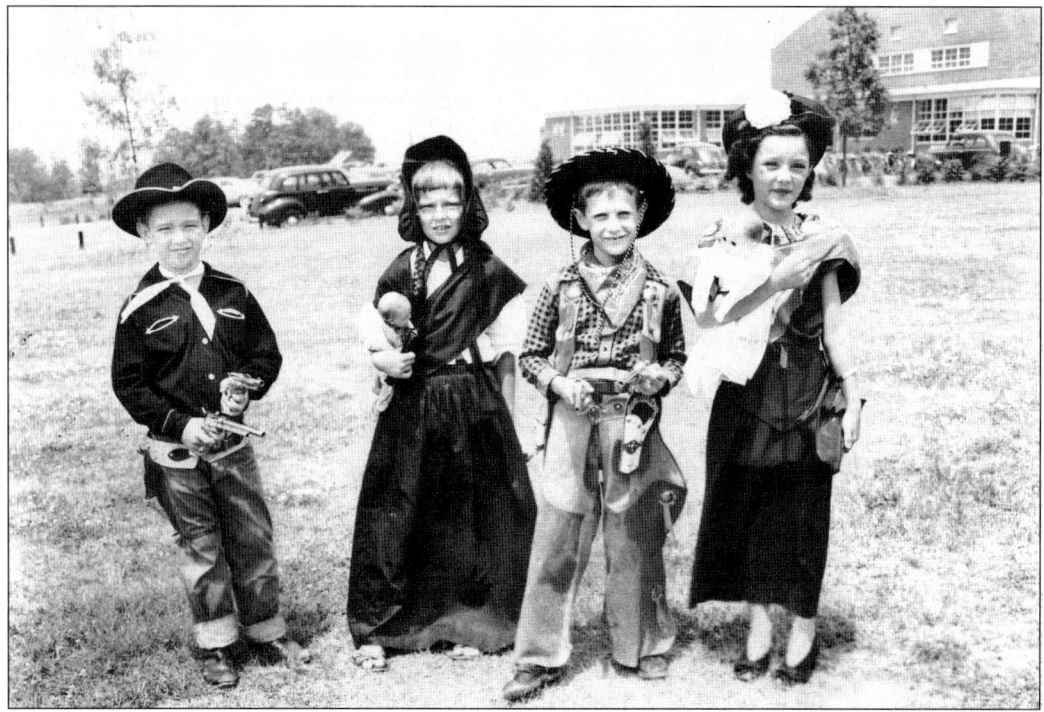
The quiz for this book is to identify these four youngsters who were specially dressed for some event at the new community center. Maybe a reader is pictured.

Three
THE ALL-AMERICA CITY

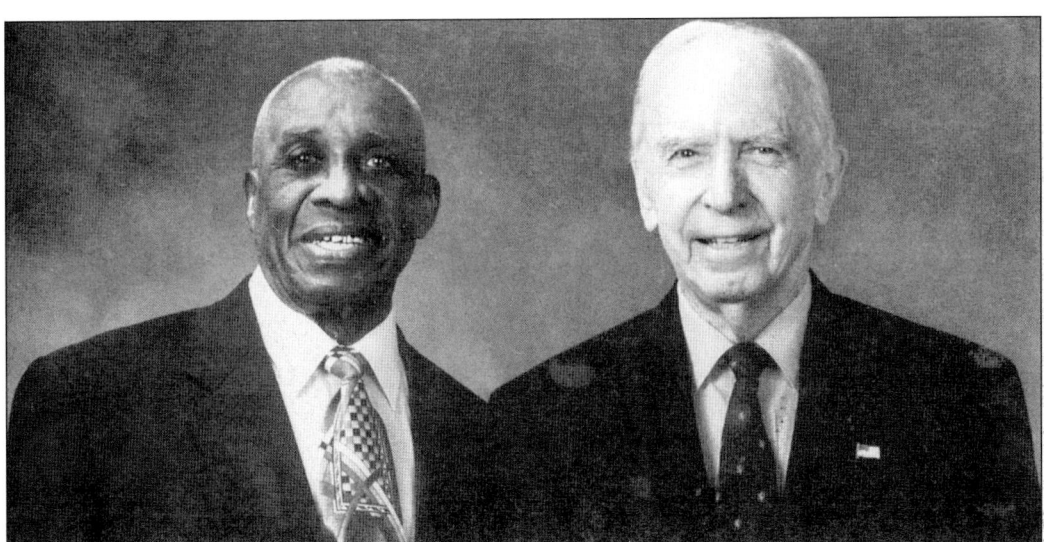

This picture is significant, for it recognizes the end of a segregated society. Lester D. Roark (right) became mayor in 1976 and recommended the Reverend Samuel Raper to fill his seat on the town council from Ward One. In 1998, Samuel Raper and Lester Roark became the first black man and white man to be cofounders of a public trust for their city. The Raper-Roark Trust Fund can be spent for appearance and beautification projects. (*The Heritage of Cleveland County*.)

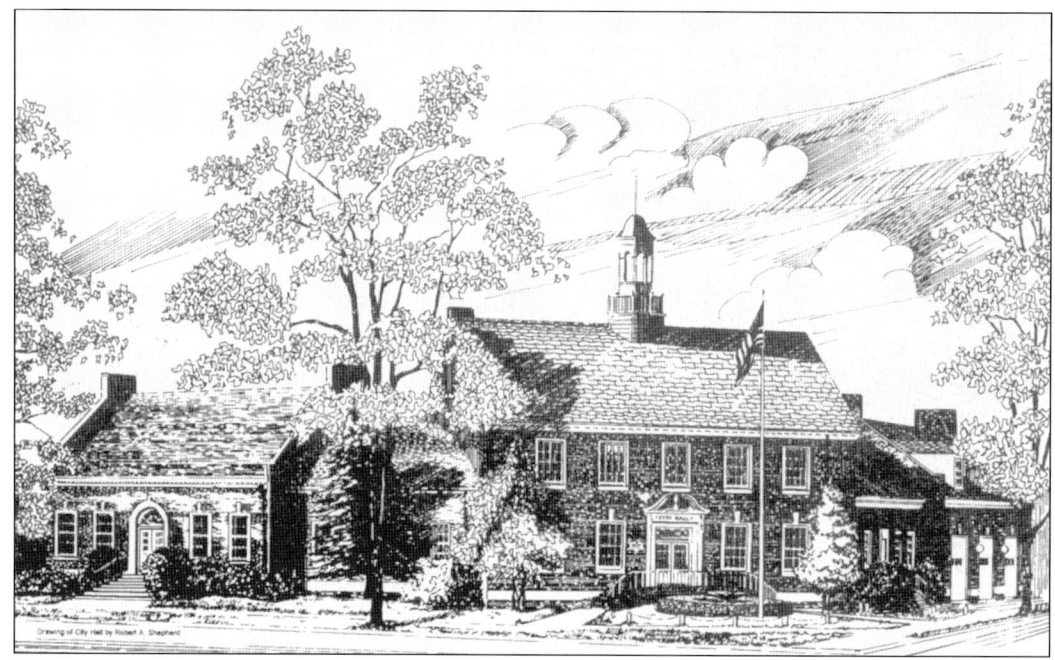

This drawing of the Shelby City Hall by architect Roger Holland shows a New Deal–era structure that has been used for over 70 years as the headquarters of Shelby's city government. At one point, the Shelby Public Library occupied the left wing of the building, and the right wing was the home of the Shelby Police and Fire Departments.

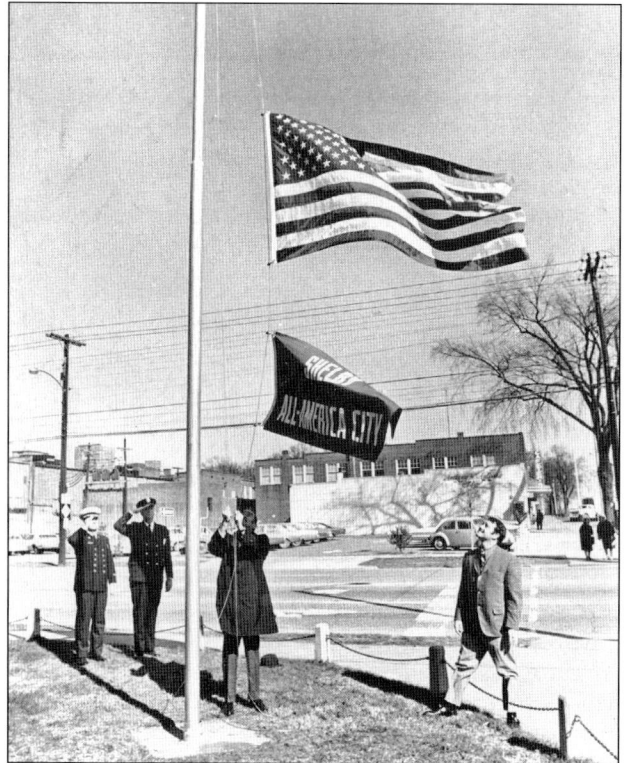

Local citizens worked hard to bring to Shelby the distinction of being an All-America City. In this photograph, the All-America City flag is raised in front of the city all by Mayor Hubert Plaster as, from left to right, fire chief Glenn Barrett, police chief Barry Lee, and All-America City volunteer Jim Toole look on. (Brendan Camp LeGrand.)

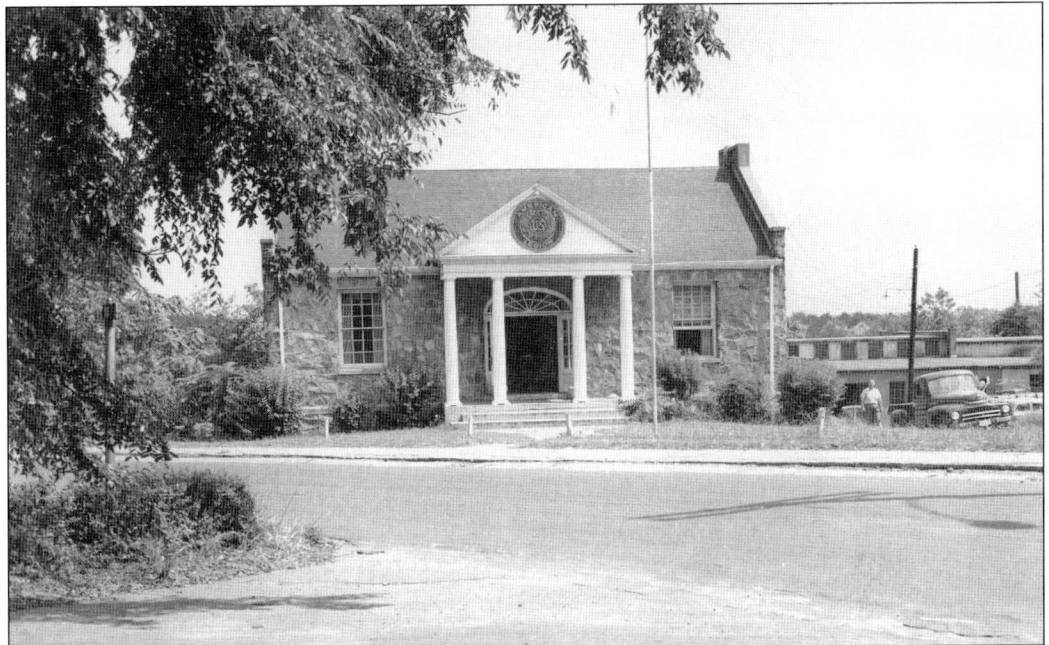

This building stood where the current Cleveland County Justice Center is located. In this picture, it is the American Legion headquarters, but it served various purposes over the years. The photograph was taken by Floyd Willis, who took thousand of pictures of the people and places in Shelby. His images are a great source of local history.

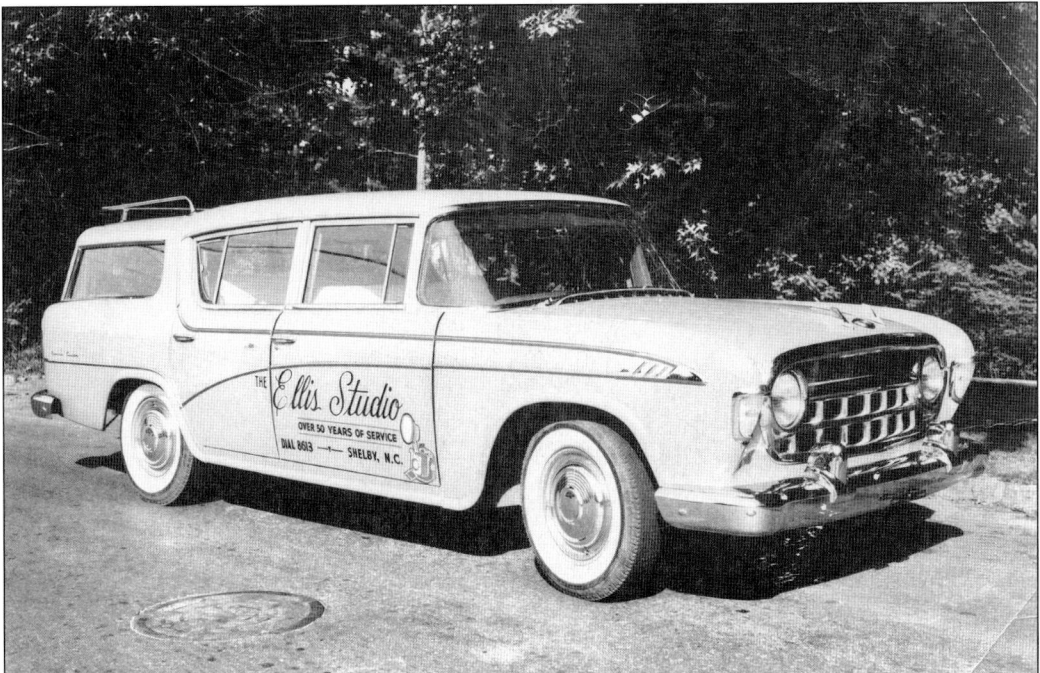

The 1960s brought the Rambler from George Romney's American Motors. This one, as the sign says, was the vehicle for Ellis Studio, which served Shelby for over 50 years. Willis and Ellis were prime recorders of the history of Shelby on film.

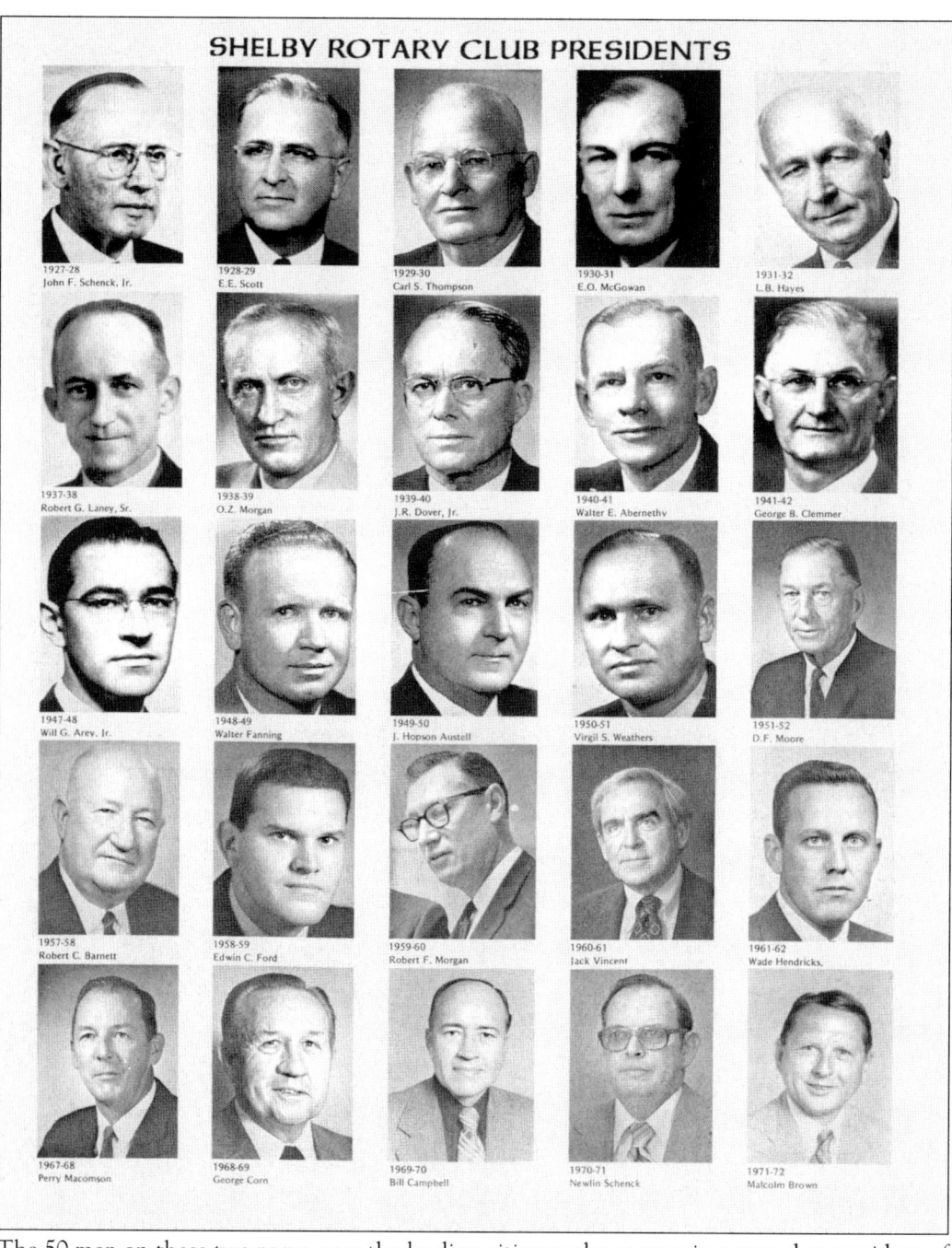

The 50 men on these two pages were the leading citizens who at one time served as president of the Shelby Rotary Club from 1927 through 1977.

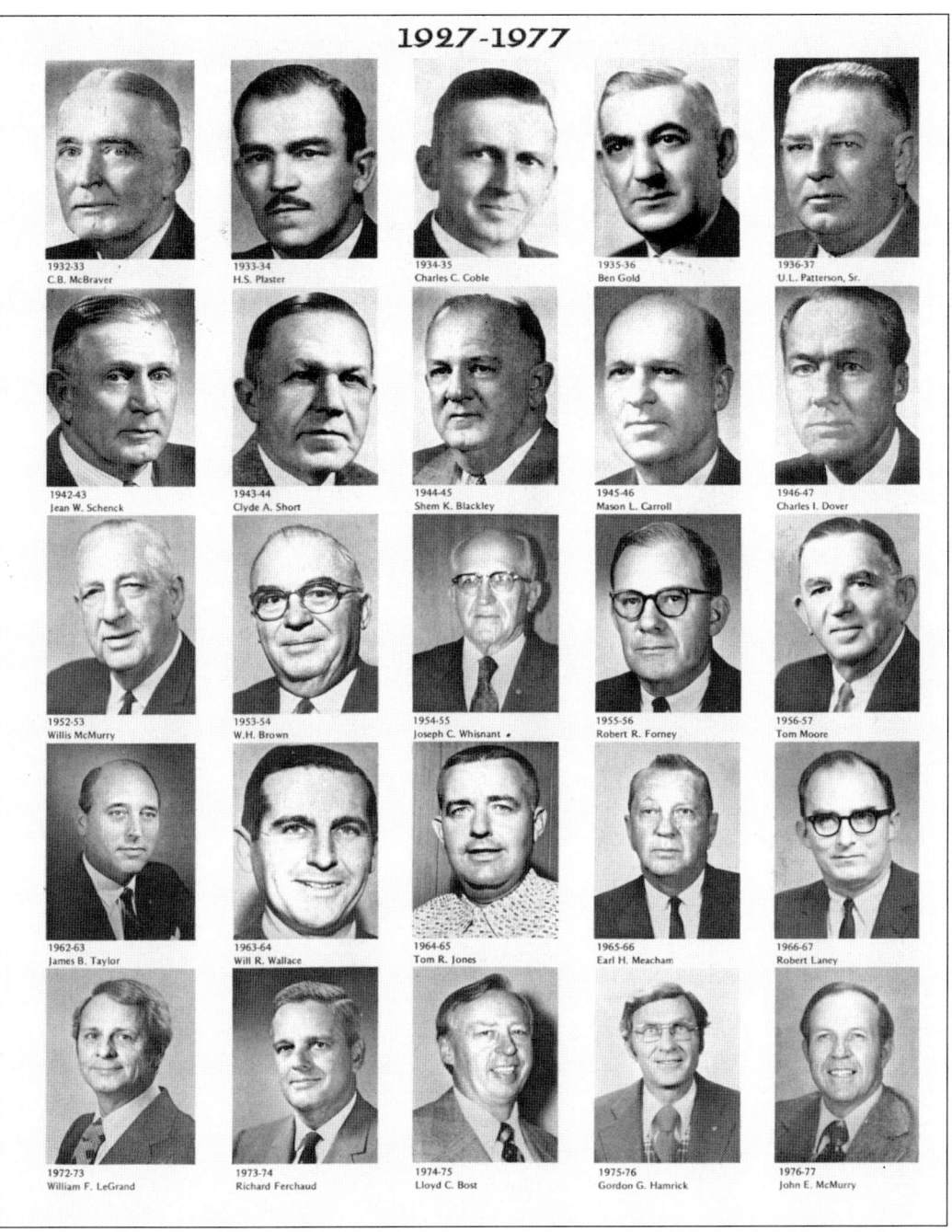

The Shelby Rotary Club is recognized as the leading civic club in the city, with over 150 members.

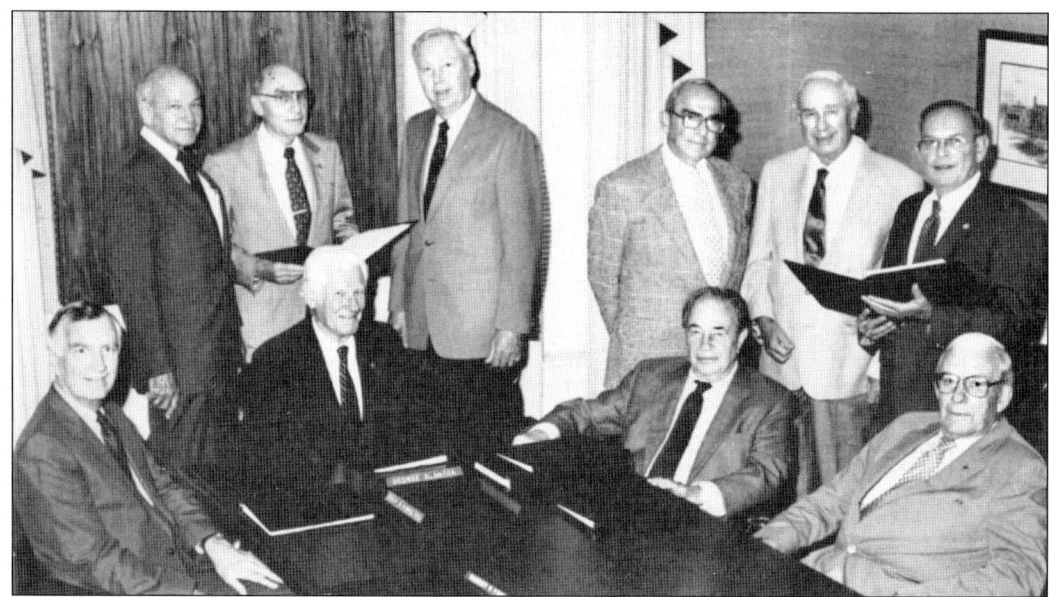

Shelby's "Hometown Bank" since 1874 has occupied the same corner location for over 130 years. The photograph of the board shows a number of local business leaders. From left to right are (seated) Edgar B. Hamilton (president and chief executive officer), George Blanton Jr., (chairman of the board), William E. Pearce (senior vice president), and Robert Forney (board member); (standing) board members R. T. LeGrand Jr., C. Rush Hamrick Jr., Lloyd C. Bost, G. J. Vincent, Henry L. Weathers, and Newlin P. Schenck. (First National Bank.)

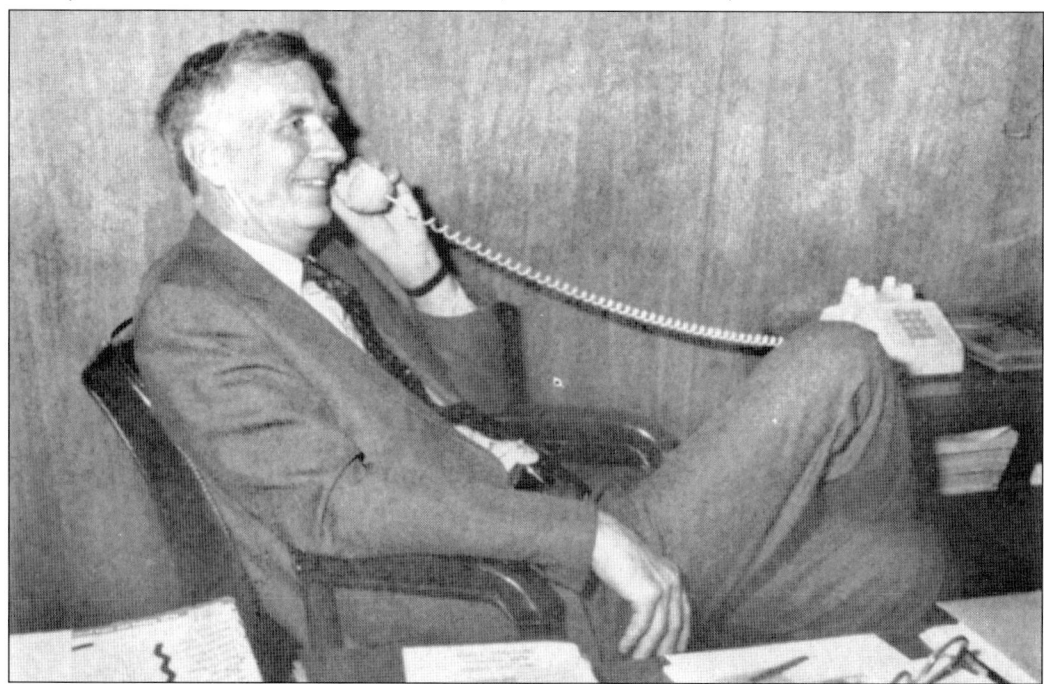

Edgar Blanton Hamilton is a descendant of Burwell Blanton, one of the three founders of First National Bank. Blanton Hamilton succeeded George Blanton Jr. as bank president. Now retired, Hamilton serves as chairman of the board of directors emeritus. (First National Bank.)

For years, Shelby's second bank was Union Trust Company (now a part of BB&T). In the 1960s, the bank opened a new headquarters at the corner of Marion and Washington Streets. This picture in the new structure shows, from left to right, Pres. Clyde Stutts, board chairman J. O. Lutz, and former president and board vice chairman Jesse Bridges.

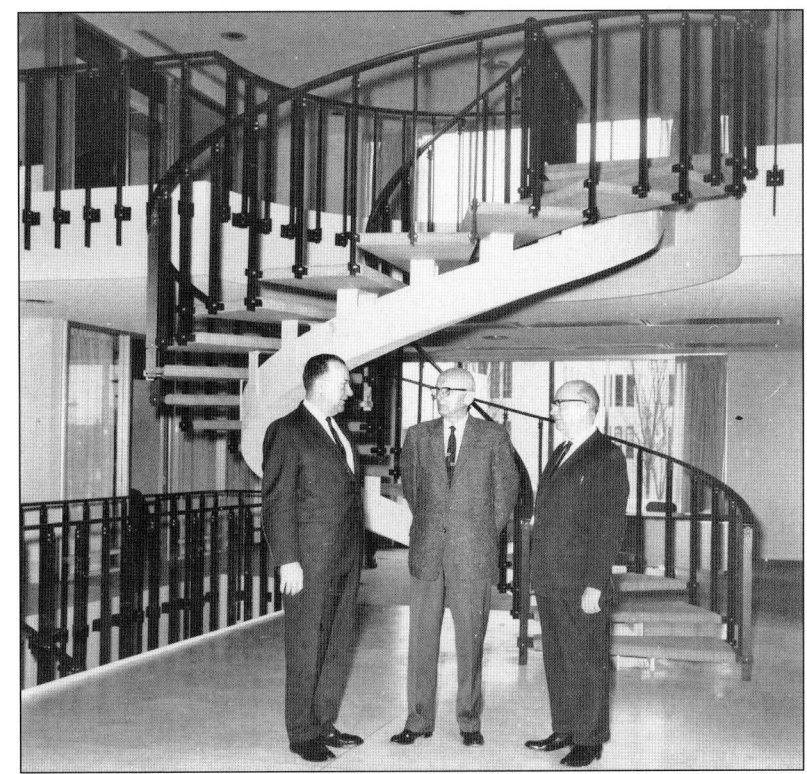

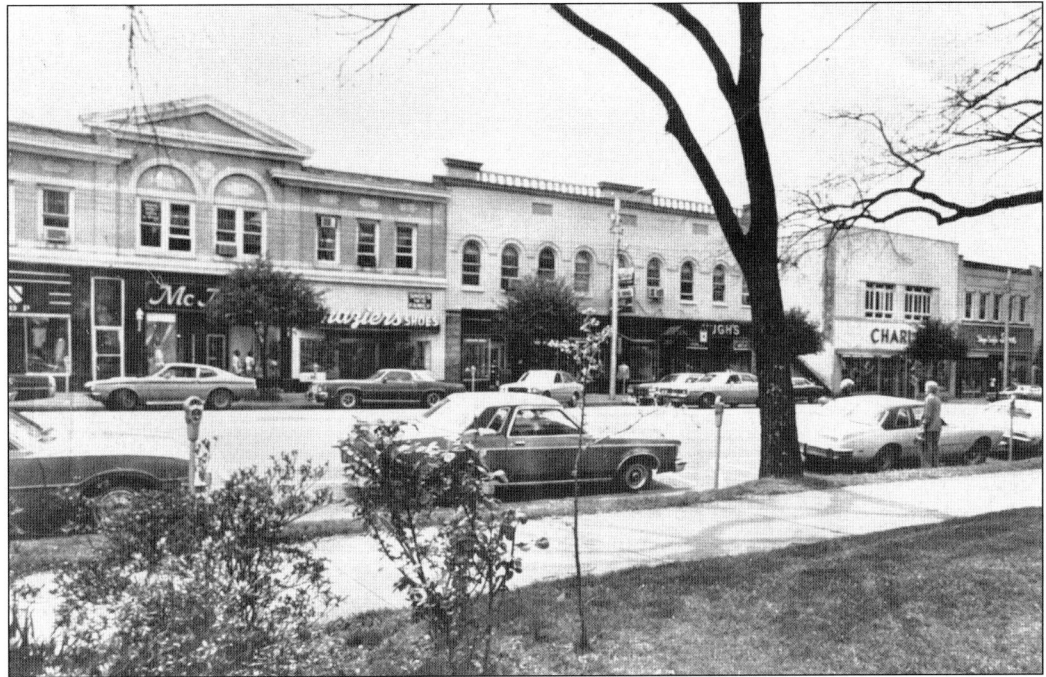

Warren Street on the south side of the square in the 1960s was a vital part of the uptown business district. Partially visible at the left (in the Royster Building) are longtime men's store Loy's Men's Shop and McNeeley's, which featured upscale women's ware.

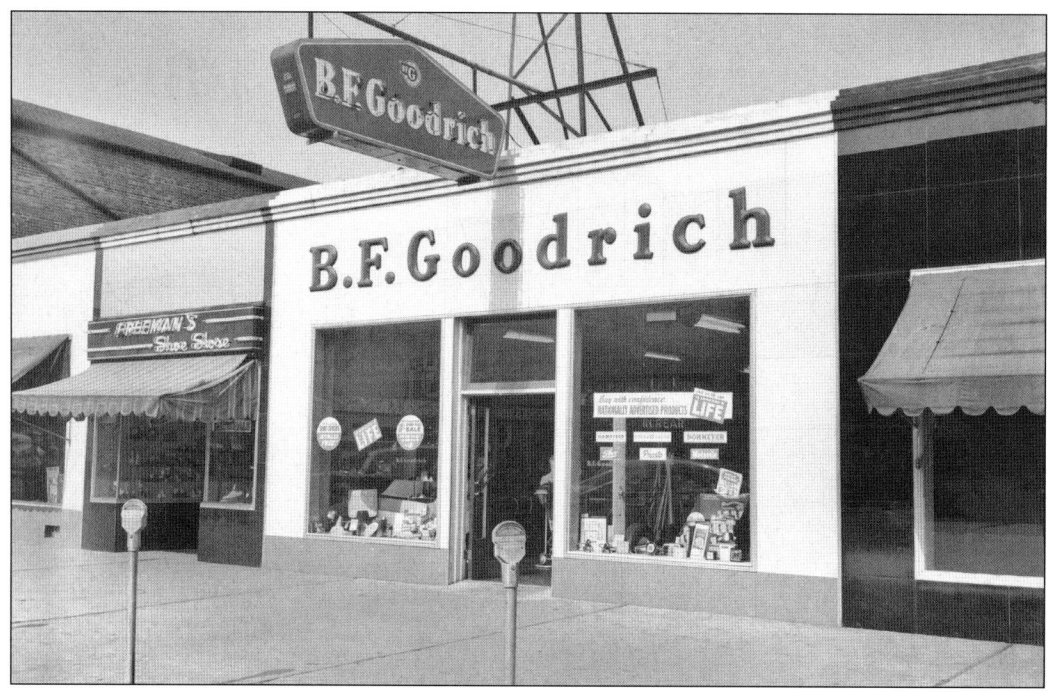

This view of South Lafayette Street across from the Belk-Stevens store shows B. F. Goodrich store and Freeman's Shoes. The black building was the Western Auto, the Shelby Newsstand, and today is a part of the Shelby Café. (Lloyd Hamrick Collection.)

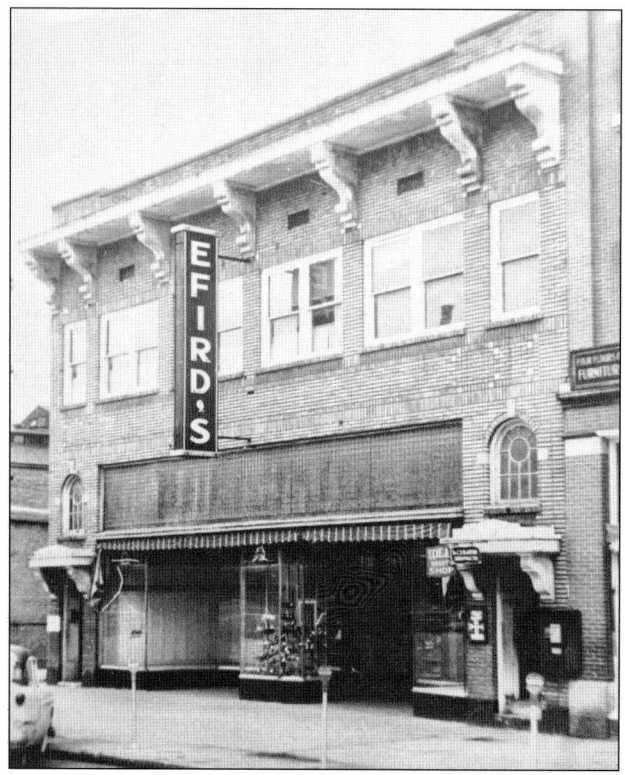

Just up the street, less than a block from the Goodrich Store, was Efird's Department Store. Efird's served Shelby shoppers during the 1940s and 1950s. (Lloyd Hamrick Collection.)

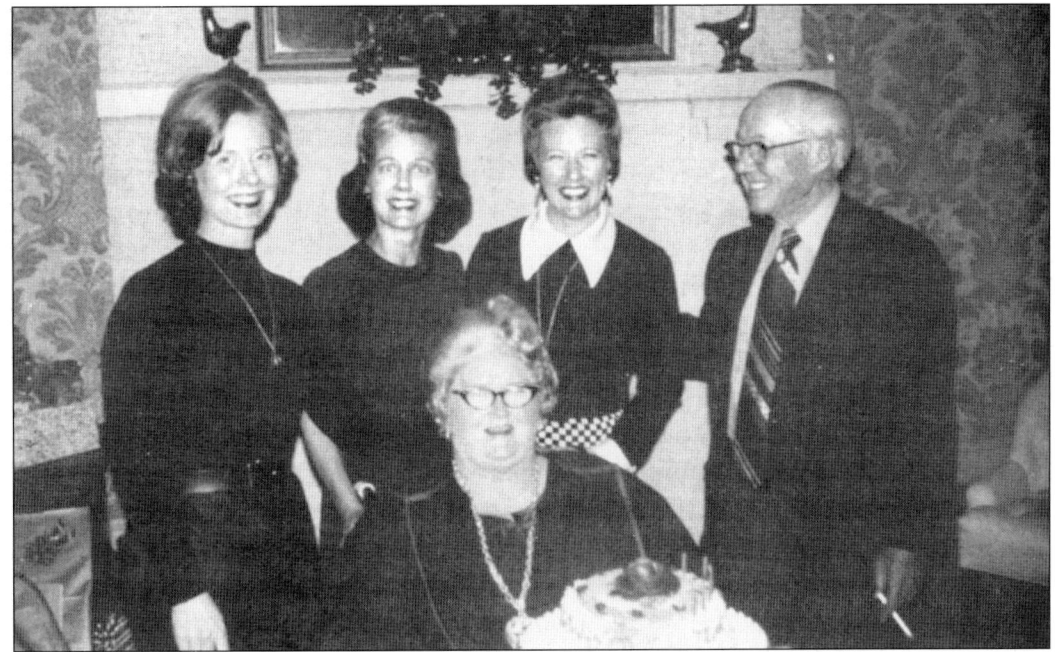

A part of 20th-century history in Shelby and Cleveland County was the Dover Textile Group, which was founded in 1907. Here the founder's son, Charles I. Dover, helps his wife, Kathleen Nolan Dover (seated), celebrate her 70th birthday. Their daughters (from left to right) Dorothy, Anne, and Kathleen look on. (*A Son Named Charles.*)

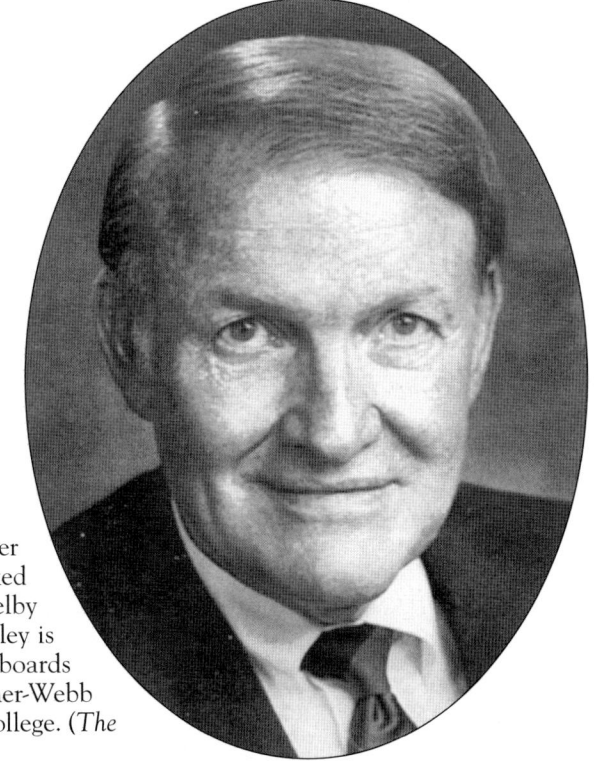

Hoyt Bailey, a son-in-law of Charles I. Dover and North Carolina State graduate, worked for J. P. Stevens before returning to Shelby in 1962 to work with Dover Textiles. Bailey is an active civic leader, having served on boards of Cleveland Memorial Hospital, Gardner-Webb University, and Cleveland Community College. (*The Heritage of Cleveland County.*)

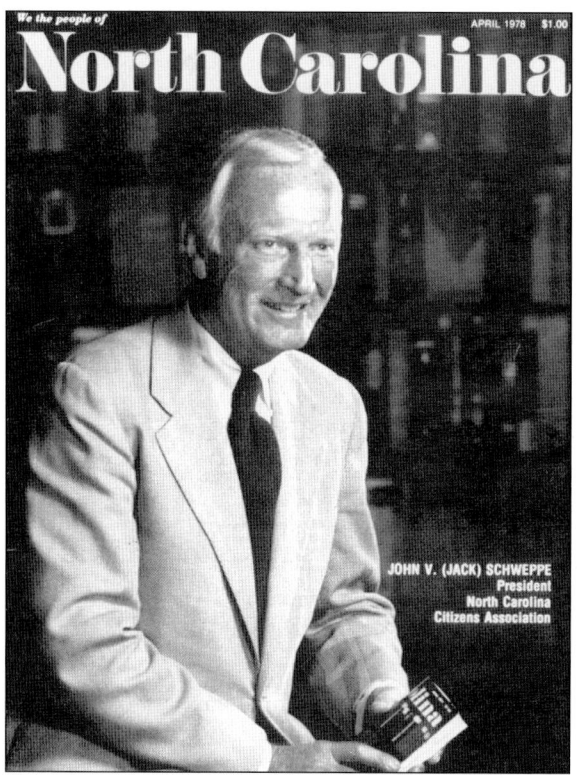

When fiberglass manufacturer Pittsburgh Plate Glass (PPG) came to Cleveland County, Jack Schweppe arrived as plant manager. He and his family became active members of the community. Here he is pictured as president of the North Carolina Citizens Association.

PPG remained a solid economic strength in the county. PPG chief executive officer Vince Sarni (center) visited the local plant. At the left is David Banks, who was the human resources manager at PPG. Local plant manager Dave Hardin is in the background. (David Banks)

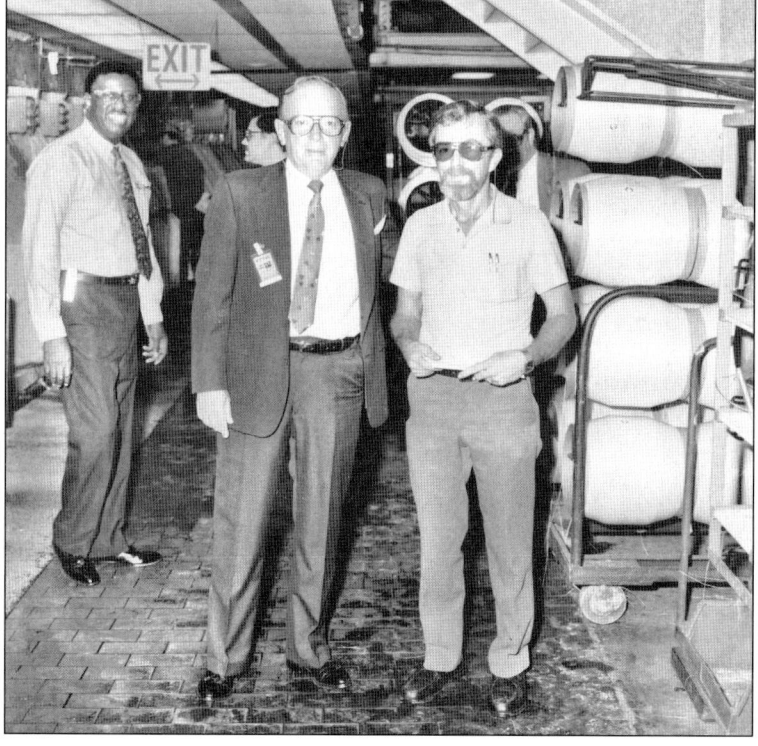

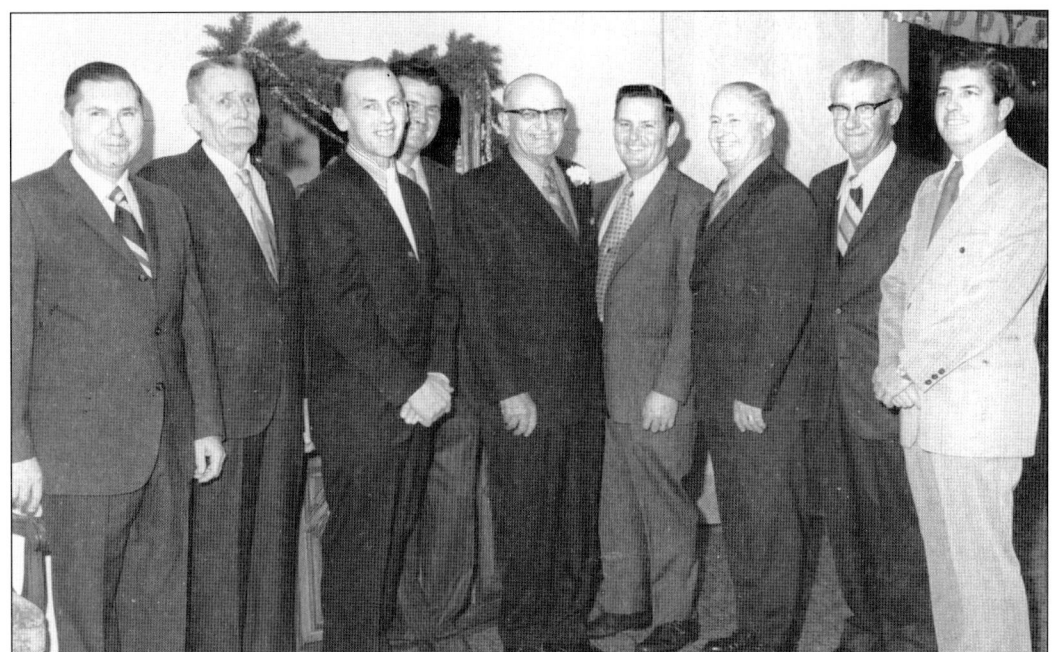

A leading local industry is Cleveland Lumber Company, located just off North Morgan Street on the Southern Railroad. Leaders of the company are pictured at a Christmas party in the early 1960s. From left to right are Wayne Hoyle, Garfield Trammel, Gene Ricker, D. L. Turner, R. J. Rucker, Jennings Brooks, Elmer Wheelus, Boyce Freeman, and Garland Johnson.

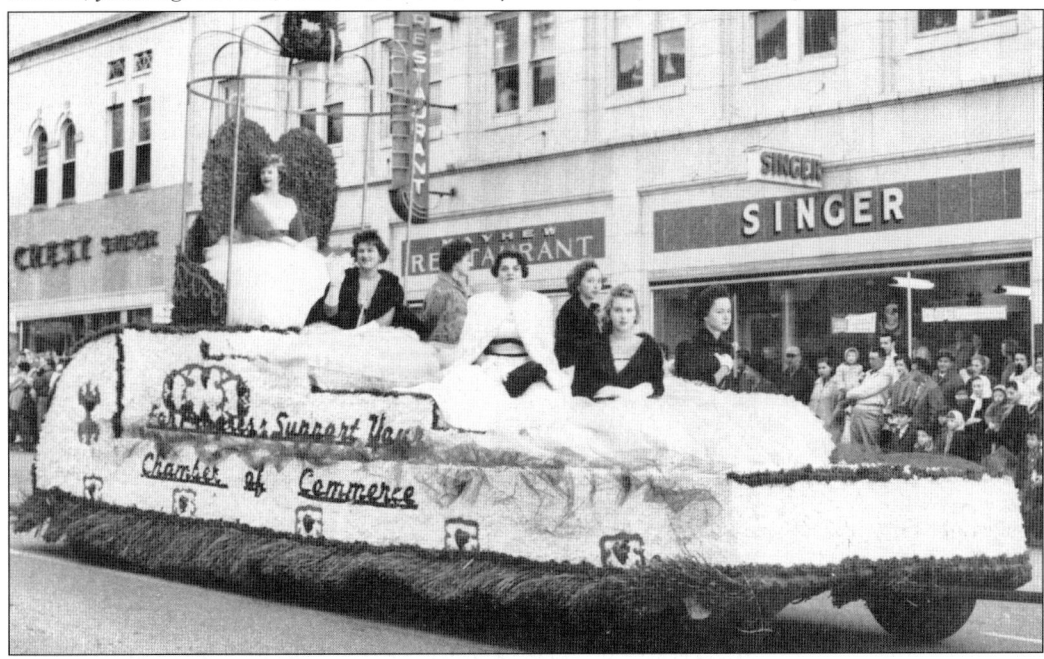

Active in promoting local business was the Shelby Chamber of Commerce (now the Cleveland County Chamber of Commerce). Behind the float is the Mayhew Restaurant, which was a leading uptown Shelby gathering place. The buildings in the background on West Warren Street were lost in the 1979 Shelby fire. (Lloyd Hamrick Collection.)

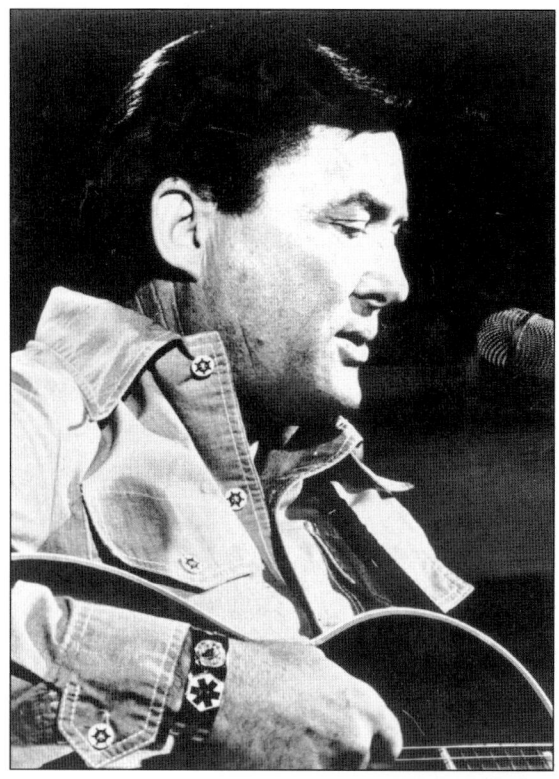

Don Gibson grew up in Shelby. After World War II, he worked for Jim and Kat Lewis at the J&K music shop before going on to Nashville and a career in country music. His country music hits included "O Lonesome Me" and "I Can't Stop Loving You," which were written in the same afternoon.

One of the most famous celebrities coming out of Cleveland County is Earl Scruggs. Scruggs grew up in the Flint Hill community near Boiling Springs and later worked and lived in Shelby. A bluegrass banjoist, Scruggs is credited with developing a unique instrumental style that helped to popularize the five-string banjo.

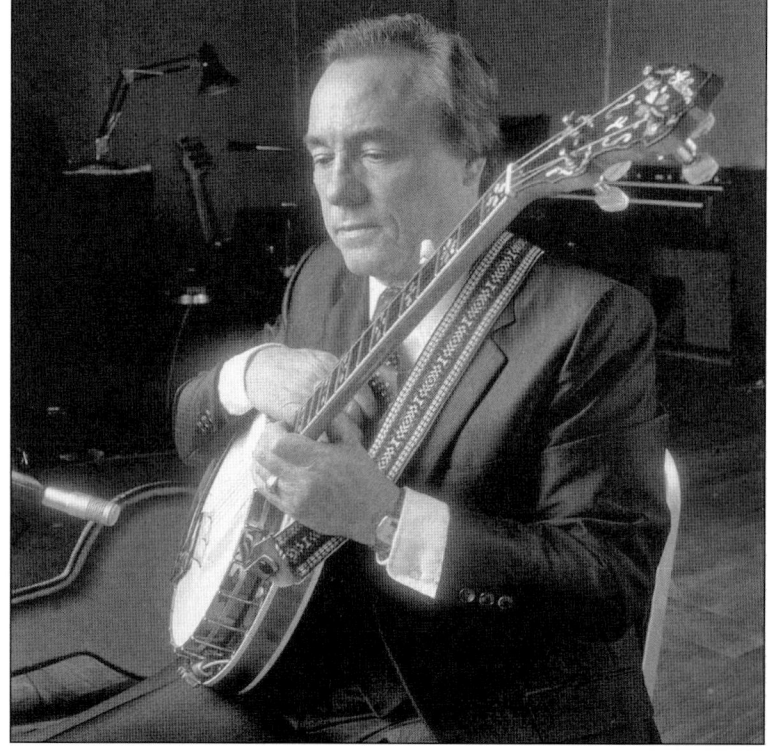

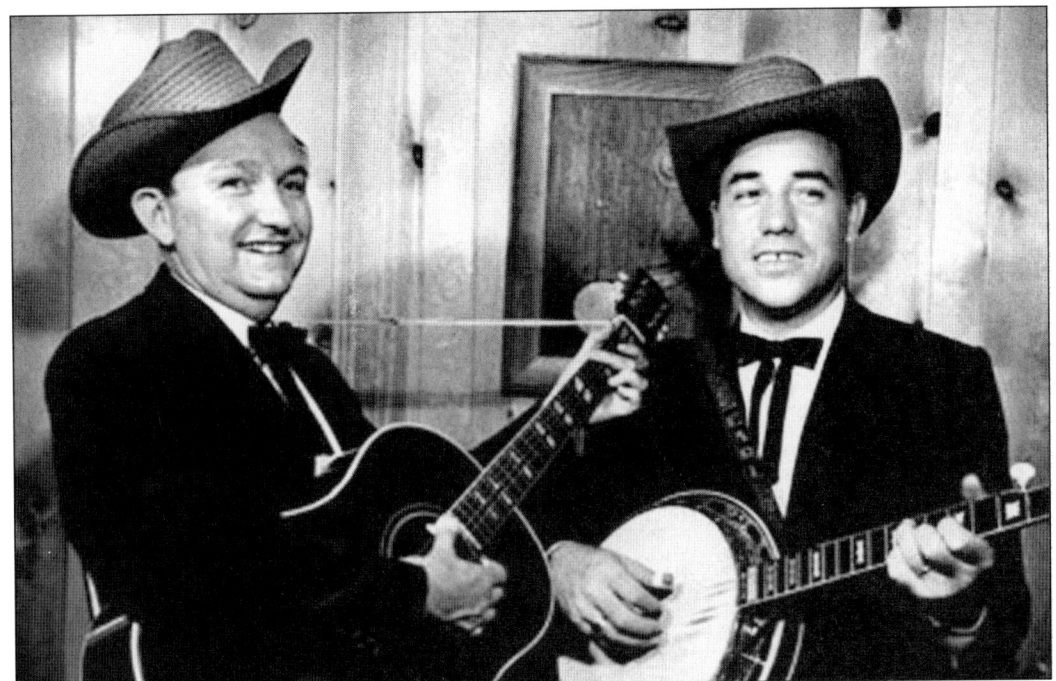

Scruggs became famous playing with his long-time partner Lester Flatt. Flatt and Scruggs sang the theme song for the hit sitcom *The Beverly Hillbillies* and appeared on several episodes of the show.

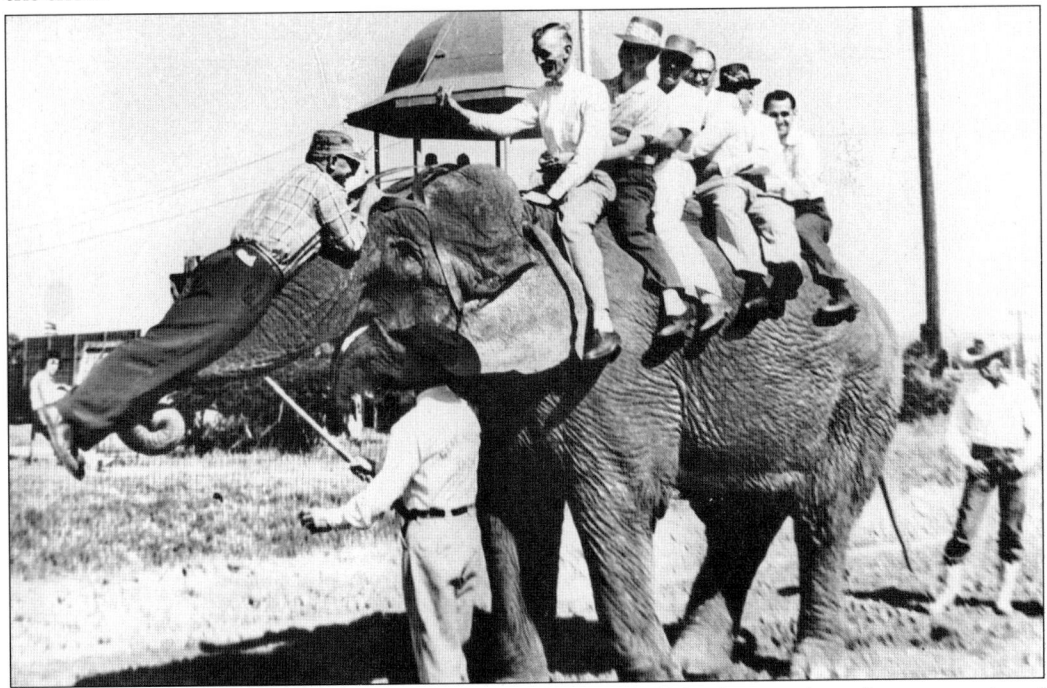

Former sheriff Haywood Allen is pictured third from left (in bow tie) in this promotional photograph taken at the Cleveland County Fair. Many musicians like Gibson and Scruggs have gotten their start playing for county fairs.

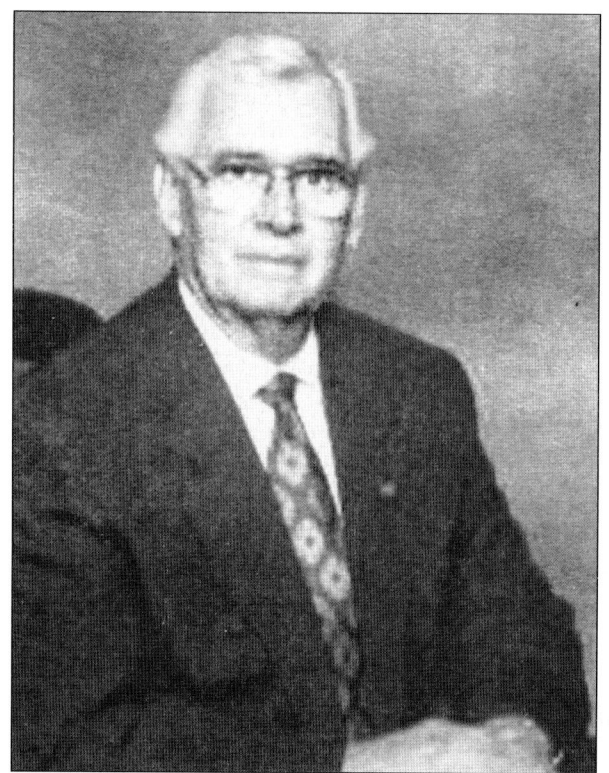

In 1960, George Clay Jr. and Bob Barnette opened a funeral home on West Warren Street in a house that had been the home of Tony Hammock. The business grew, and in 1998, Clay built a modern facility on West Dixon Boulevard. Clay served as mayor of Shelby.

W. Hugh Dover became a well-known local voice of radio station WOHS. People woke to his weather, business news, stories, and general all-round discussions. From 1960 to 1968, he served on the Cleveland County Board of Commissioners.

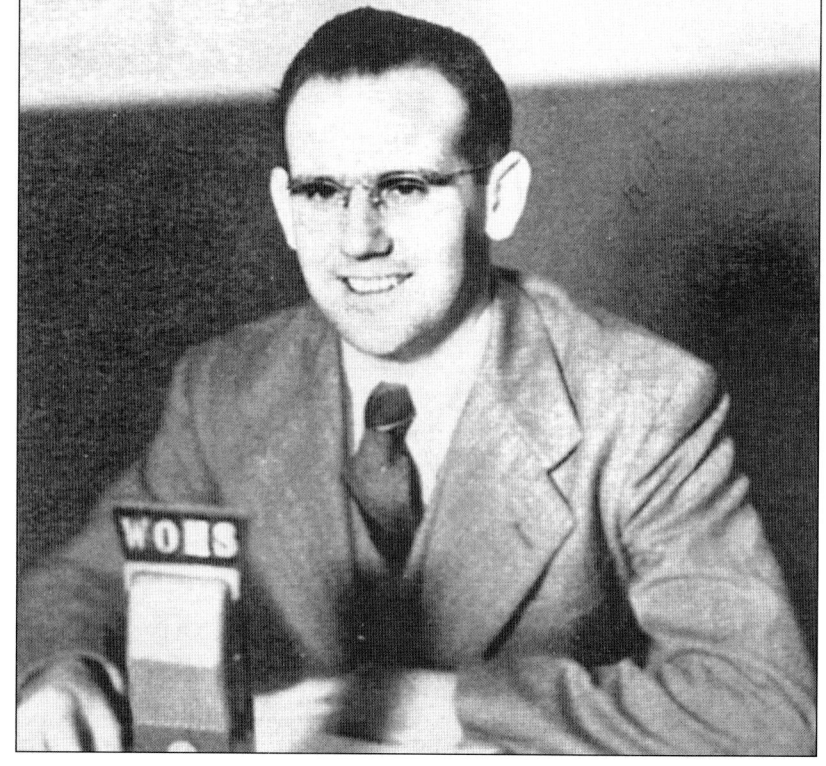

Almost any resident of Shelby from the 1950s to the 1990s should recognize the name of Ralph Gilbert Jr. Gilbert lost an arm when he was young, but this never seemed to slow him down. For years, he was associated with Gilbert-Jones Realty. He served for over 20 years as the chairman of the Cleveland County Board of Elections and was a county commissioner from 1990 to 1999.

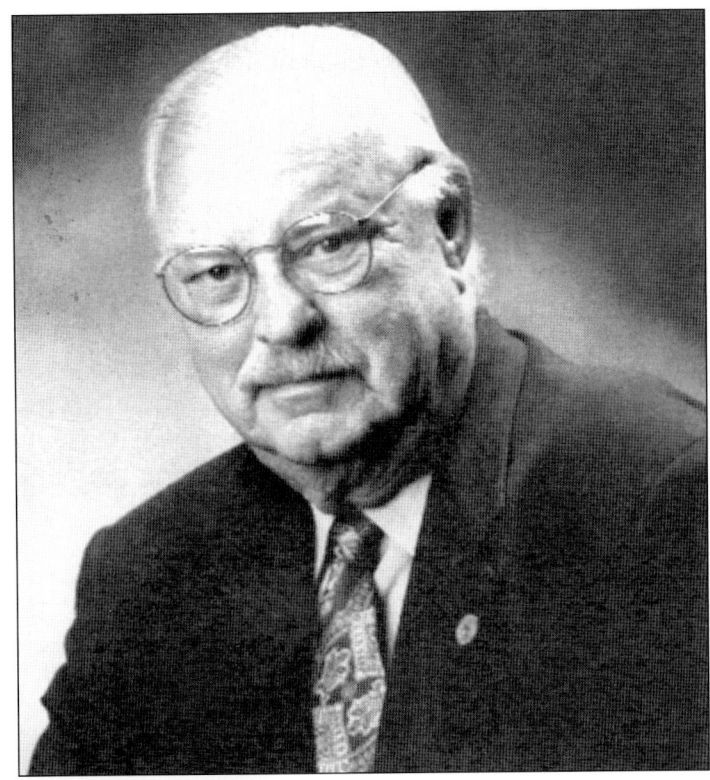

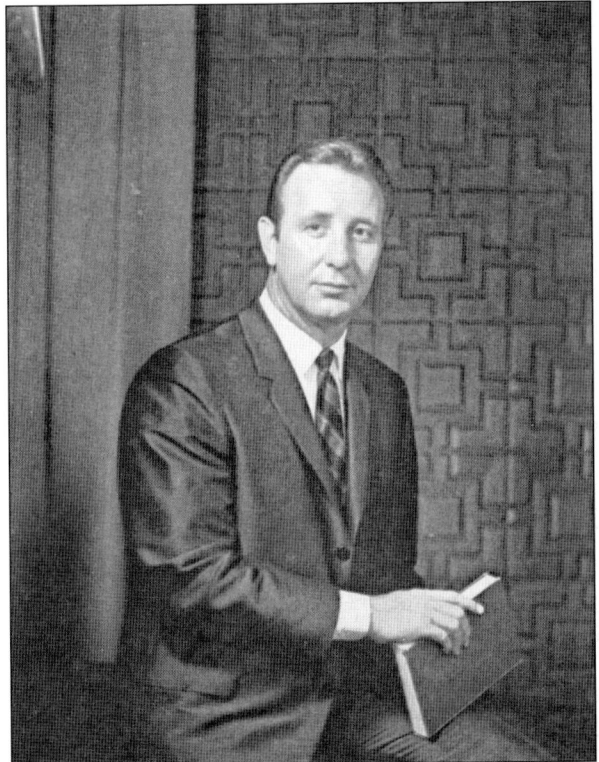

Not all community leaders were in business or politics. In 1969, Dr. Gene Watterson became the pastor of Shelby's First Baptist Church. Dr. Watterson led the church for a record 25 years, and today in retirement he is still serving churches.

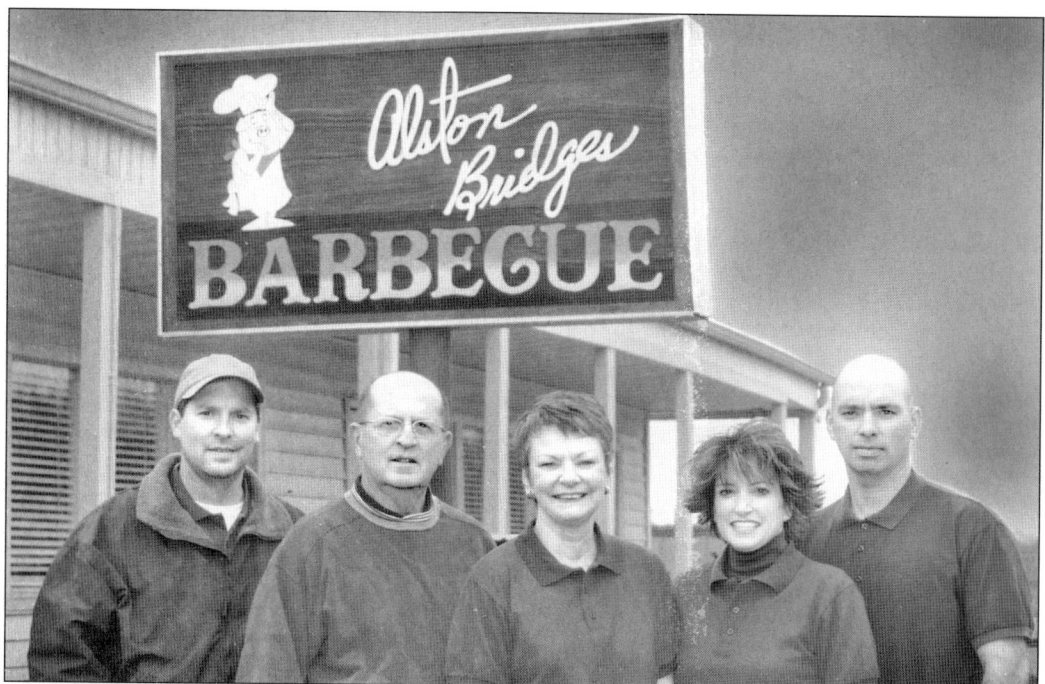

This picture shows that the Alston Bridges Barbeque is truly a family business. Alston Bridges's son Kent is shown with his wife and three of his children. All five of them work five days each week providing food and fellowship for scores of customers.

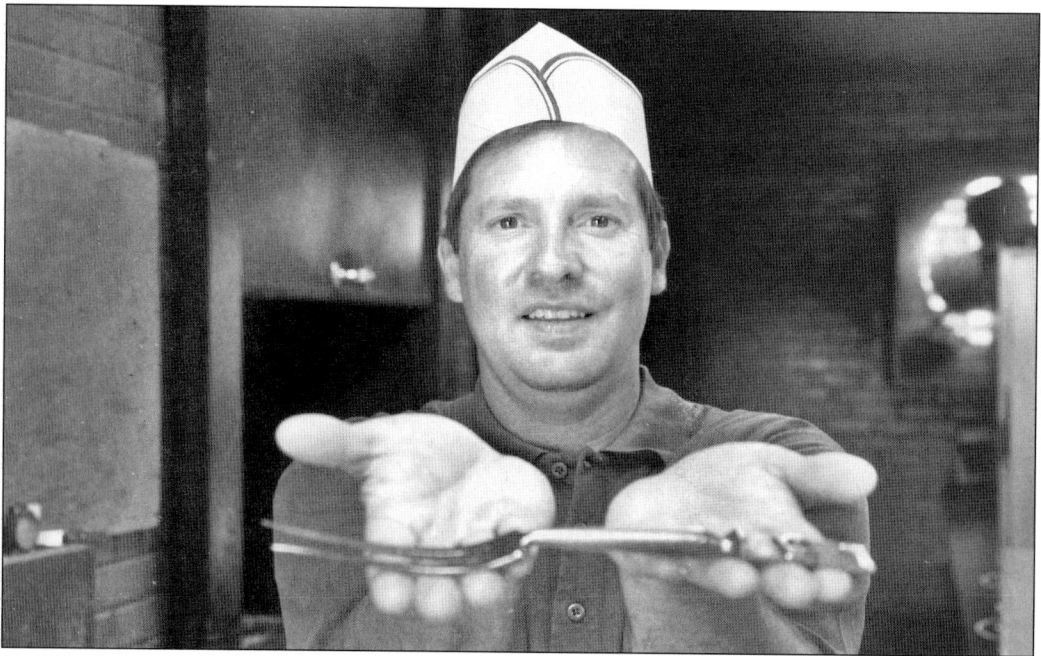

Reid Bridges is seen holding the fork used to test to see if the meat is properly cooked at Alston Bridges. The fork has been handed down through the generations at Alston's. When misplaced, the family has had sleepless nights and even a trip into the garbage dumpster to retrieve their special fork. (Margaret Patterson.)

Grace Rutledge Hamrick was an author and journalist. She wrote for the *Cleveland Times*, and during World War II, she served as managing editor. She became the editor of the paper in 1960. In 1982, she joined the *Shelby Daily Star* as a columnist. She authored several local histories, including *Miss Faye* a biography of Mrs. O. Max Gardner, a history of First Baptist Church for its 125th anniversary in 1972, and a history of the Cleveland County Fair.

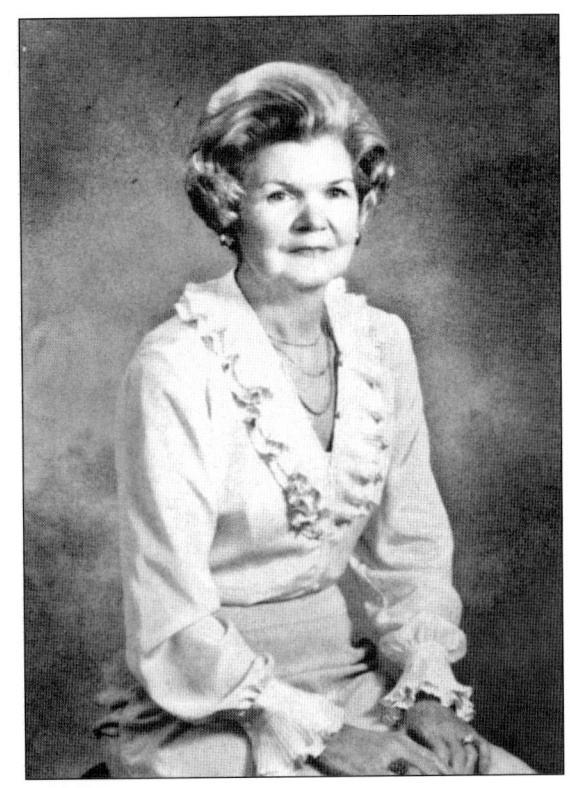

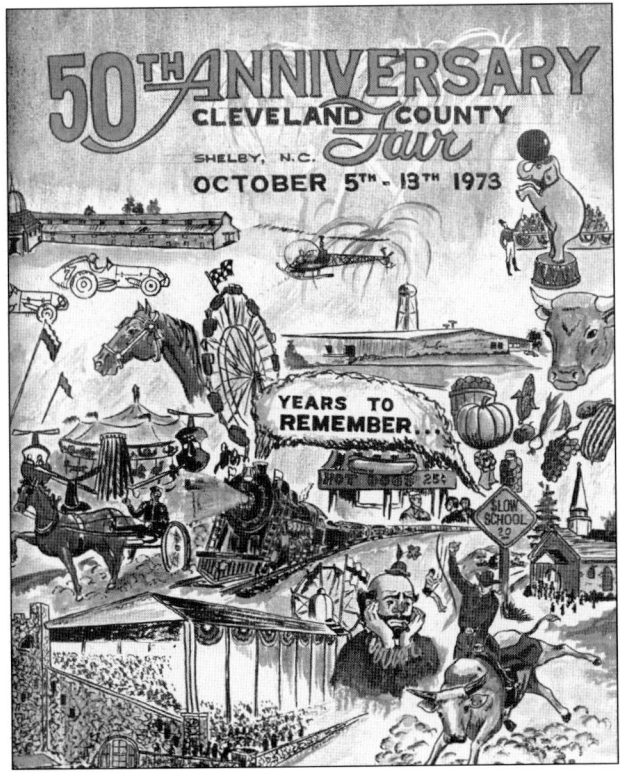

No Shelby story is complete without a view of the Cleveland County Fair. Begun in 1924, it is referred to in advertising copy as "the biggest annual event ever held in Cleveland County" and remains the largest county fair in North Carolina.

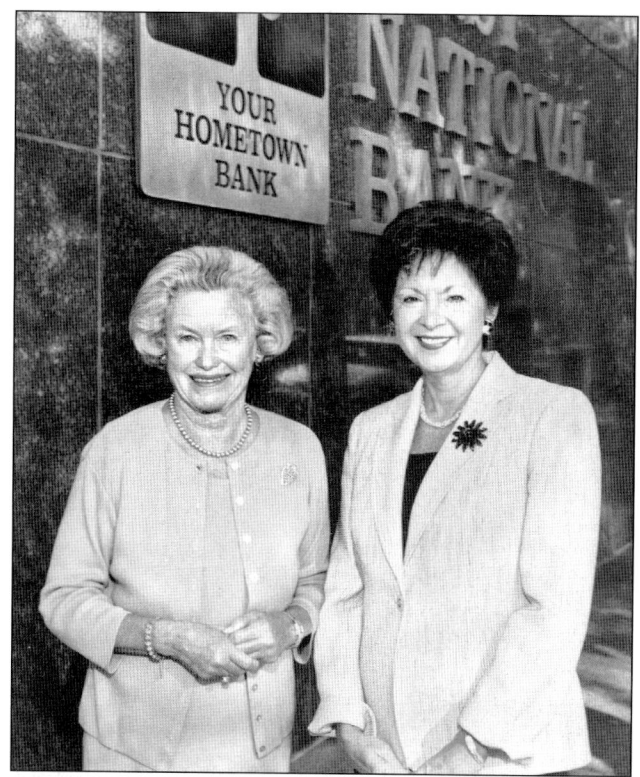

Shelby's First National Bank ("Your Hometown Bank") has been the subject of the Arcadia title *First National Bank: Hometown Banking Since 1874*. The 133-year-old financial institution has been led in recent years by Adelaide A. Craver (left) who is now chairperson of the board and chief executive officer. Helen Jeffords (right) is president, chief operating officer, and chief financial officer. (First National Bank.)

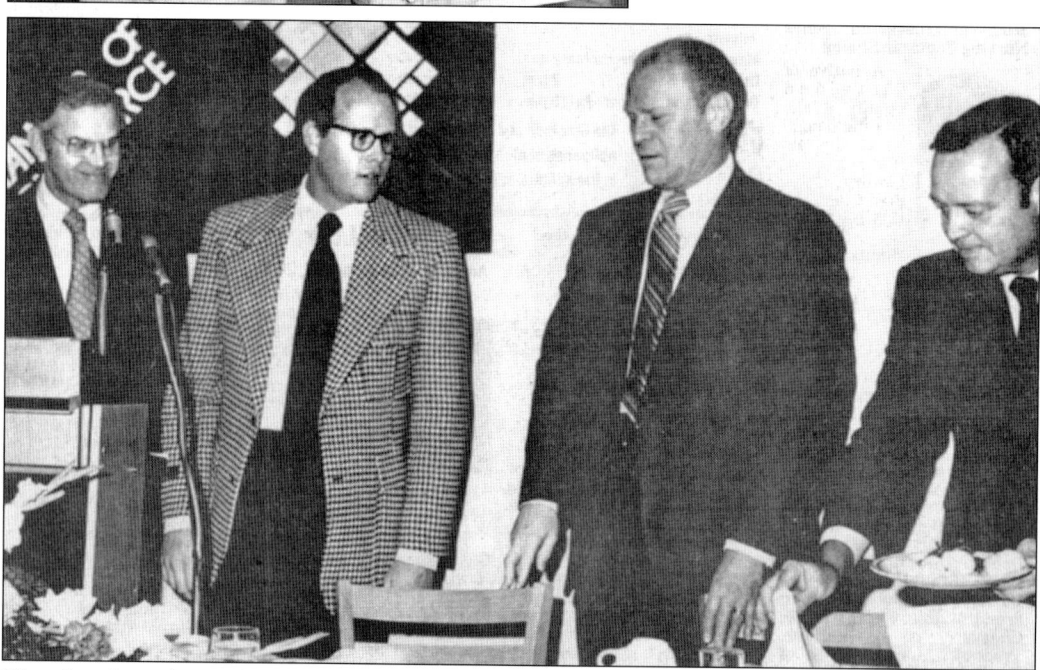

The chamber of commerce worked with the longtime congressman from the district, Rep. James T. Broyhill of Lenoir. In 1973, soon-to-be vice president Gerald R. Ford appeared at a chamber event. From left to right are businessman Edwin Ford, then–chamber president and local business leader Litton Suttle, Gerald Ford, and James Broyhill.

One of Shelby's leading families for several decades was that of J. L. Suttle Jr. (pictured). Suttle's father served as mayor around the time of World War I. Suttle Jr. was a leading executive with a savings and loan association and also a leading tennis player. Mrs. Suttle, the former Sara McFarland, was a community leader. (*The Heritage of Cleveland County*.)

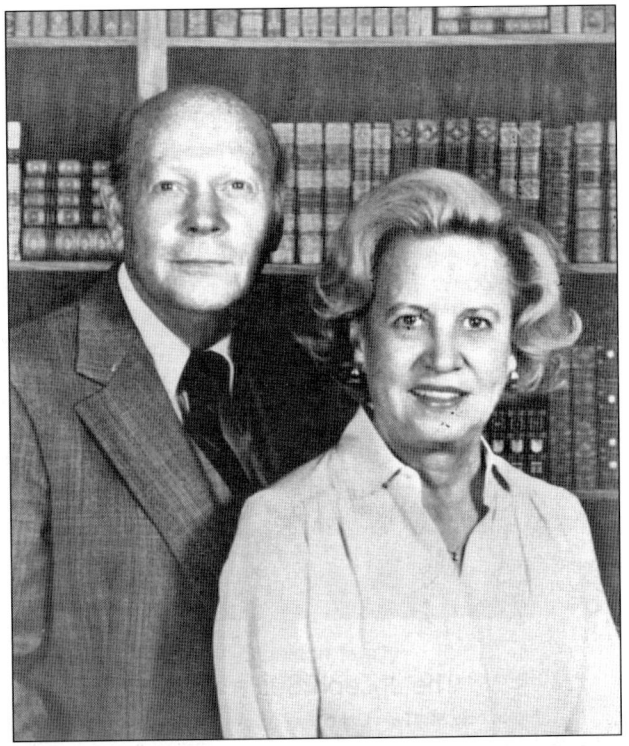

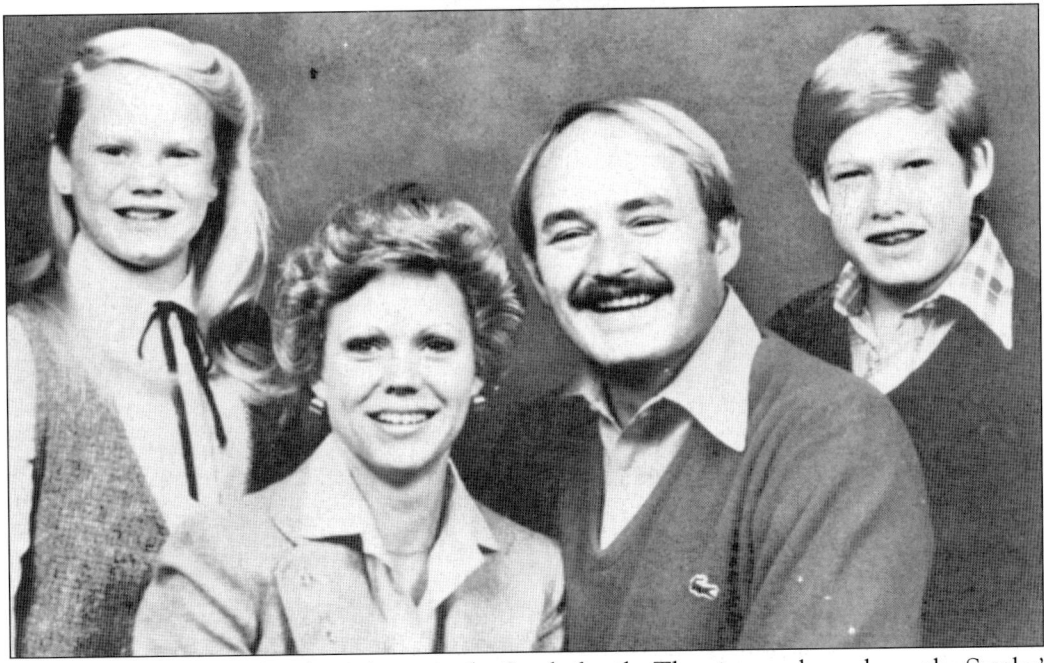

Civic involvement is a family tradition in the Suttle family. The picture above shows the Suttles' daughter Carole and her husband, W. Jack Arey, with their children, Mildred Carole (left) and W. J. Jr. (right). The Areys have also been community leaders, and their daughter, Millie Arey Wood, is a leader in the Destination Cleveland County Revitalization Committee. (*Cleveland County Heritage*.)

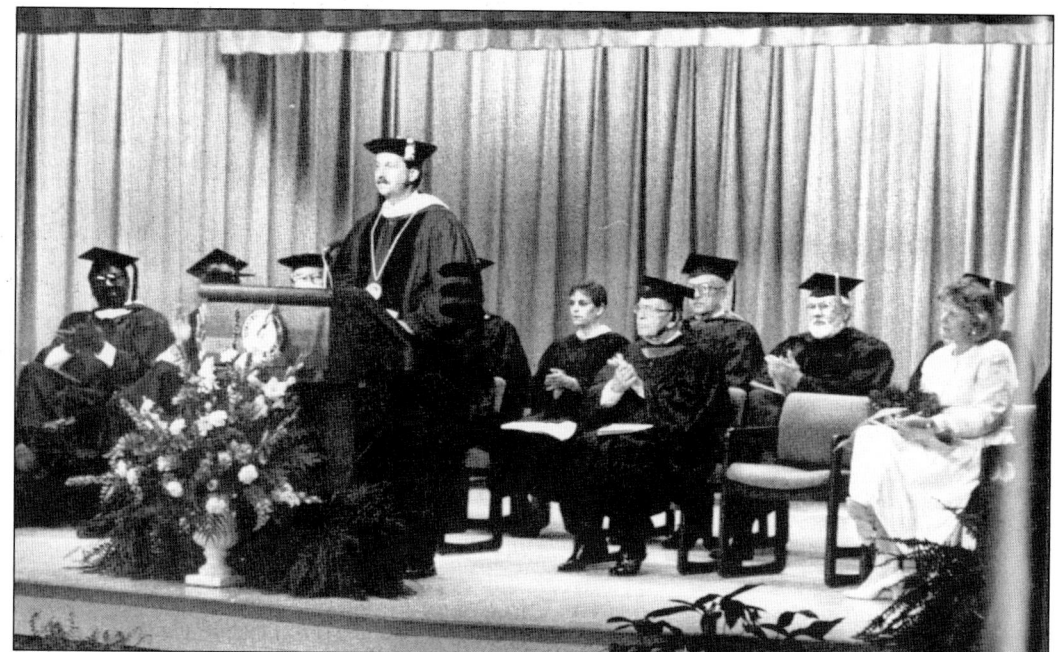

Located at the eastern edge of Shelby is Cleveland Community College, one of North Carolina's leading community colleges. Dr. Steve Thornburg is pictured speaking at his 1991 inauguration ceremony. Under the leadership of only its second president in its 41-year history, the college is growing in facilities and in academic excellence.

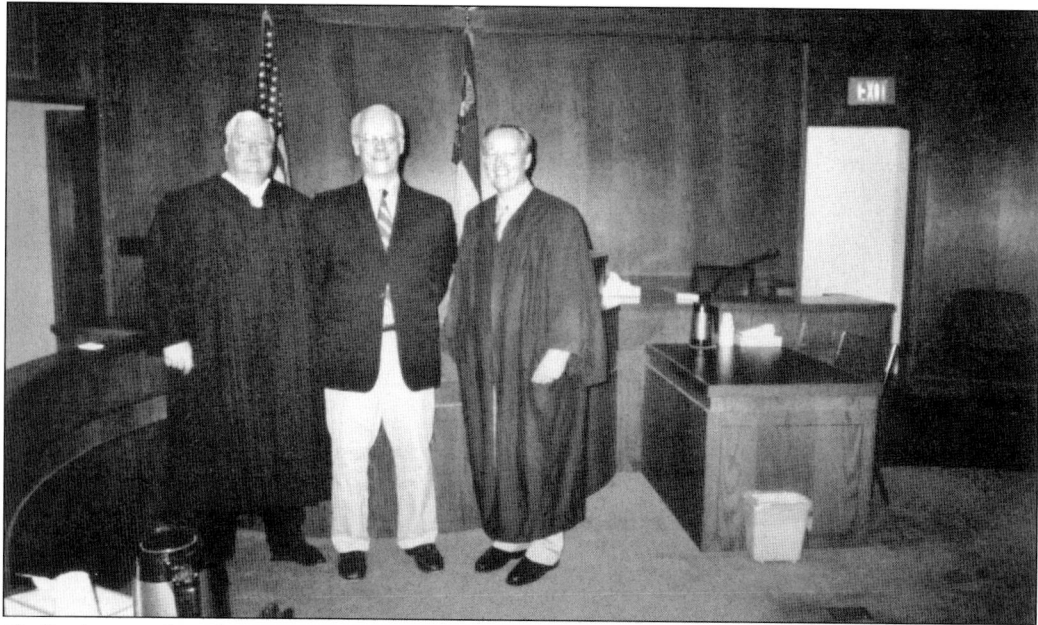

Shelby has produced many outstanding judges through the years. Pictured in the courtroom are, from left to right, James W. Morgan, district court judge from December 1990 to March 2000 and superior court judge from March 2000 to present; John Mull Gardner, superior court judge from December 1987 to March 2000; and Forrest D. Bridges, superior court judge from 1995 to present. (June Albright.)

Four
SHELBY CITY SCHOOLS

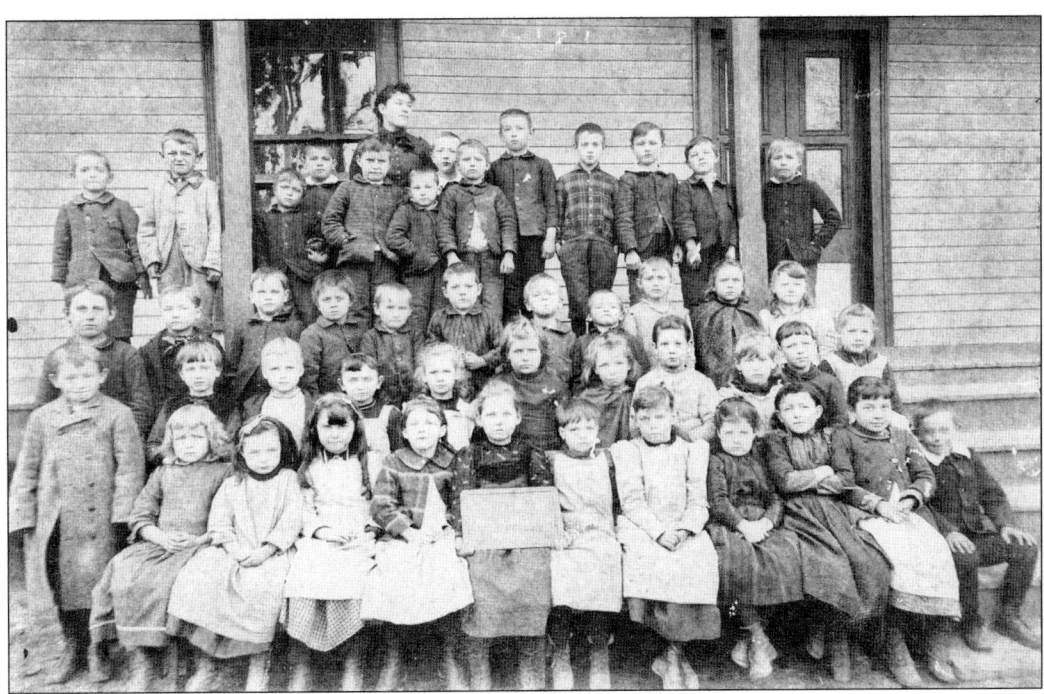

Public schools in the United States were largely a product of the 19th century. The South was slow to build or support a public school system. Poverty and a rural population were two reasons for this slow growth. The town of Shelby would create its own school system, which would operate as a separate system for over 100 years. This 1893 picture shows young children by the front entrance of the graded school.

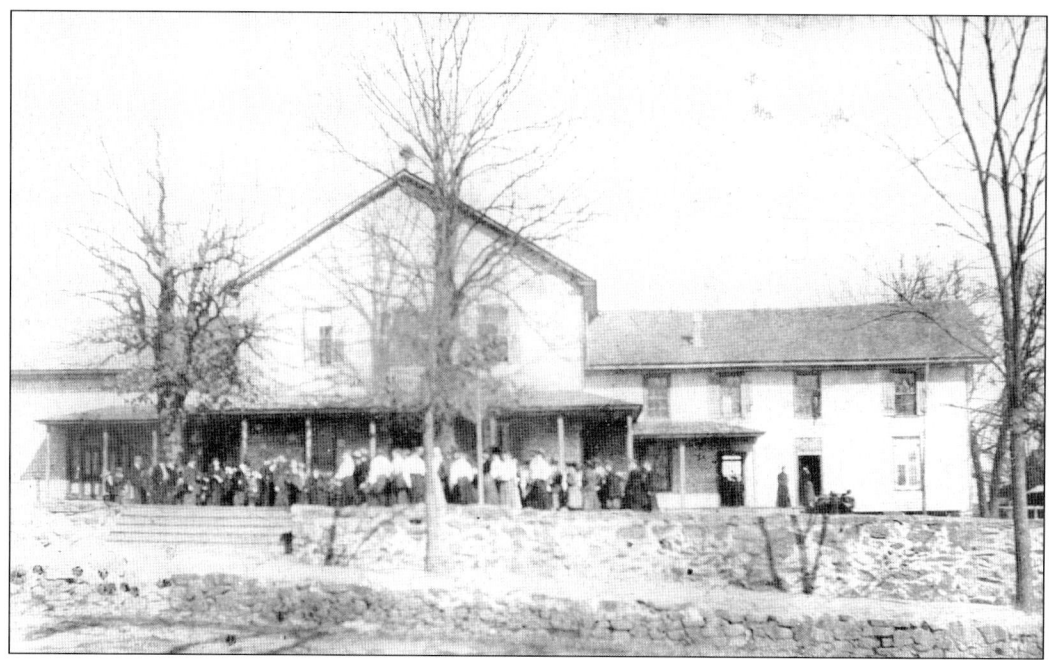

Several private schools existed for various groups at various times in Shelby. Originally formed as a private school, this building served as Shelby's first public grade school. The structure burned on October 13, 1905. For the next year, classes were held in a variety of places, including in the courthouse and on the second floor of the Shelby National Bank.

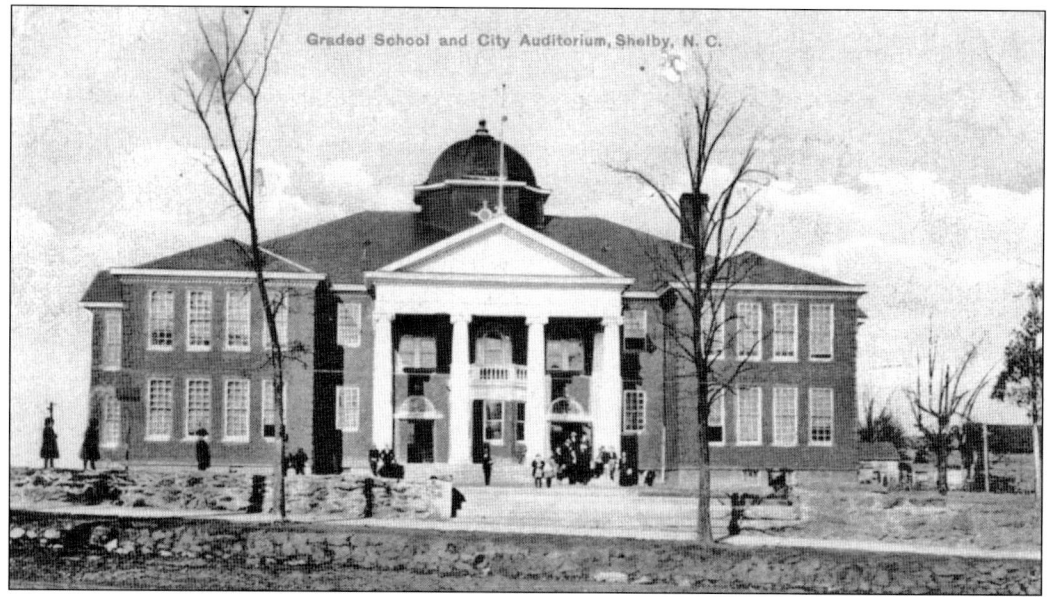

An early postcard pictured Shelby's modern graded school, which opened in January 1907 at a cost of $30,000. The word "graded" appeared on postcards, meaning that the school was not a one-room school where all students met together. For nearly three quarters of a century, all of Shelby's white children (and some black children in the later years) attended some grades in this building. Note the wall in front of the new school; the stone wall in front of the school remains on the site today as a reminder of the buildings that once stood there.

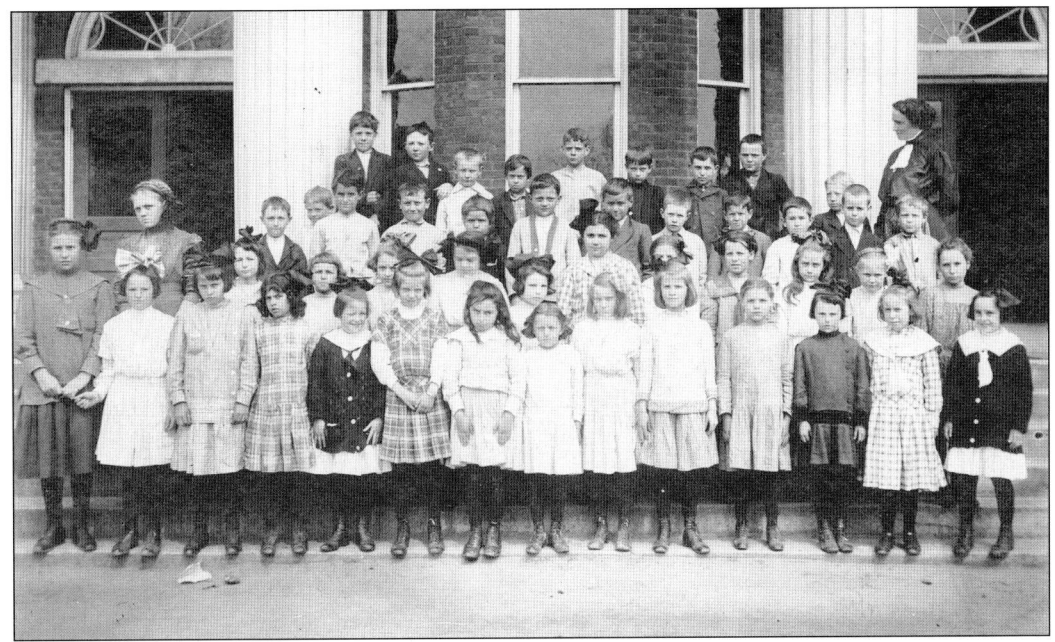

This group of second-grade students poses in front of the new school in 1909. The students are dressed up for a special occasion, possibly for the group photograph.

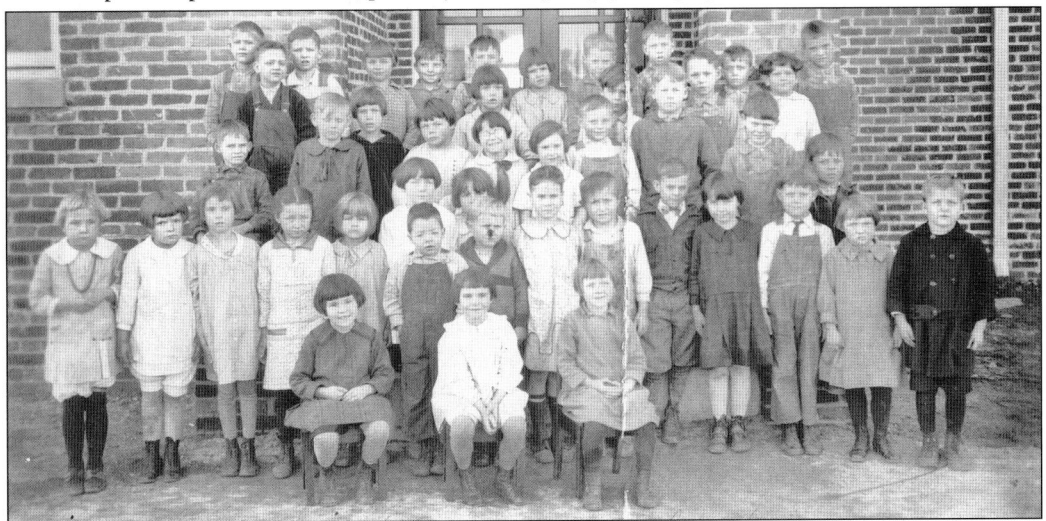

As the early years of the century passed, the school system built six elementary schools, which would serve Shelby for decades. Graham School was built on West Oak Street in 1927 and is the only one of the six buildings that is still standing. This 1927 photograph shows a first-grade class. From left to right are (first row) Edith Abernathy, Martha Ann Eskridge, and Louise ?; (second row) Vera ?, Dora McSwain, Annie Sweezy, Gladys Green, Ruth Cline Thompson, Pansy Jones, Louise Webb, Elizabeth Falls, Jack Jones, G. L. Gaffney, Addie Lee Hambright, Clyde Wilson, Nancy McSwain, and Thomas Henderson; (third row) John ?, Lillian Bridges, Evelyn ?, Lillian Pruett, Theo Jarrett, Gary Hefner, unidentified, A. C. Bridges, Flay Taylor, and Flecther Queen; (fourth row) D. Wright, ? Price, Earline Pruett, A. V. Queen, Forrest Glass, Helen ?, ? Blanton, A. C. Canipe, Carol Stanley, Lucile Wright, Annie Bell Hollifield, Arnold Vaughn, Grady Dover, Fred Champion, Bruce Morgan, and Jack McSwain.

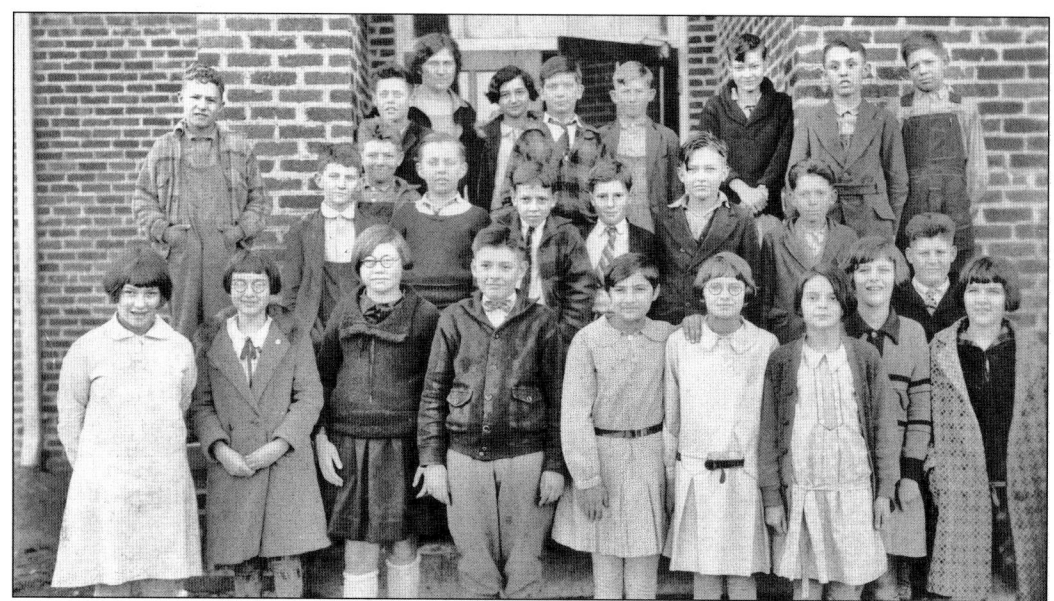

This 1927 picture shows a group of sixth-grade Graham School students. From left to right are (first row) Sarah Lee Norman, Ethel Alexander, Pauline Baker, William A. Broadway Jr., Gwendolyn Dellinger, Isabel Lackey, Rachel Connor, Helen Smith, and Gene Moore Thompson; (second row) Bruce Putnam, unidentified, James Eskridge, John McClurd Jr., Stuart James, Zeb Mauney Jr., C. B. Poston, and J. L. Dover; (third row) Hugh Peeler, teacher Helen Dickson, Annie Ruth Dellinger, Pete O'Shields, unidentified, Hester Lee Lackey, George Norris Dover, and Vernon Mode.

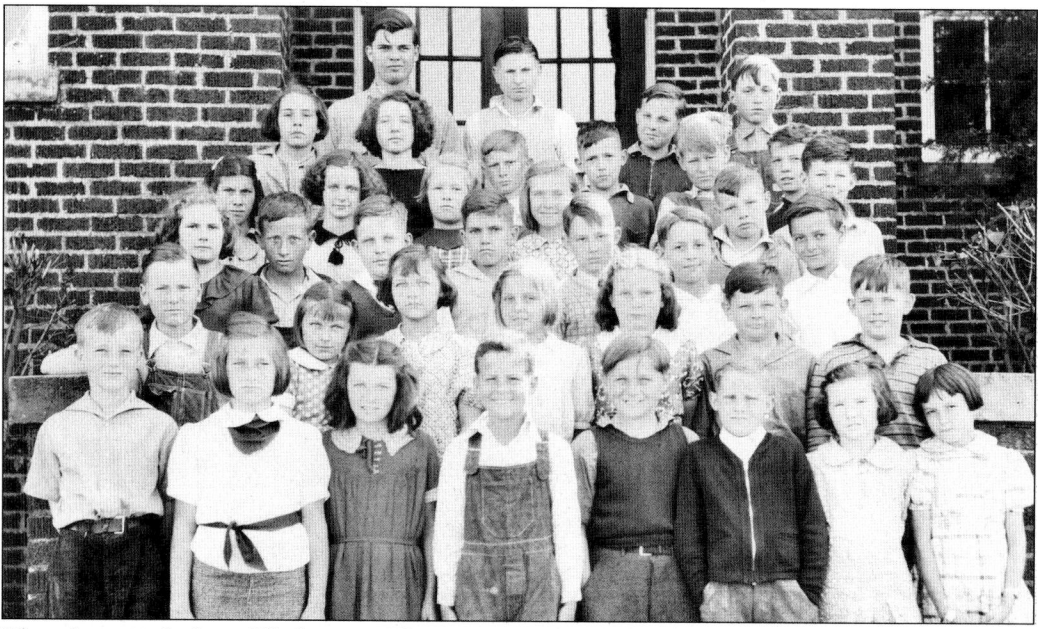

This photograph shows Washington Elementary students who were members of Ruby McDonald's class. They included Jimmy Cline, Jack Suttle, Carver Wood Jr., Bobby Parris, Harrell Green, Thomas Kirry, Russell Ropp, Billy Spake, Pat Patterson, Dick Arey, Newlin Schenck, Buddy Spangler, Hoke King Jr., Charles Maynor, James Reep, J. Hardin Lee Jr., Roy Stockton, Beryl Heffner, Jack Dover, Ralph Mauney Jr., and Doris Bowling.

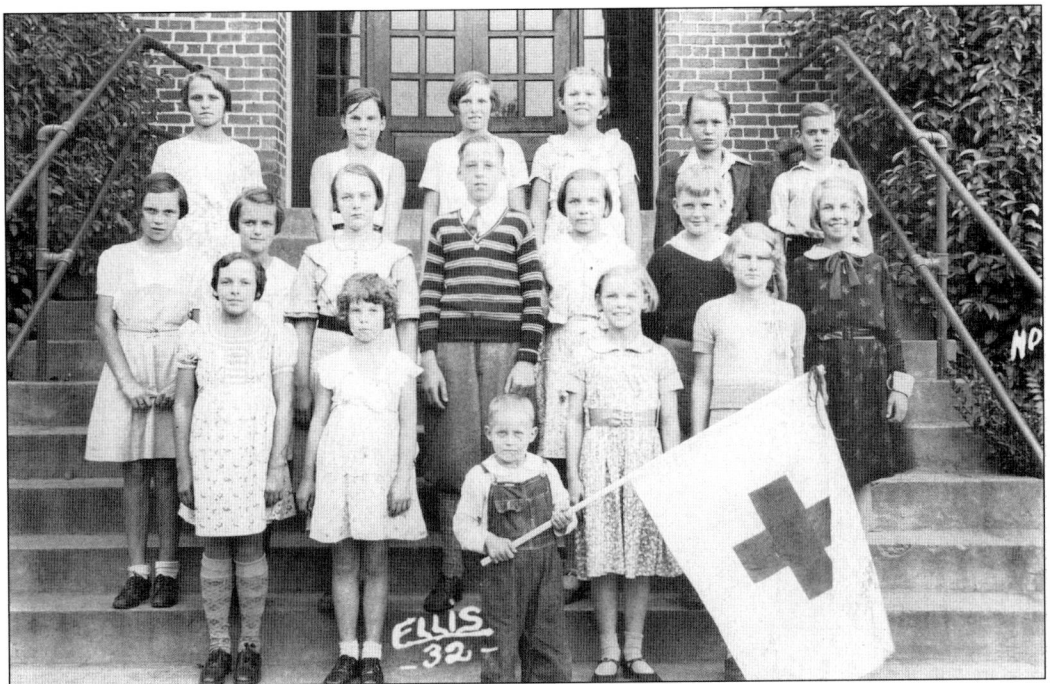

This is another example of a photograph made by the Ellis Studio. The 1932 picture depicting donors at a Red Cross fund-raiser seems to be at Washington School. The boy in the middle with the striped shirt is future baker Floyd Bost. (Uptown Shelby Association.)

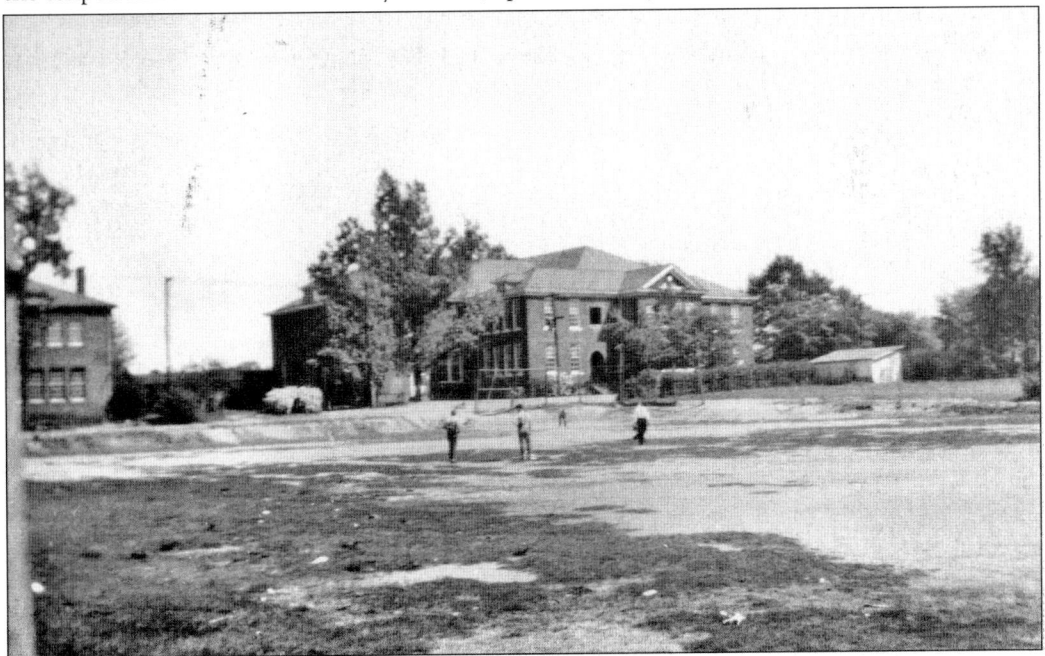

This c. 1950 view shows Shelby Graded School at a time when it had become the Shelby Junior High School, with grades seven and eight. The building at the left served as a band building for both junior- and senior-high students. The well-used playground was also a parking lot for events at the Shelby baseball field on West Sumter Street.

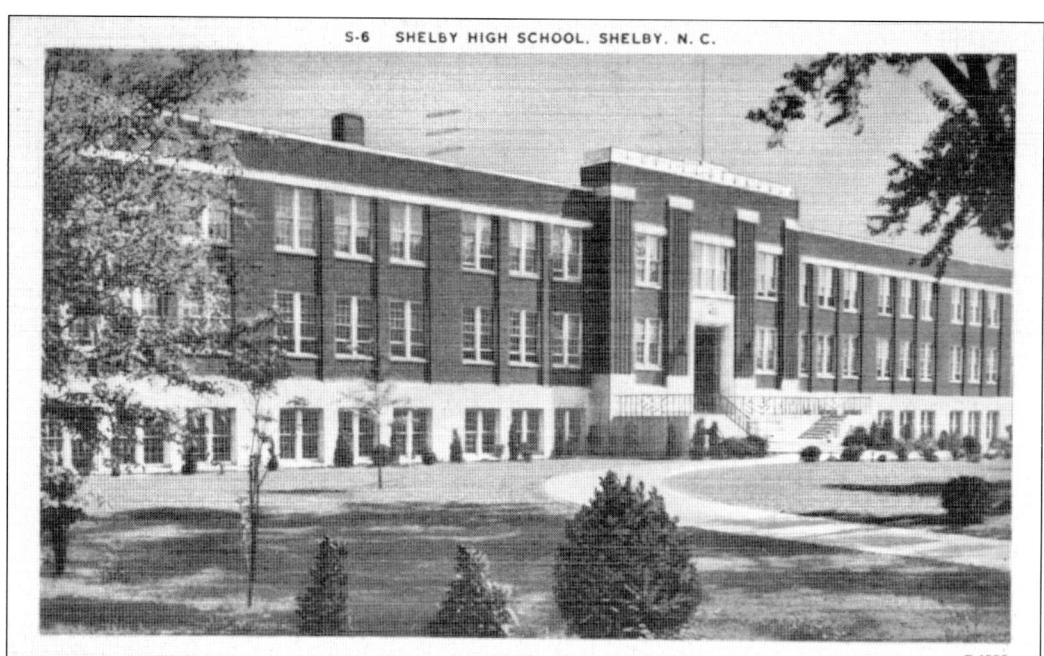

In 1937, a new Shelby High School (SHS) was built, leaving the old graded school for junior-high students. The postcard view shows a building that looks much like it does today after it was remodeled for the Shelby Middle School.

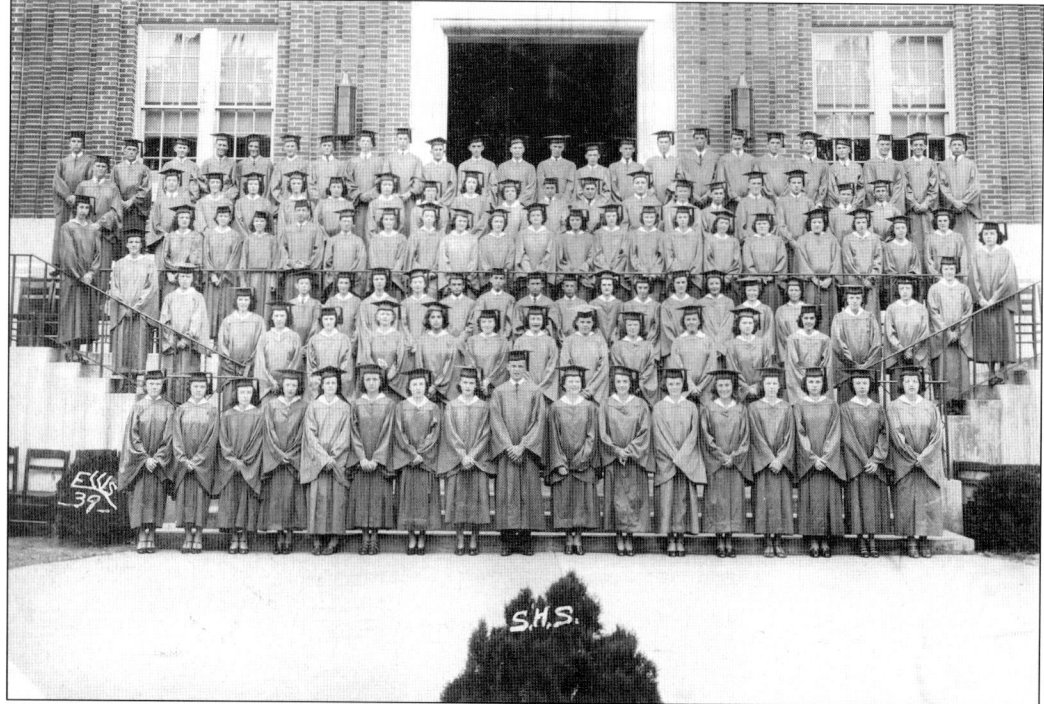

For years, all SHS graduating classes were pictured standing on the steps of the building. The class of 1939 was one of the early groups, and they had the opportunity to spend almost three years in the new building. (Uptown Shelby Association.)

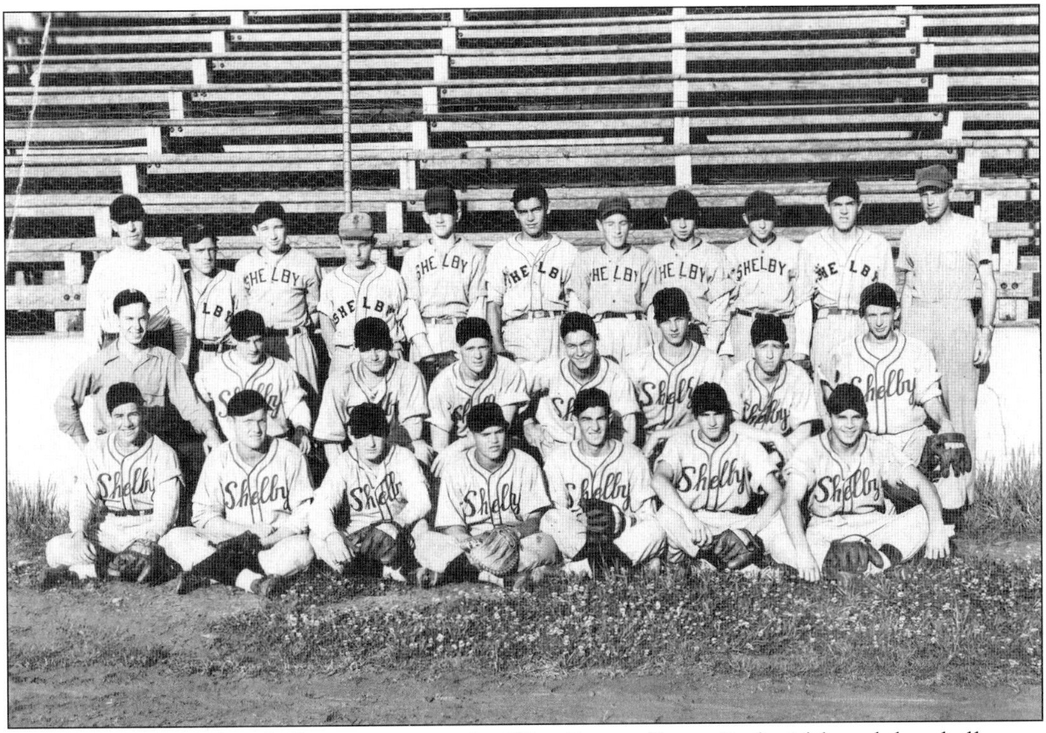

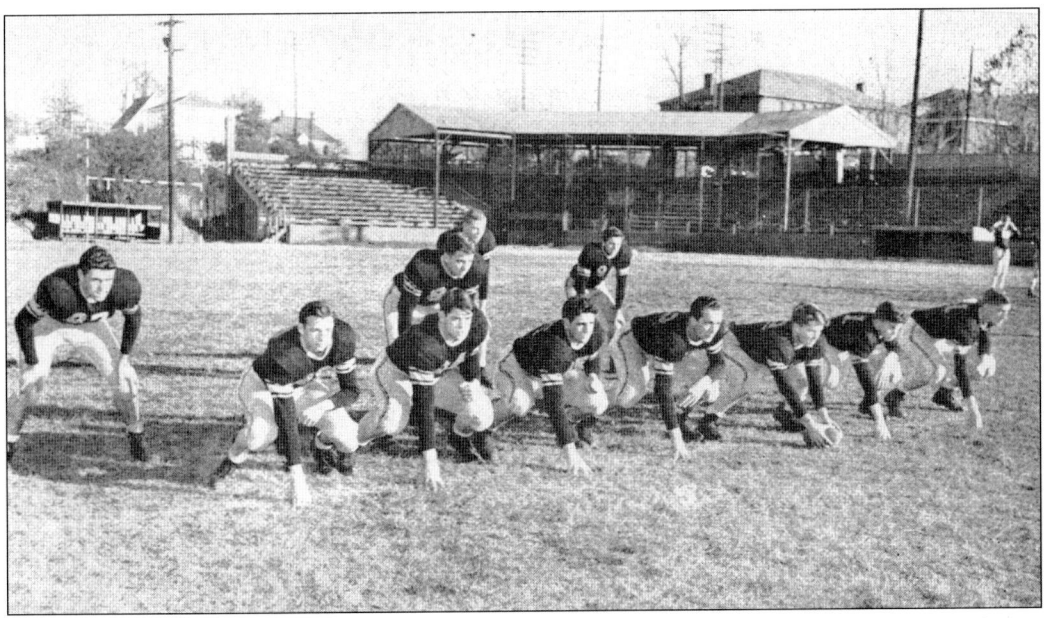

Shelby High's 1944 baseball team poses at the West Sumter Street Park. Although baseball was a major sport in Shelby at the time, uniformity of uniforms seems not be a requirement. (Uptown Shelby Association.)

Members of the 1948 Shelby High football team line up for an offensive play. The Sumter Street Park was really a baseball field, but a 120-yard football field (including the end zones) was just possible between the dugout and the hill in left field. (Patrick McMurry.)

FACULTY

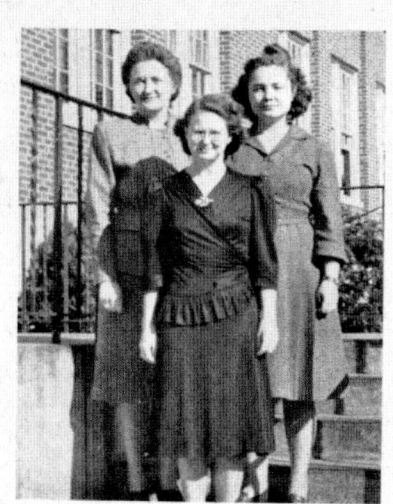

Mrs. Robert Doggett
Mrs. T. A. Parker
Mrs. Inez Connor

Mr. Marion Bird
Mr. Lloyd Little
Mr. Roy W. Morris

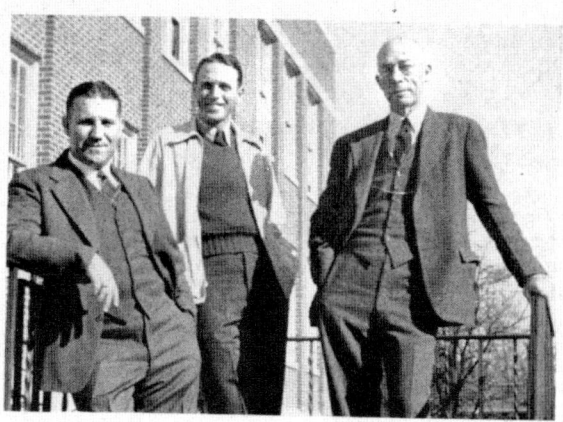

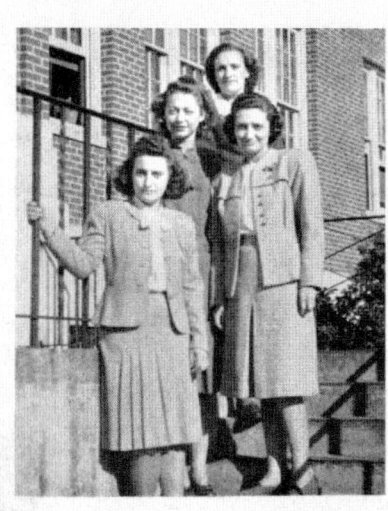

Miss Rachel Smith
Miss Sara Mundy Hamrick
Miss Dorothy King
Miss Mamie Lou Forney

This page from the 1947 Shelby High annual shows 10 teachers, many of who were longtime educators and are remembered by hundreds of former SHS students. (*Cruiser*.)

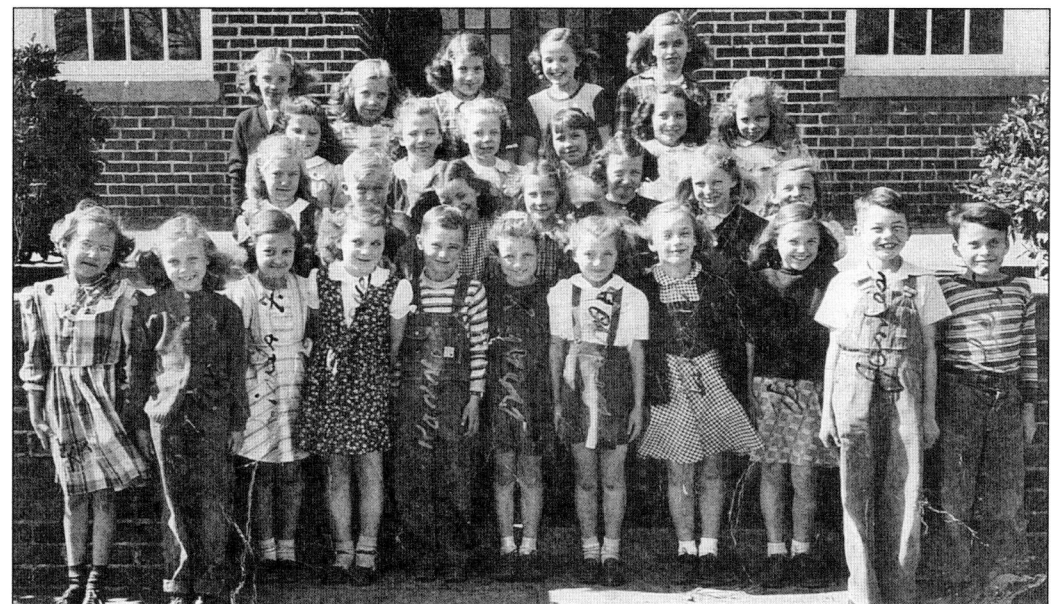

These members of the Shelby High classes of 1958 and 1959 are pictured in their elementary days at Morgan (or South Shelby) School. They are, from left to right, (first row) Kay Hollifield, Fay Bowman, Linda Fortenberry, Sue Jane Barkley, Ronald Vaughn, Mary Waters, Brenda Hollifield, Kay Duncan, Valarie Revels, James Turner, and Robert Camp; (second row) Harriet Hamrick, Jean Philbeck, Sarah Morrow, Pat Moffett, Linda Petty, Suzanne Putnam, and Wynette Fisher; (third row) Loratte Brooks, Ima Jean McAbee, Juanita Ester, Frances Bell, Libby Putnam, and Fredia Deaton; (fourth row) Brenda Gamble, Jane McCurry, Barbara Taylor, Joan Tessner, and Glenda Surratt.

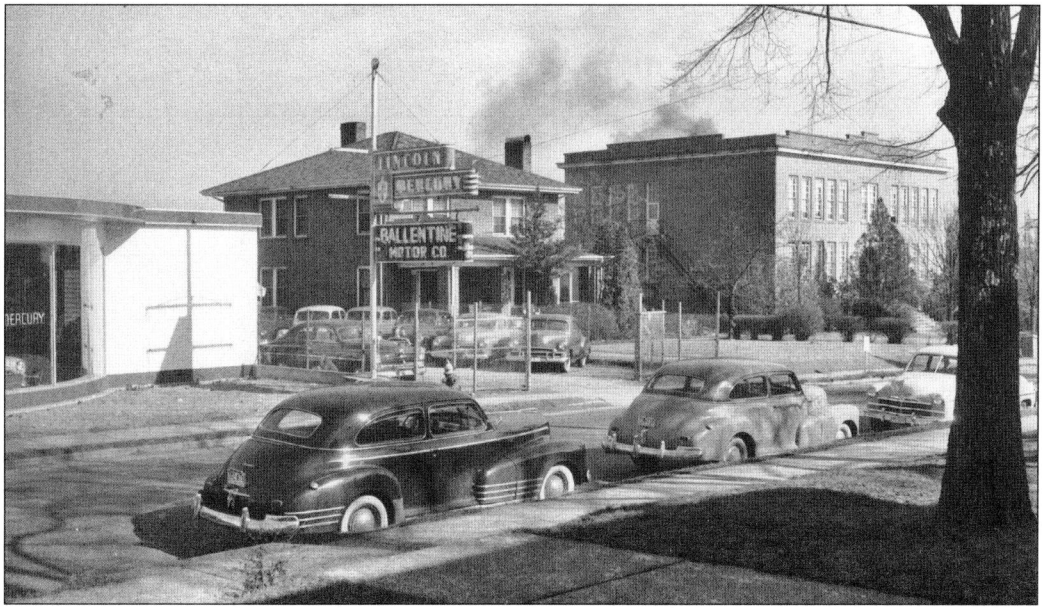

Three of the original six elementary schools were two-story buildings. This c. 1950 photograph shows Marion School on East Marion Street (site of the current Eckerd's Drug). The building would soon become the first of the six to be torn down. (Lloyd Hamrick Collection.)

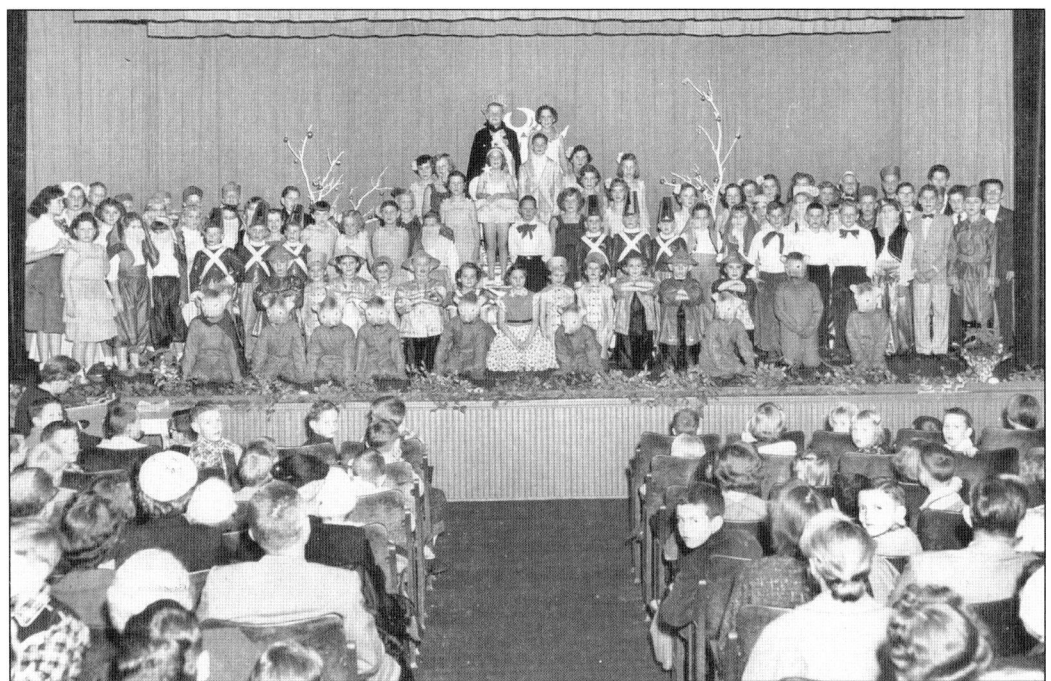

Dozens of Shelbians at Washington School participated in the *Nutcracker Suite* in December 1954. In the photograph one can find Charlie Magness, Montrose Meacham, Joann Freeman Surratt, Julian Wray, Jay Vincent, and Pat Rogers. (Joann Freeman Surratt.)

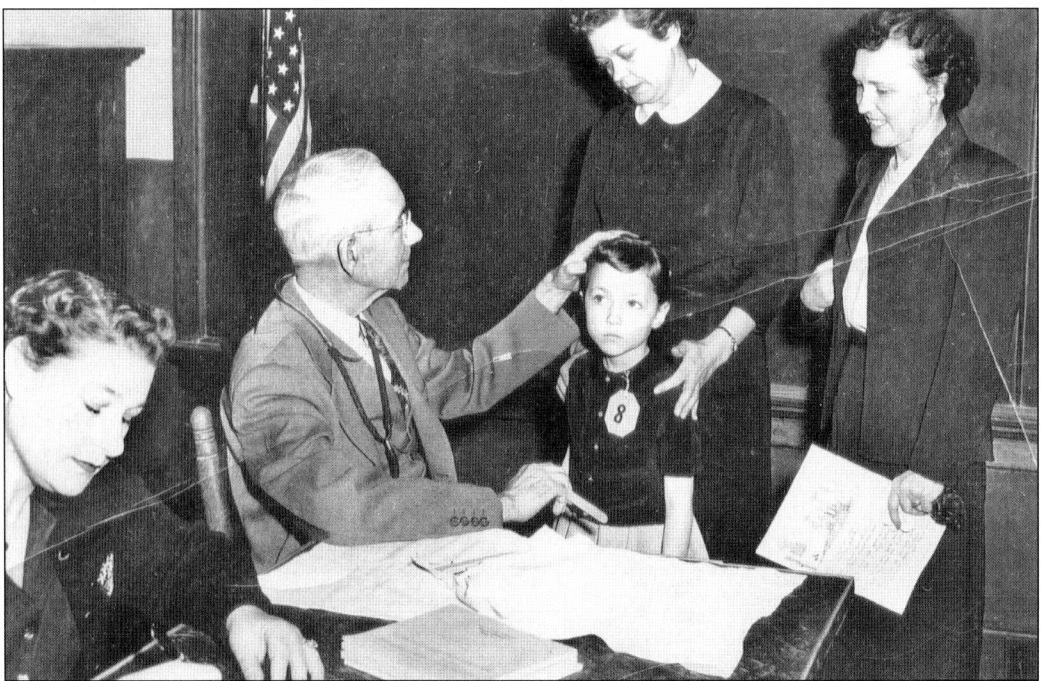

A familiar figure to students in 1954 was Dr. Z. P. Mitchell of the Cleveland County Health Department, who often gave vaccinations. Student Melba Smith Edwards is next in line for a shot. (Brendan Camp LeGrand.)

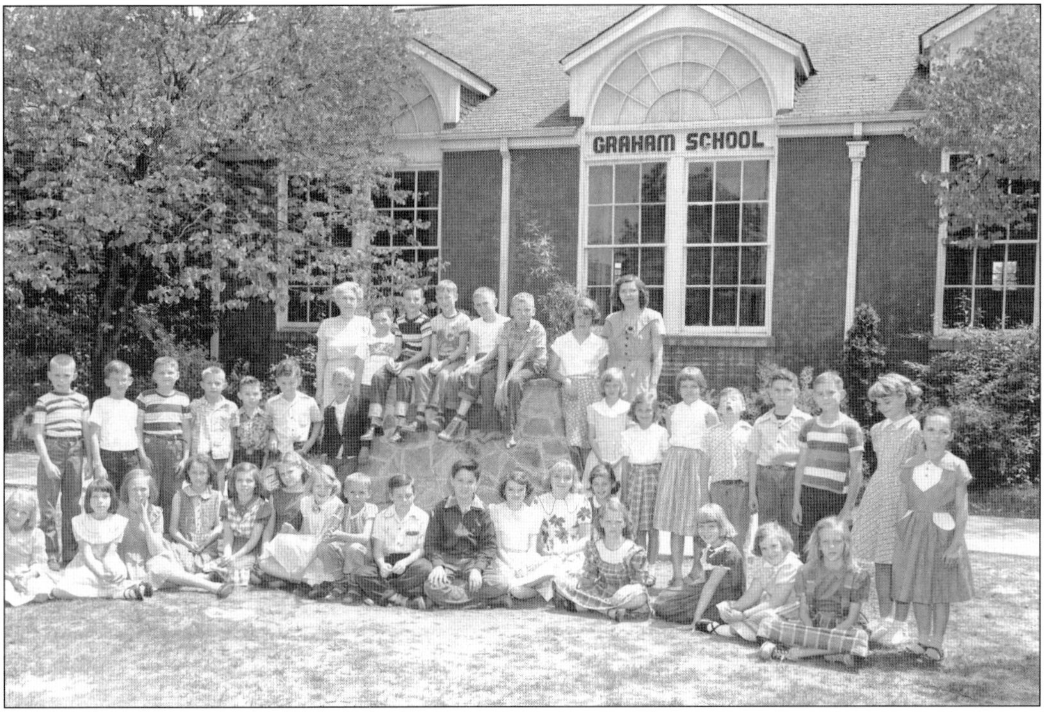

A clear view of the front of Graham School in the 1950s shows young students with longtime principal Ruby T. Hudson (top left).

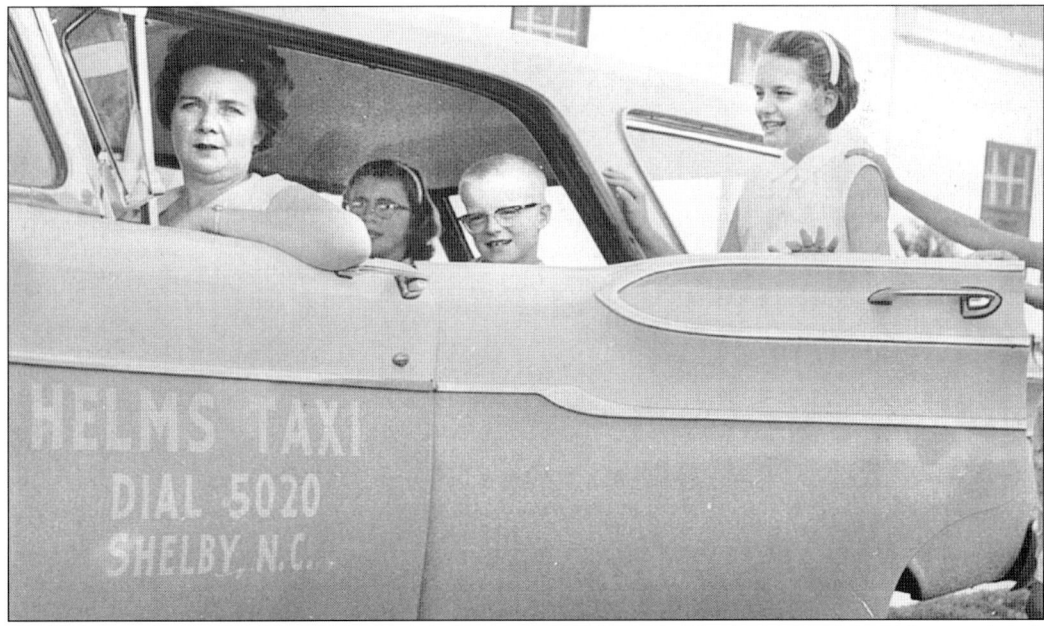

Few buses ran in the Shelby City Schools. Most students walked or rode a bicycle to school. However, some came in taxis. Mrs. Helms was one of many who operated a taxi service to school. (Brendan Camp LeGrand.)

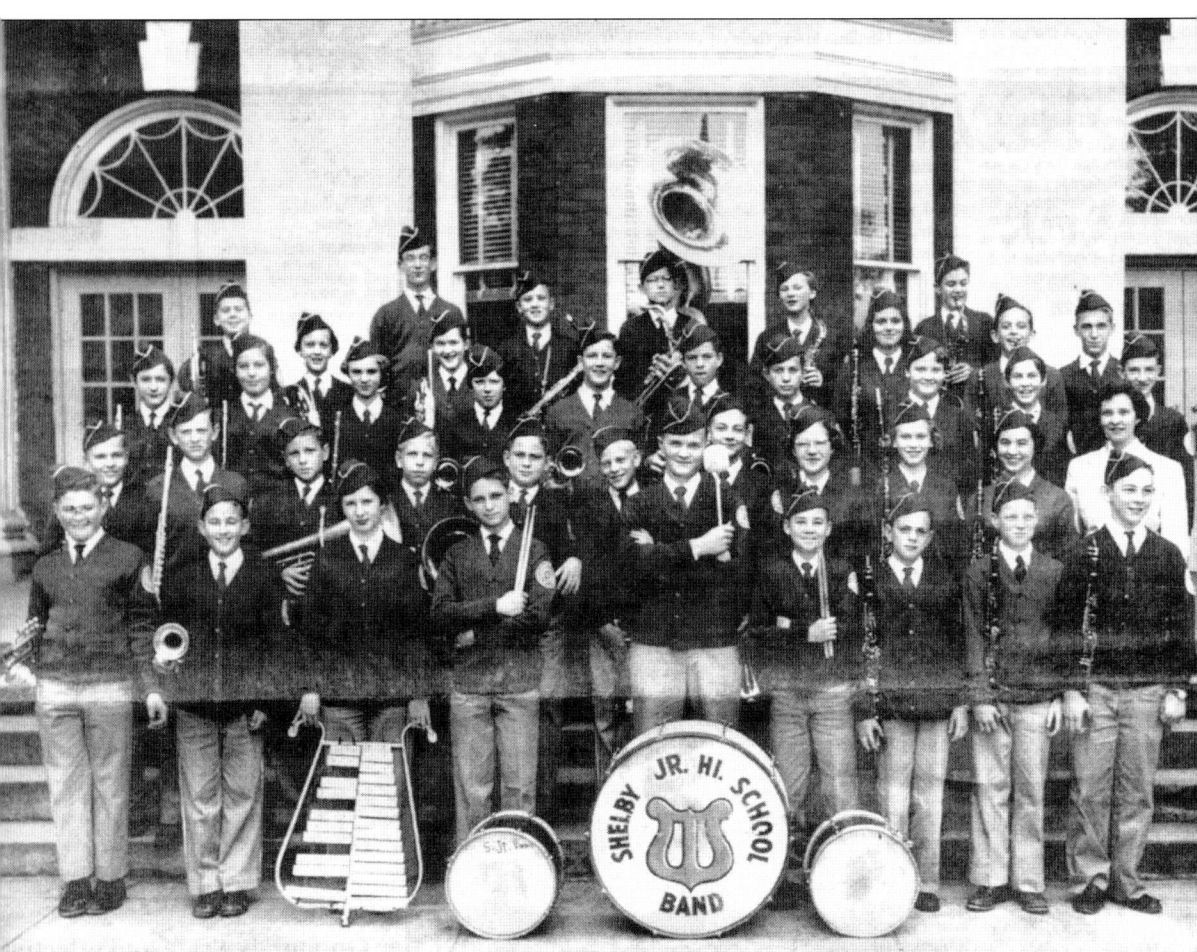

The 1955–1956 Shelby Junior High band poses in front of the Shelby Junior High building. Pictured from left to right are (first row) Mark Carr, Ben Gilliatt, Linda Shuford, Johnny Faison, Larry Allen, Dean Howard, Athos Rostan, Jimmy Toole, and Johnny Church; (second row) Conrad Martin, Harry Nolan, Flay Carpenter, Hill Hudson, Jimmy Macomson, Ronnie Canipe, Kenneth Ledford, Katherine Oehler, Adelaide Austell, Jane Dale White, and band director Miss Hord; (third row) unidentified, Wanda Lee Barger, Martha Blanton, Dianne Canipe, Nancy Bennet, Suzanne Chambers, Don Loftis, Billy Carpenter, Don Edmunson, Sandra Wright, Omega Waldrep, Victor Wray, Mae Moorehead, Robert Sills, and Gus Sanders; (fourth row) Charlie Rose, Buddy Young, Oakie Canipe, Mike Trioano Jr., Reanza Waldrep, and Johnny Carpenter. (Judith Parker-Procter.)

Decisions, Decisions... Our Administration

The School Board along with Malcolm Brown, Superintendent; Boyce Morrison, Supervisor; and Dan Moore, Principal, are actively concerned in providing SHS with an outstanding curriculum.

The Administration decides on important issues affecting each student, the academic courses, and outside activities connected with Shelby High School.

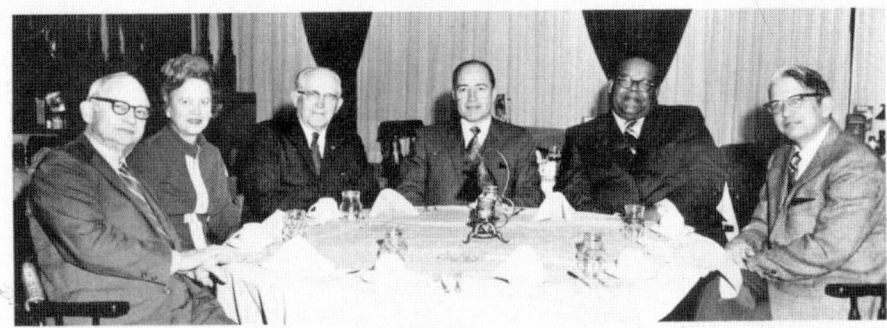

Mr. Cecil Gilliatt, Mrs. J. L. Suttle, Jr., Mr. Joe Whisnant (Board Lawyer), Mr. William Campbell, Mr. Clarence Palmer, Mr. Lamar Young.

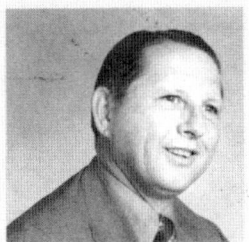

Mr. Malcolm Brown
Superintendent

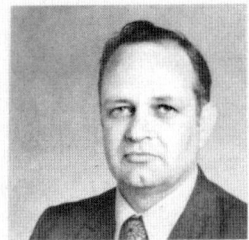

Mr. Hale Bryson
Assistant Superintendent

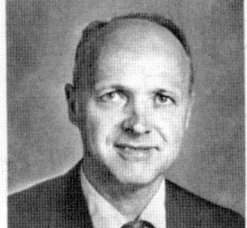

Mr. Boyce Morrison
Supervisor

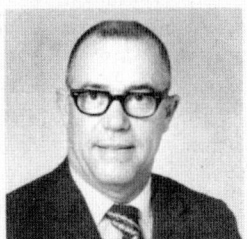

Mr. Dan Moore
Principal

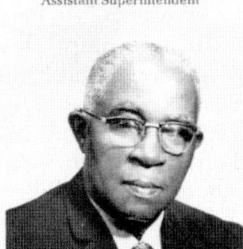

Mr. Jethro Henry
Assistant Principal

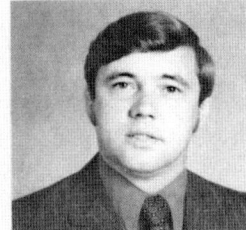

Mr. Frank McDaniel
Assistant Principal

14

The leaders of the Shelby City School System in 1972 are named above. (*Cruiser.*)

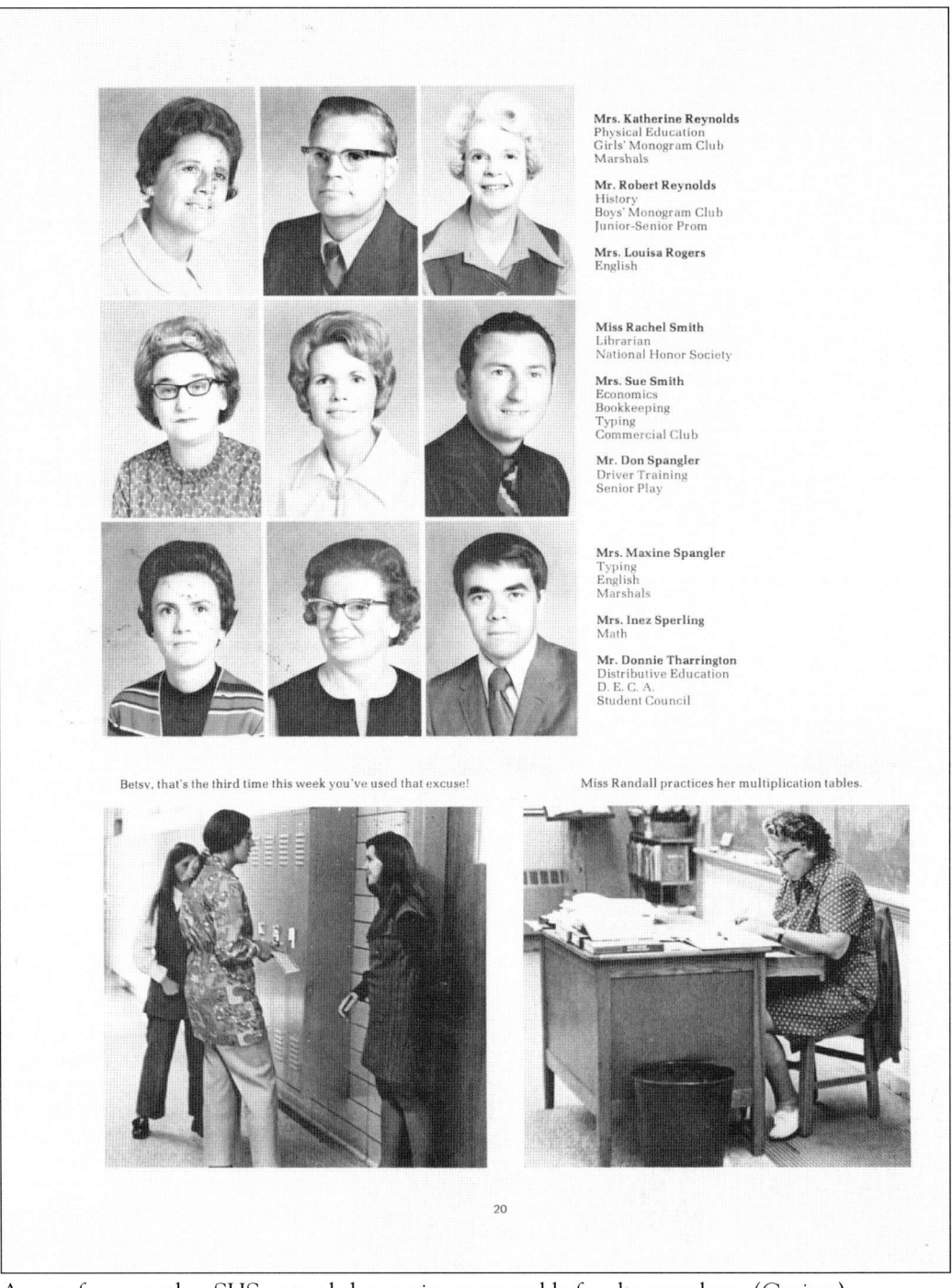

A page from another SHS annual shows nine memorable faculty members. (*Cruiser.*)

A truly memorable experience was learning algebra with Stella Randall. Randall arrived at SHS in the 1950s and survived hundreds of young scholars as they met her demands to master her subject. She is remembered for her witty quips, including asking a student caught watching the clock, "Time will pass, will you?" (*Cruiser.*)

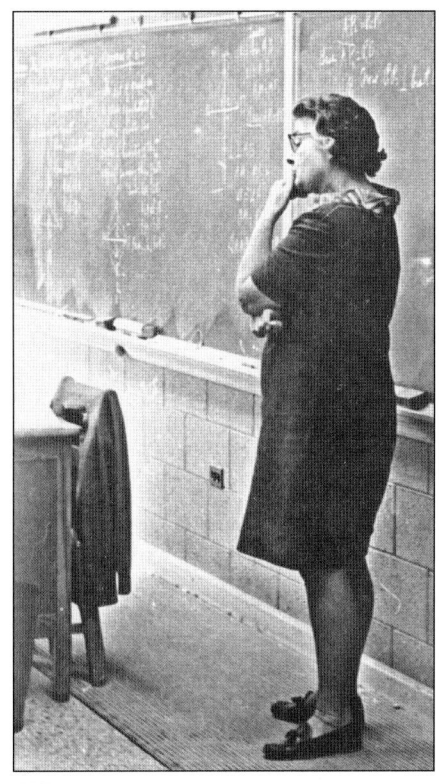

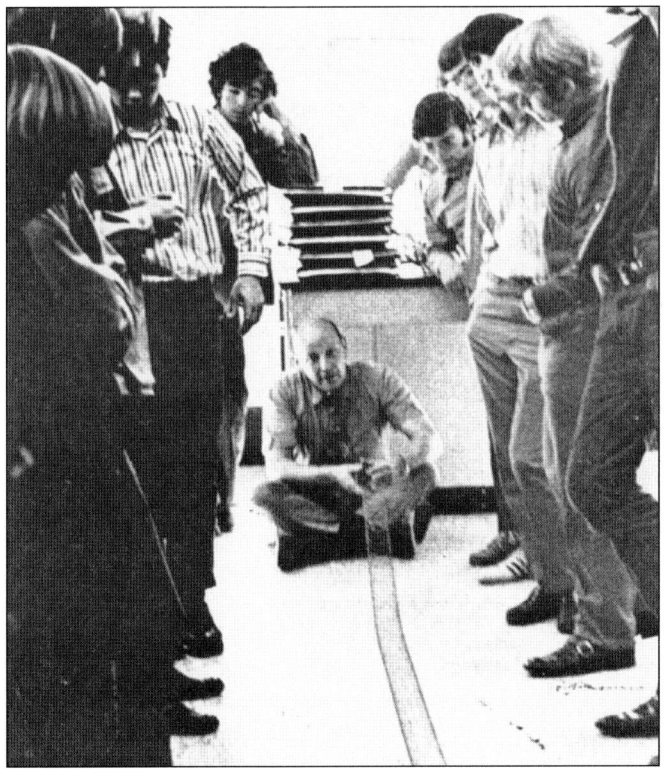

Shelby High math and physics teacher Bill Davis is remembered for his experiments and getting students involved in the subject. (*Cruiser.*)

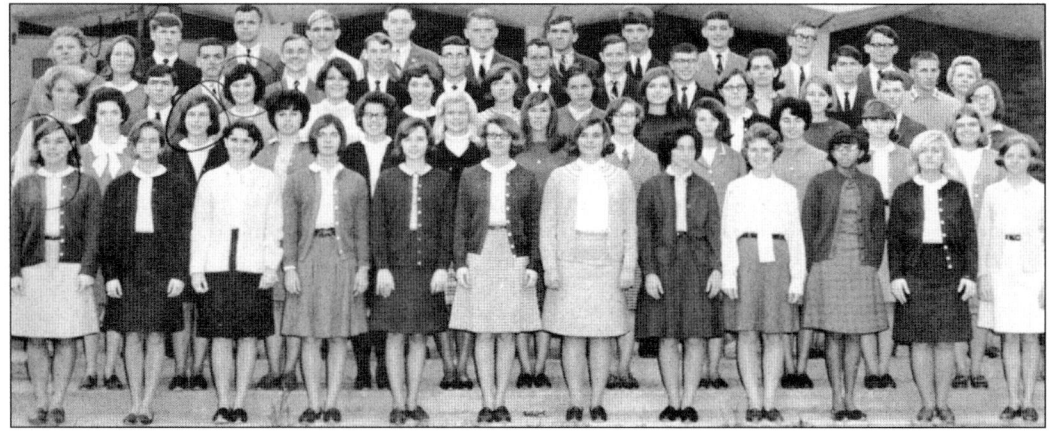

Beta Club arrived at SHS when the first members, the class of 1959, were sophomores. This group of Beta Club scholars is from 1966. (*Cruiser.*)

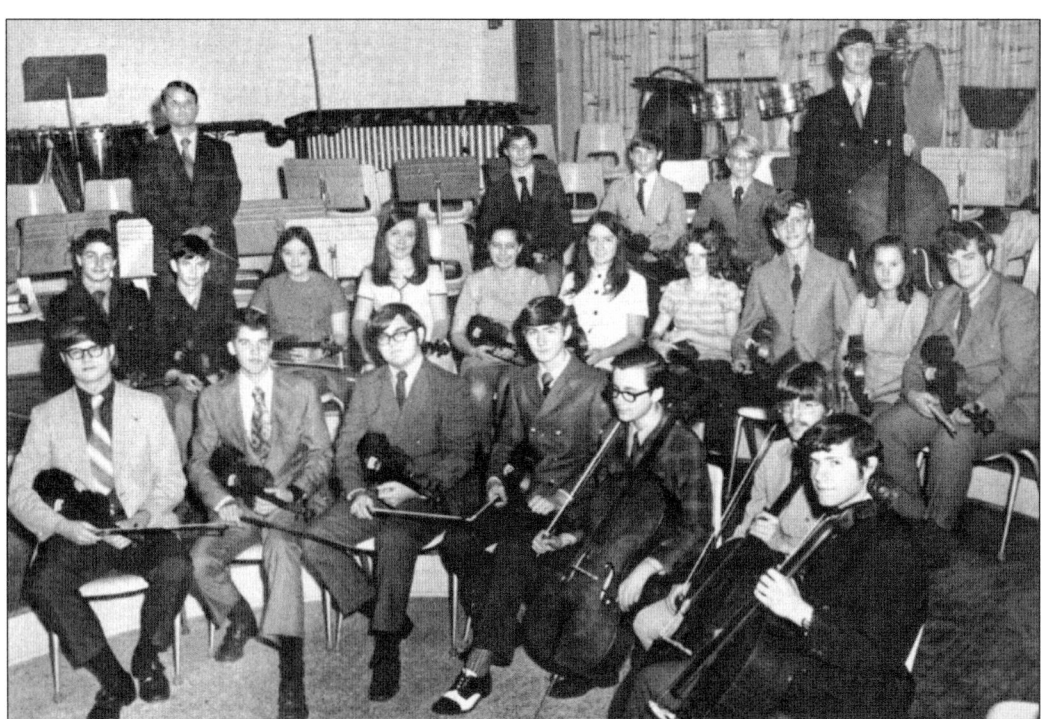

Orchestra was added to the Shelby Highs program of study in the 1960s. Pictured in the 1972 group from left to right are (first row) Bill Claytor, David Best, Barry Bridges, Eddie Cash, David Lykins, Donald Johnson, and John Rossi; (second row) Cutler Ferchaud, Bob Hearn, Debbie Beasley, Suzanne Sherrill, Mary Phillips, Geri Mauney, Karin Chadwick, Lyn Thompson, Melinda Watterson, and Duane Bradley; (third row) director Gene Ellis, Bob Burris, Bryant Scism, Jody Kendrick, and Wesley Lee. (*Cruiser.*)

The present SHS facility opened in the fall of 1961. This photograph shows the first football game of the 1961 season. Forty-six years later, fans have experienced thrills, championships, and only one losing season. (Patrick McMurry.)

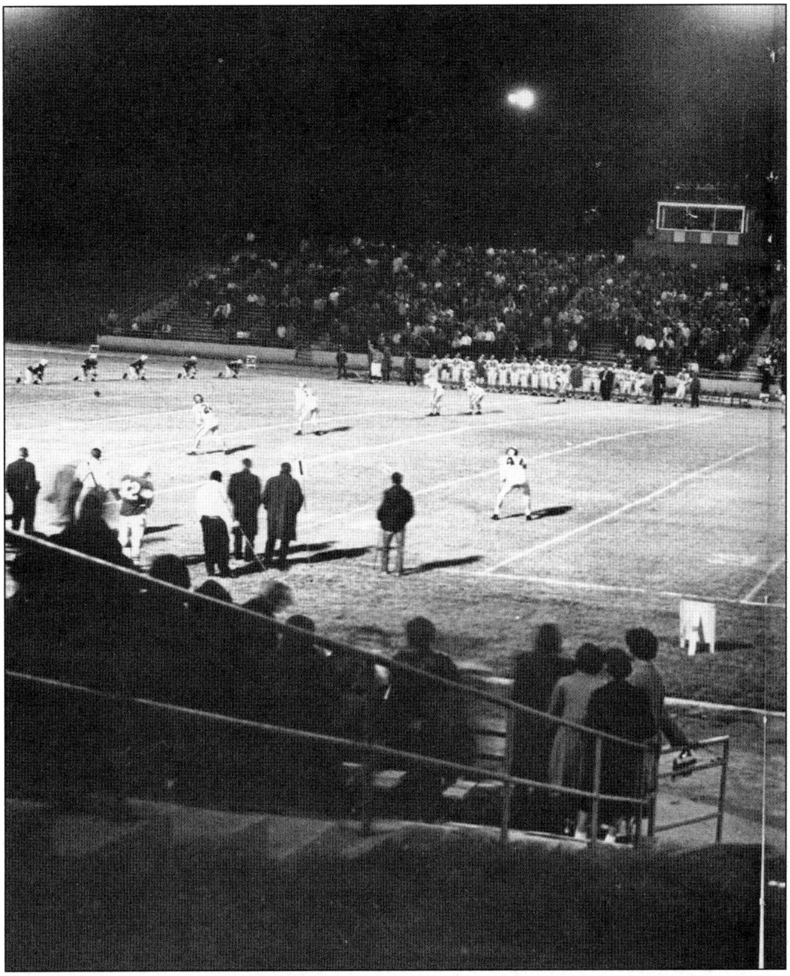

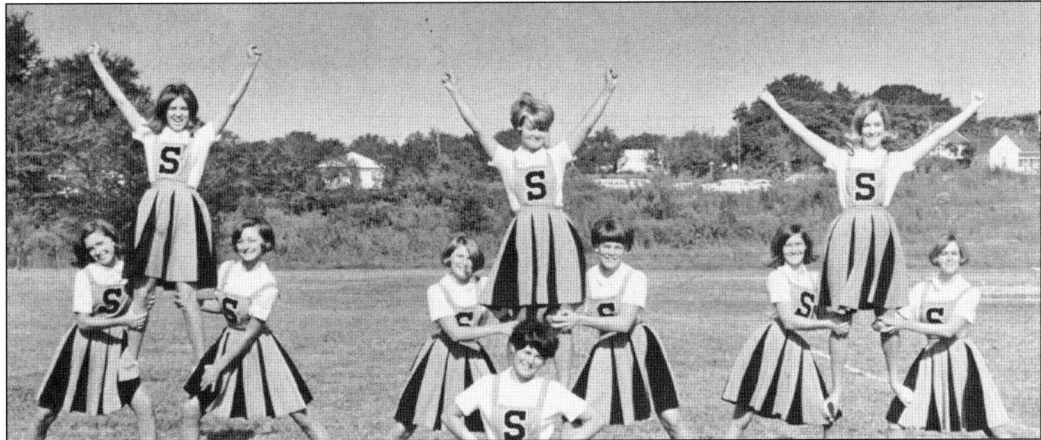

These 10 young ladies are representative of the dozens of students who have cheered the Lions to victory in football and basketball. Pictured from left to right are Billie Keeter, Nancy Brice, Carol Crump, Sue Strickland, Beth Stutts, Debbie Cloninger, Stephanie Cloninger, Susan Seal, Lee Ann Gray, and Gail Davis. (*Cruiser.*)

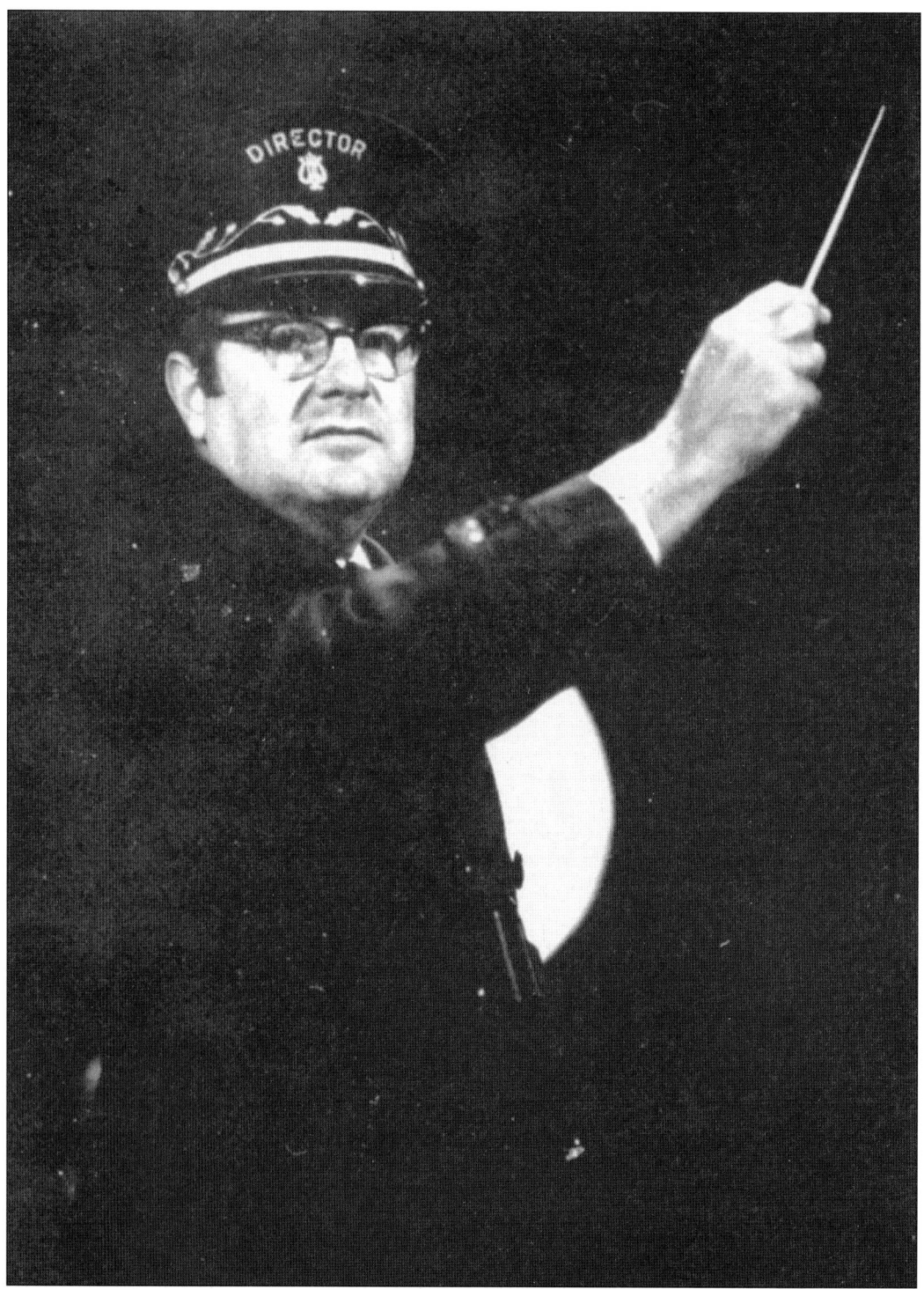
Bands members from the 1950s to the 1970s will remember Homer F. Haworth, who was, as his hat proclaims, director of the band. (*Cruiser.*)

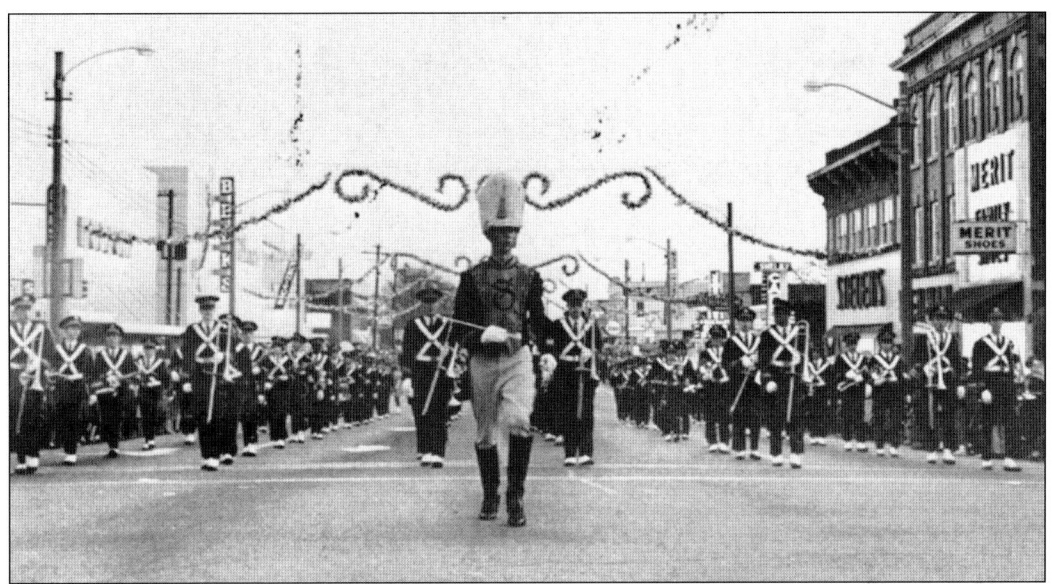

Every Shelby Christmas parade includes the Shelby High Marching Band. This c. 1965 band is marching north on Lafayette Street. (*Cruiser.*)

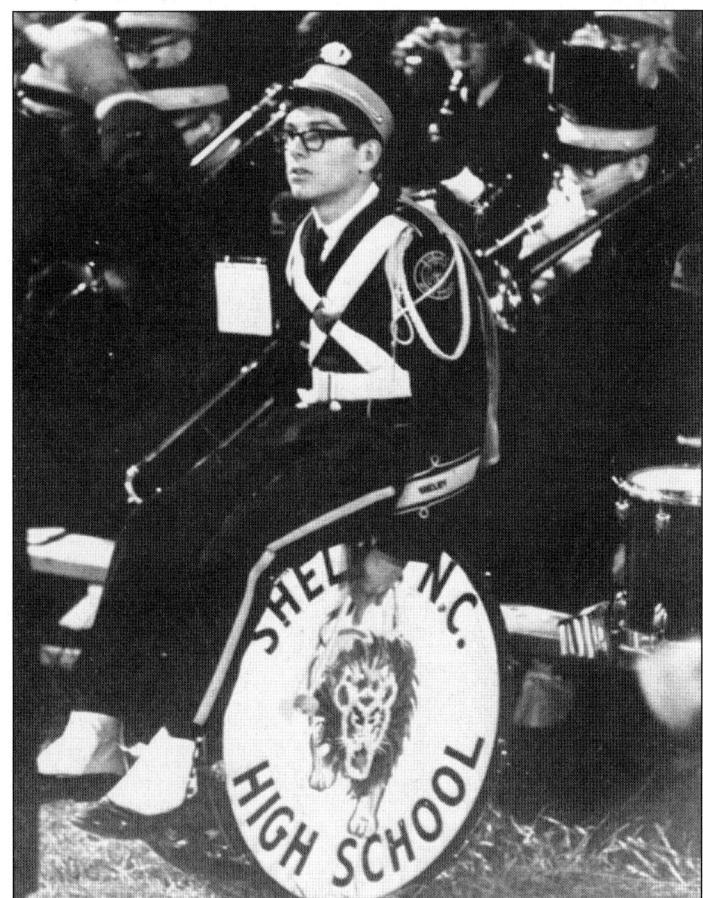

The SHS band works countless hours each fall practicing its marching routines. The band presents excellent concerts in the spring, but in the fall, the band is seen weekly at football games. Here Lee Eskridge's expression shows the disappointment as the Lions loose a close, well-fought game. (*Cruiser.*)

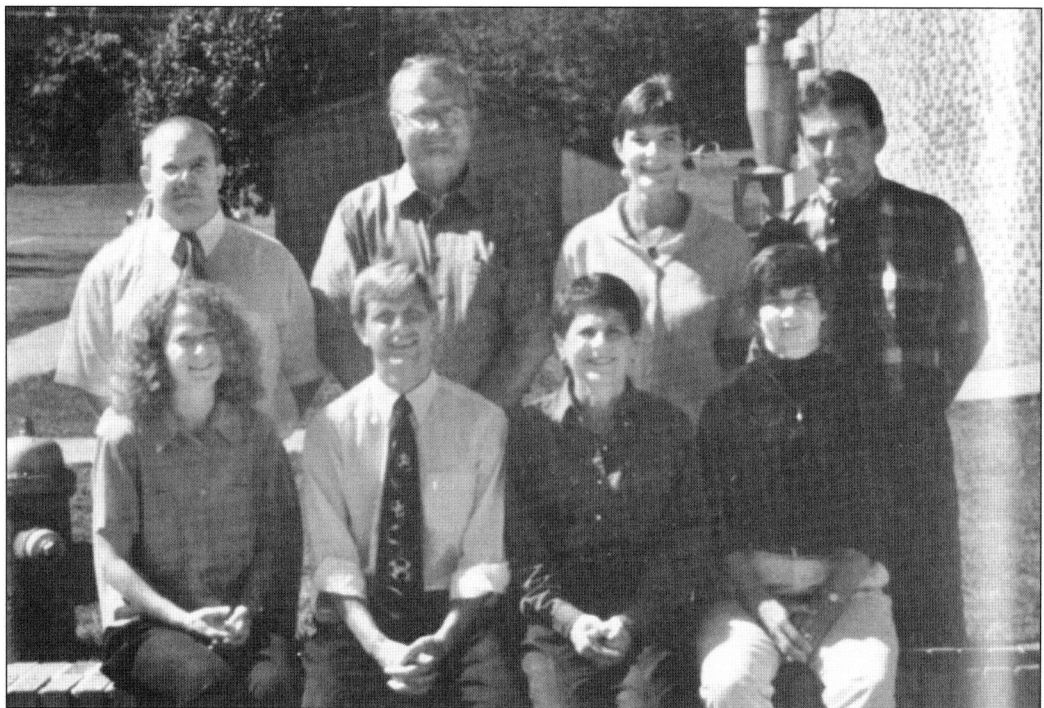

These examples of the fine SHS faculty are members of the Math Department. From left to right are (first row) Debra Crombez, David Steeves, Flossie Bonner, and Brenda Goforth, (second row) Perry Price, Art Moss, Susan Jones, and George Hall. (*Cruiser.*)

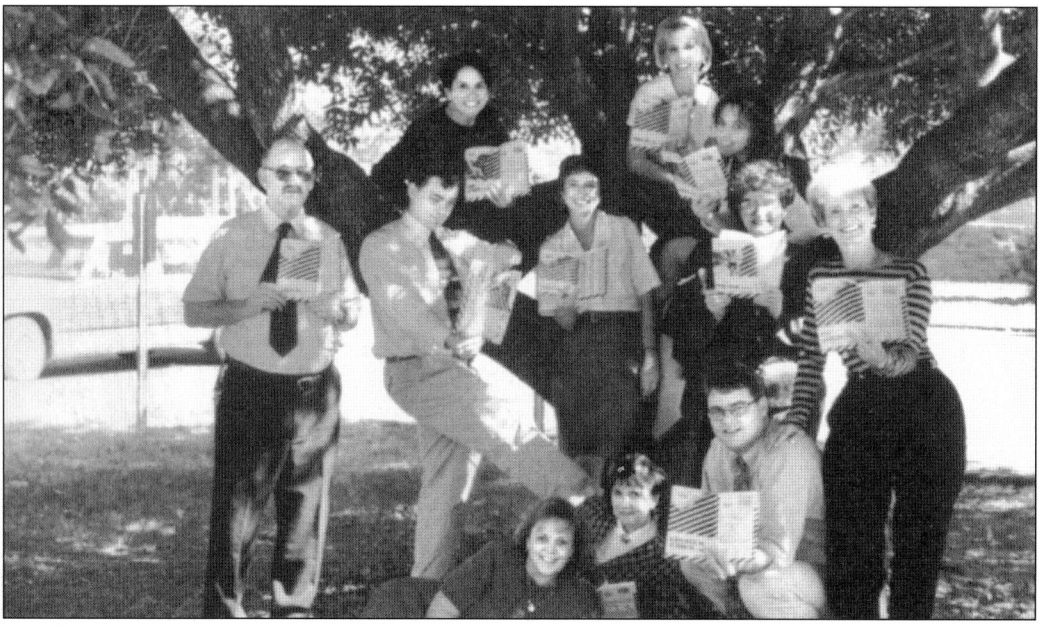

Members of the SHS English Department are known for their commitment to academic excellence. From left to right are Bob Scoggins, Jason Lineberger, Martha Strain, Glenda Self, Martha Moore, Phyllis Bumbaugh, Rhonda Wesson, Dawn Blackburn, Maria Hamrick, David Allen, and Linda Horn. (*Cruiser.*)

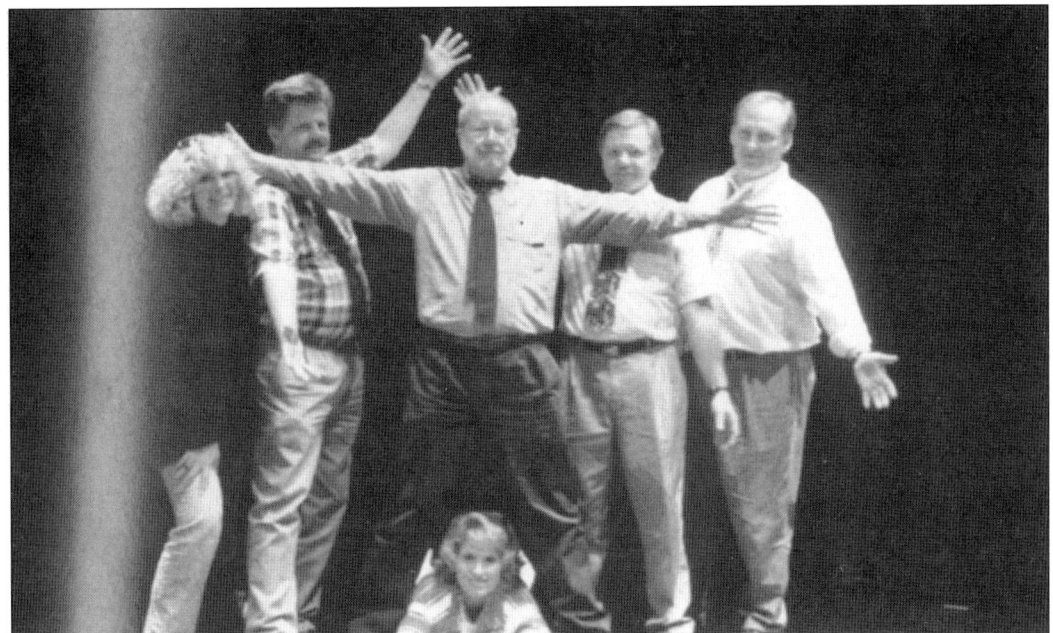

The SHS Fine Arts faculty are the geniuses behind years of award-winning student performances. Pictured from left to right are (first row) Traci Eaves (chorus); (second row) Kathy Burgin (drama), John Mode (band), Ford McDonald (art), Ed Allison (orchestra), and Steve Padgett (drama). (*Cruiser.*)

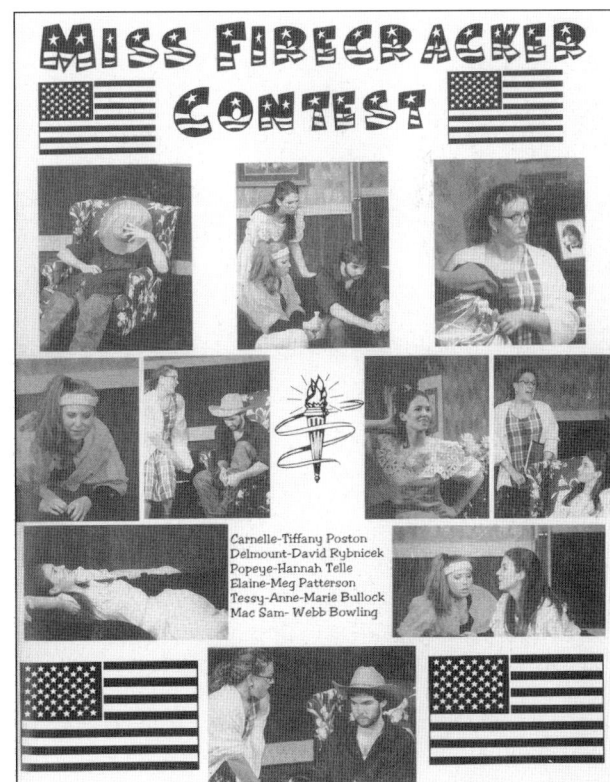

Shelby High has a history of award-winning theater productions with numerous victories at state and regional competitions. Pictured is the cast from a production of *Miss Firecracker Contest*. (*Cruiser.*)

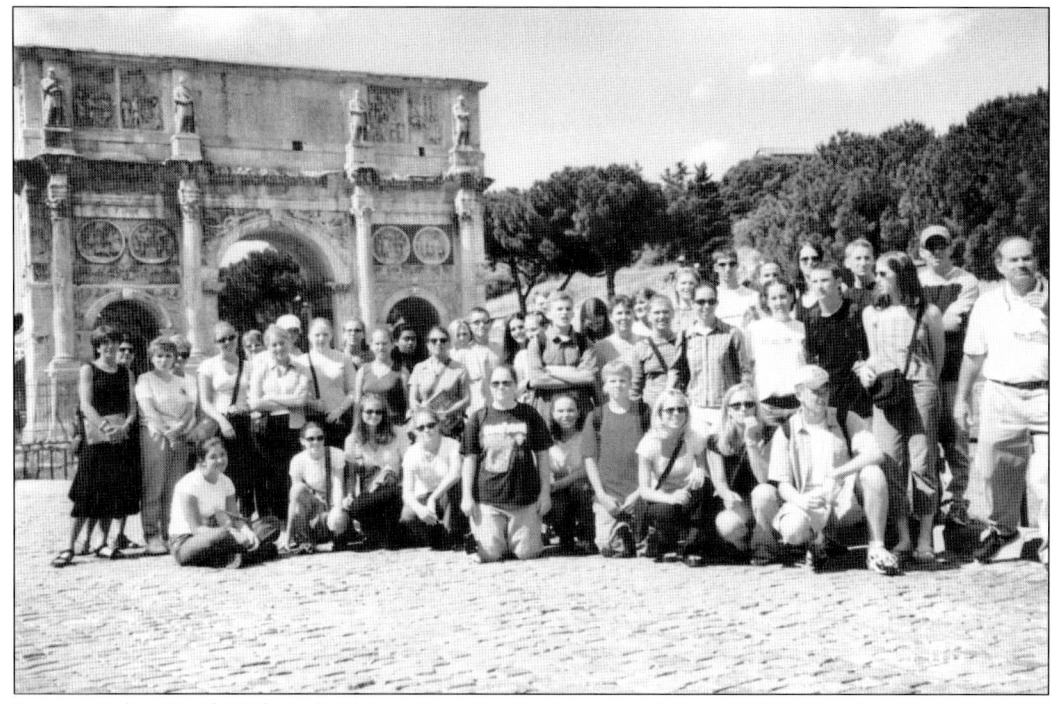
Latin teacher Emily Yelton leads a tour every three years of Europe. The students on the 2000 trip stop for a group picture in Rome.

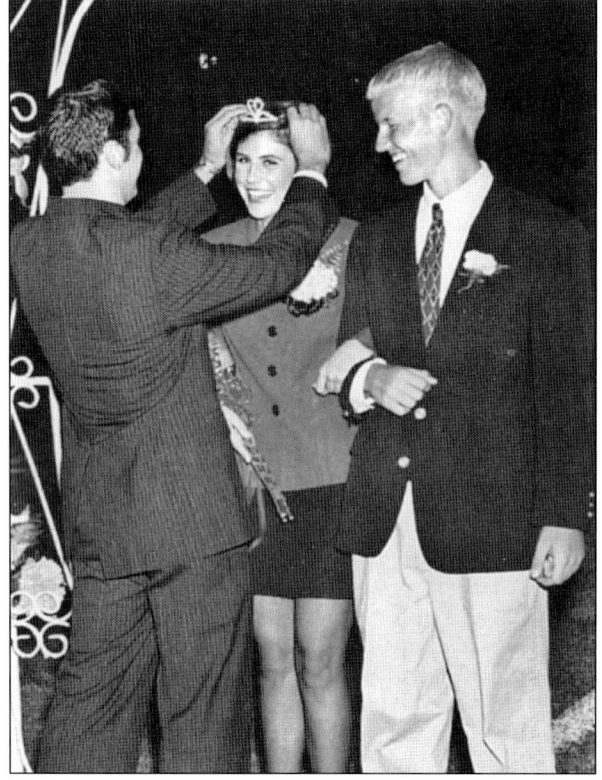
Rachel Smith is escorted by her cousin Jonathan Bridges as she is crowned 1998 Homecoming queen by class president Matt Borders. (*Cruiser.*)

Five
THE SPORTS TOWN

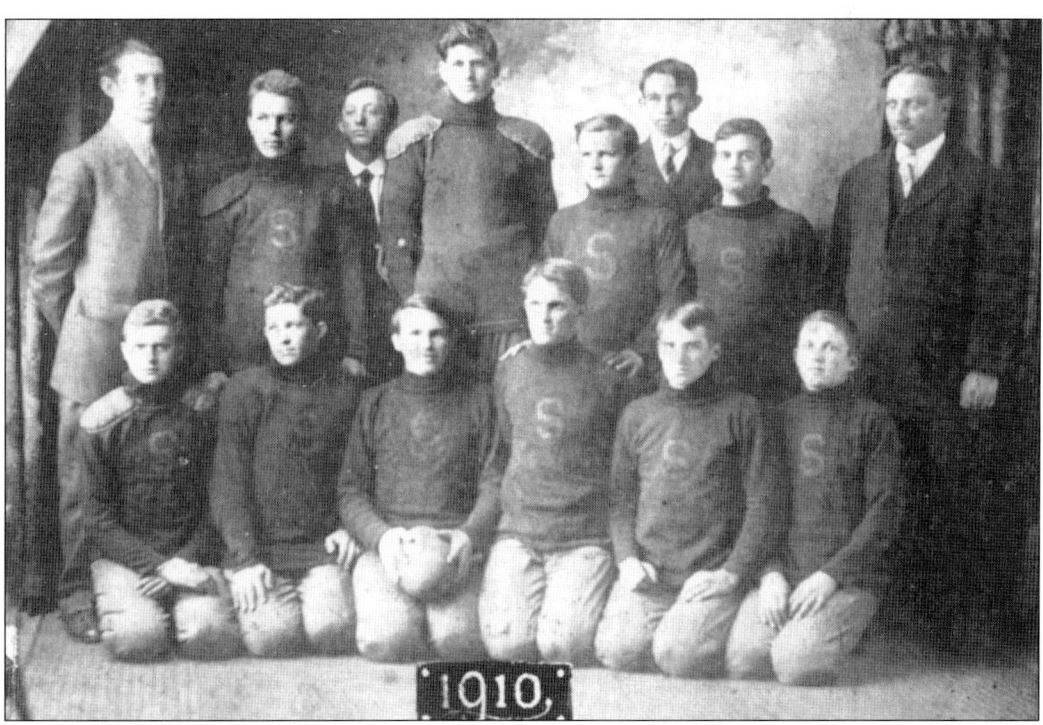

Shelby has a long heritage of fielding championship teams. Baseball, football, basketball, golf, tennis, swimming, and soccer teams from Shelby have made their mark in sports history in North Carolina. Many individuals have continued on to participate in sports at the college and professional level, some as players, others as coaches. This chapter serves as a representation of some of the players and teams that have made Shelby a sports town. Pictured above are members of the Shelby High School 1910 football team. From left to right are (first row) are Louis W. Gardner, Robert Doggett, Hilary Hudson, Ben Roberts, Harry Hudson, and Crawly Hughes; (second row) coach R. T. Howerton, Oliver S. Anthony, Alger Hamrick, George Moore, Frank Shaw, D. W. Royster, A. W. Archer, and coach S. N. Lattimore.

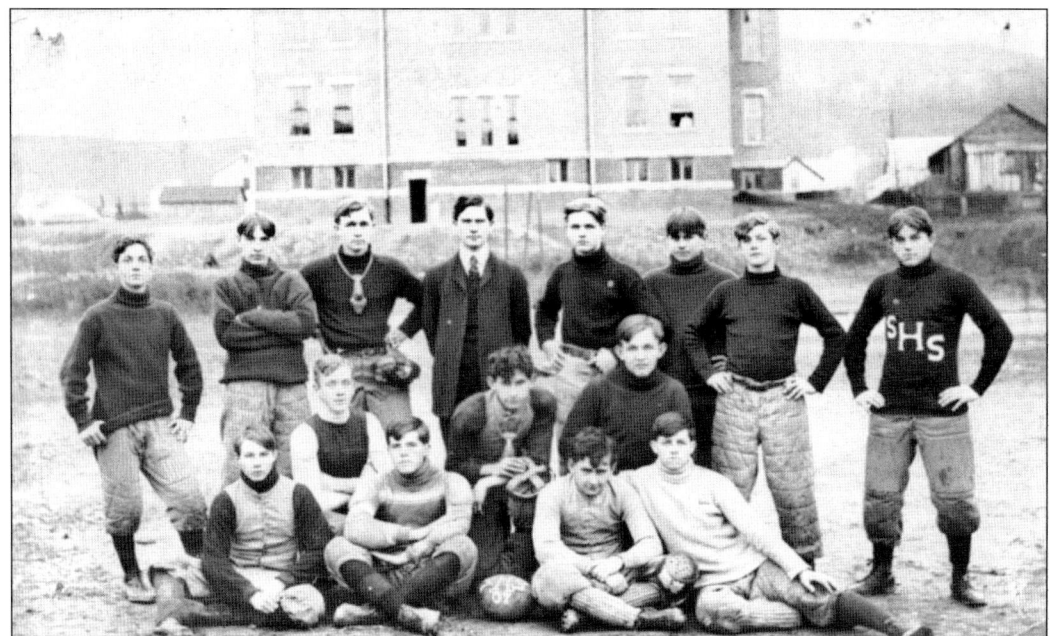
This postcard shows the Shelby High School football team of 1907 led by coach L. L. Ledford. The picture contradicts the record books that indicate football was first played in Shelby in 1910.

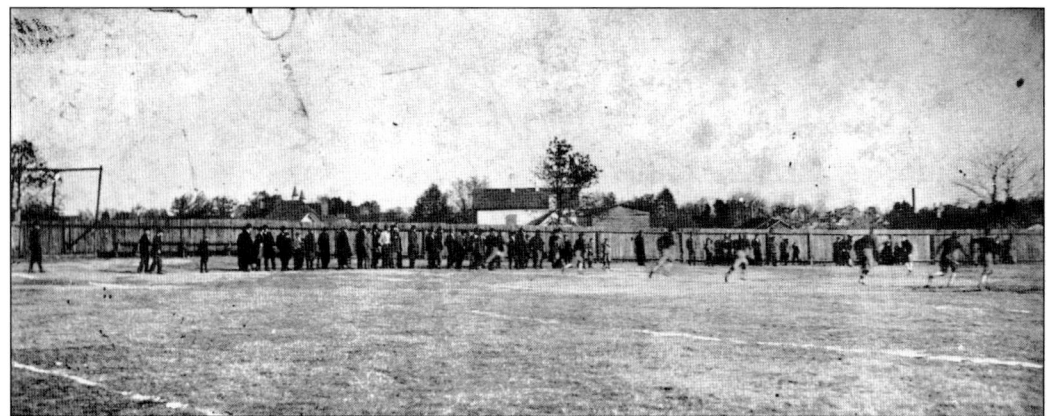
Shelby High School first played football on a field at the corner of Martin and West Graham Streets. This 1910 photograph shows fans standing by the sideline as the players take the field. (*A History of Cleveland County.*)

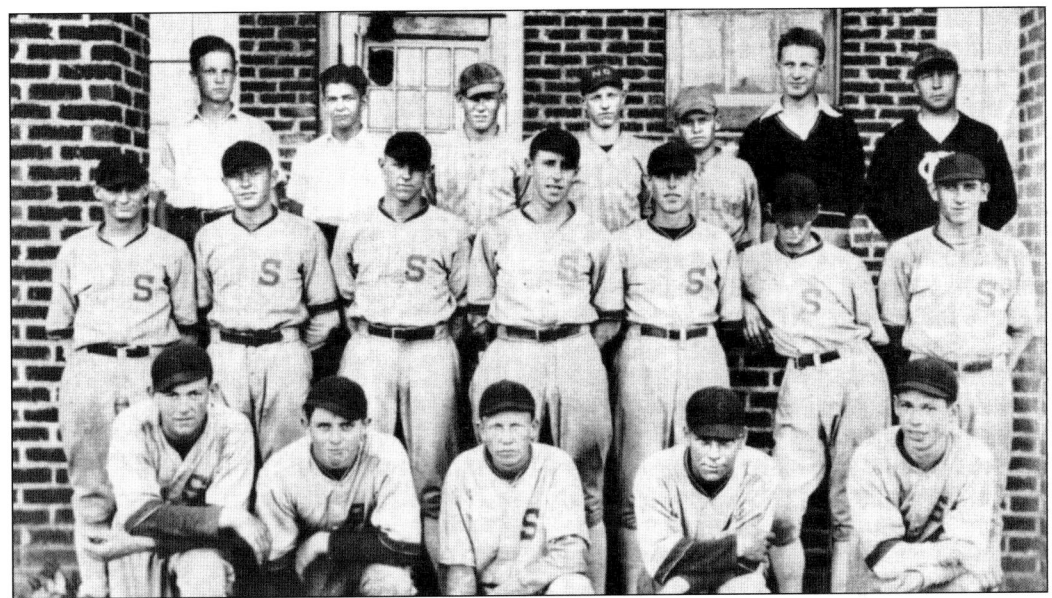

The 1929 Shelby High baseball team is pictured after winning the school's first state championship. Pictured from left to right are (first row) Frank Harrelson, Donnie Hulick Jr., Palmer McSwain, Carl Queen, and Guy Bridges; (second row) Thurston Bumgardner, Hal Farris, Marshall "Lefty" Moore, Milton Gold, Sherrill Hamrick, Clay "Mud" Poston, and Cline Owen Lee; (third row) Allen Suttle, Charles Switzer, an unidentified player, Sam Dayberry, an unidentified player, manager Ralph Gardner, and coach R. W. "Casey" Morris. (*A History of Cleveland County*.)

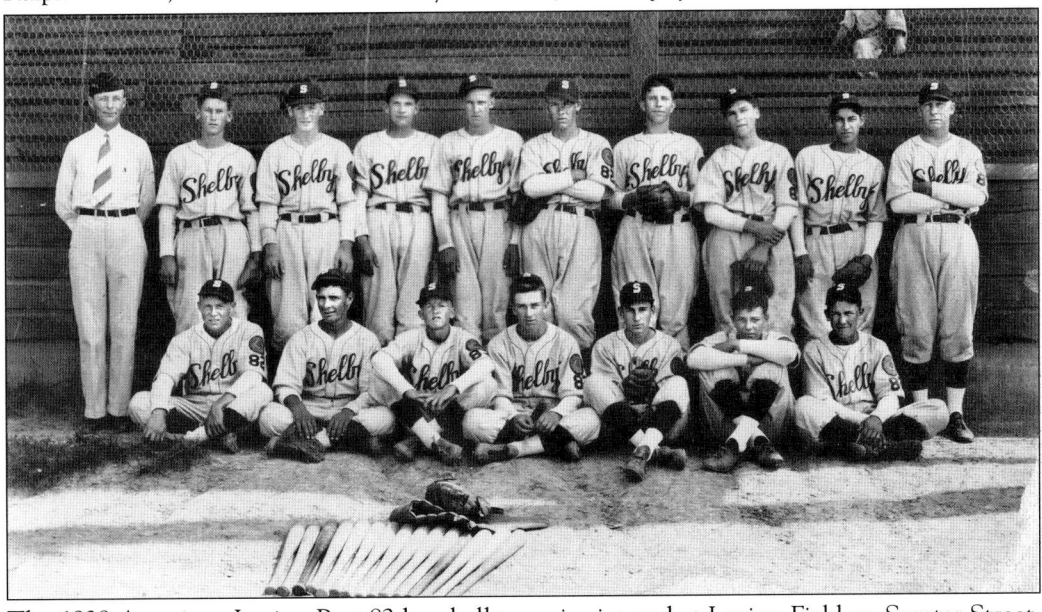

The 1938 American Legion Post 82 baseball team is pictured at Legion Field on Sumter Street. Pictured from left to right are (first row) Joe Lane, Don Gold, Bud Hardin, Sam Crawley, ? Morrison, Charlie Ballard, and Hal Dedmon; (second row) athletic director Mr. Hamrick, Bob Brooks, Red Christopher, Elly Grant, John B. Roberts, Richard Branton, Jack Whetside, Sleep Gibson, Archie Bridges, and coach Casey Morris. Post 82 would go on to win state championships in 1942, 1945, 1951, 1957, 1958, and 2001. (Uptown Shelby Association.)

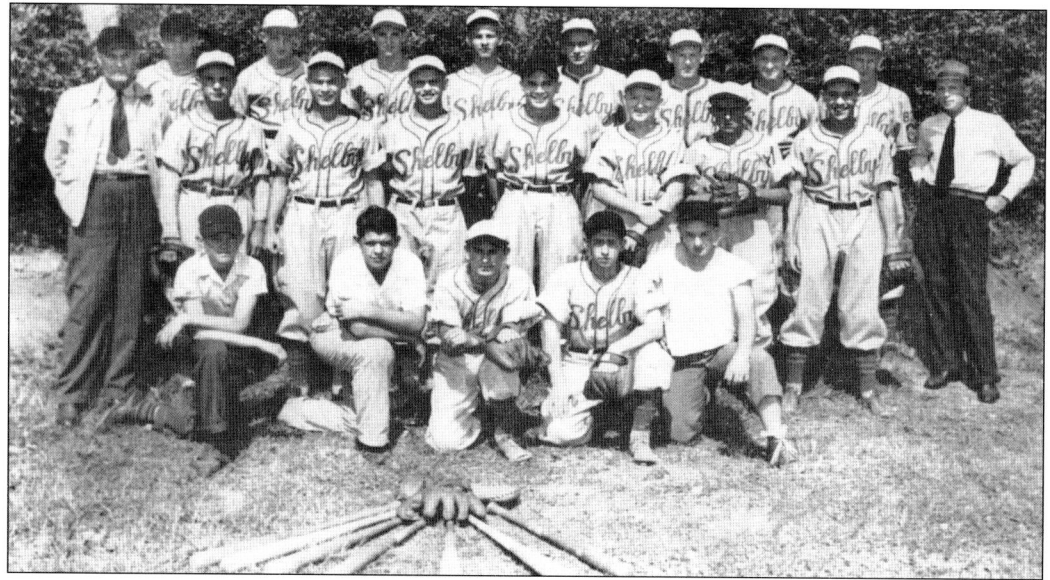

In 1945, Post 82 won the Legion Little World Series, played in Charlotte, North Carolina, and claimed the title of National Champions. Pictured from left to right are (first row) Babe Hamrick, Benny Allen, B. C. Wilson, Furman Webber, and Norris Jones; (second row) Lefty McGraw, Boots Kent, Jack Bridges, Allan Washburn, Bill Megginson, Floyd Cook, and Mack Poston; (third row) coach Pop Simmons, A. J. Bumgardner, Charlie Hutchins, Loy Paige, Don Cheek, Bill Weaver, Gene Hastings, Harvey Brown, Bob Cabaniss, and coach Lloyd Little.

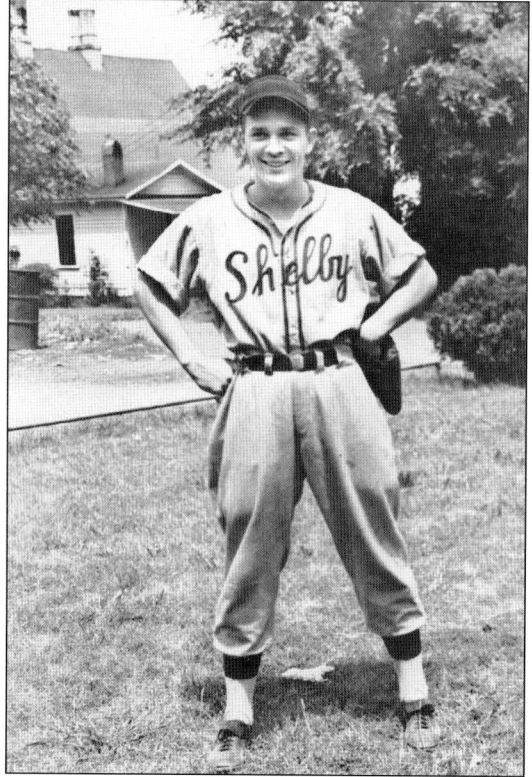

Allan Washburn was a star on the 1945 American Legion championship team. Washburn went on to play minor-league baseball. (Uptown Shelby Association.)

Rogers Hornsby "Lefty" McKee played two seasons with the Philadelphia Phillies in 1943 and 1944 before entering military service. At the time, McKee was the youngest pitcher to play in the major leagues.

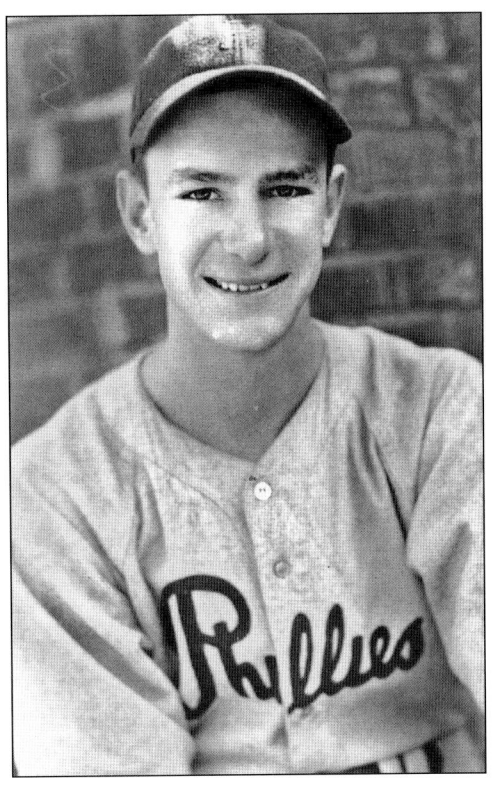

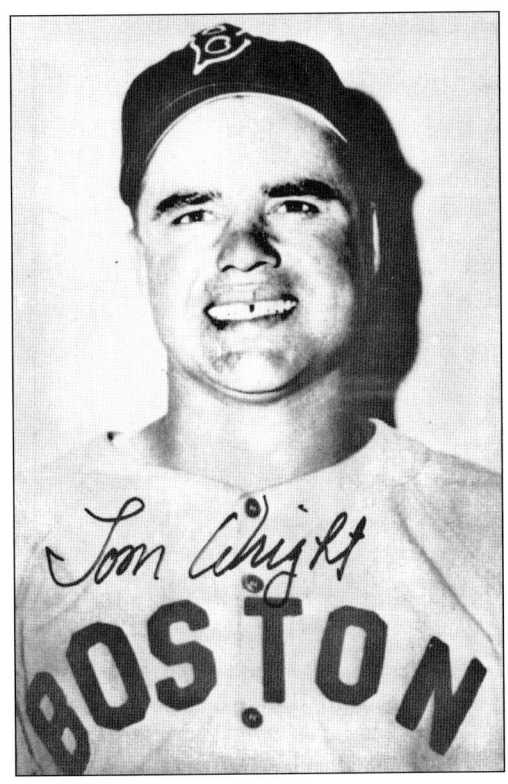

Tom Wright played outfield for seven seasons in the major leagues. He played for the St. Louis Cardinals, Boston Red Sox, and later with the Washington Senators.

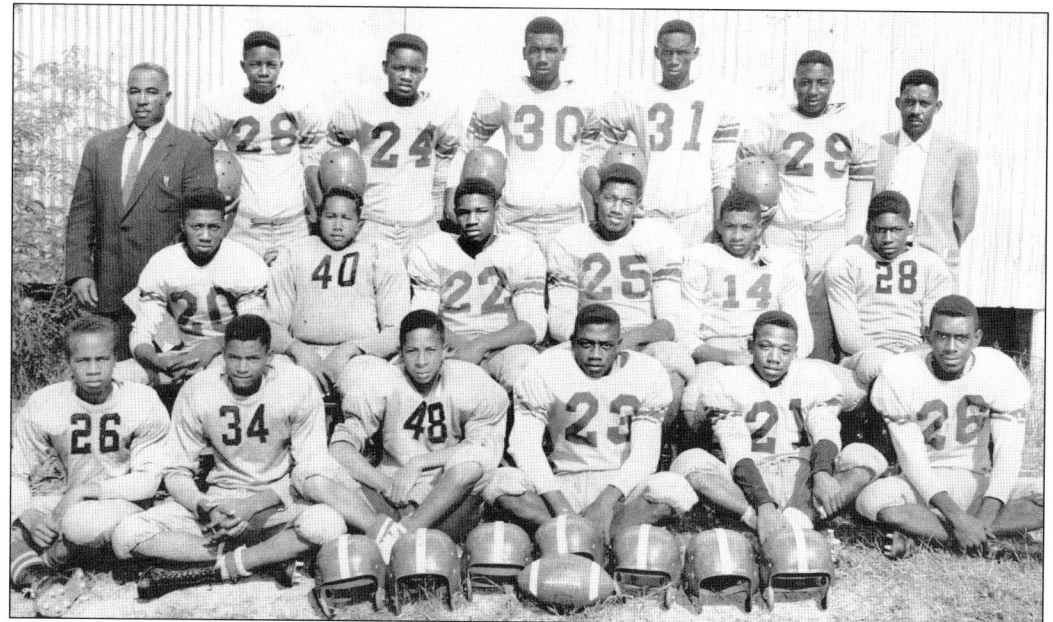

The Cleveland High School Tigers are pictured in the late 1950s. Members from left to right included (first row) Johnny Brown, Jeremiah Wilson, Leon "Pop" Cunningham, James McConnell, James Cherry, and J. C. Berry; (second row) Sam Cherry, Billy Bridges, Harvey Keaton, Bobby Bell, Sam "Sonny" Raper, and Hubert Brantley; (third row) assistant coach Henry, Irving Toms, Ben Toms, Pink Bell, Jimmy Hartgrove, Robert Lee McConnell, and head coach John Winston.

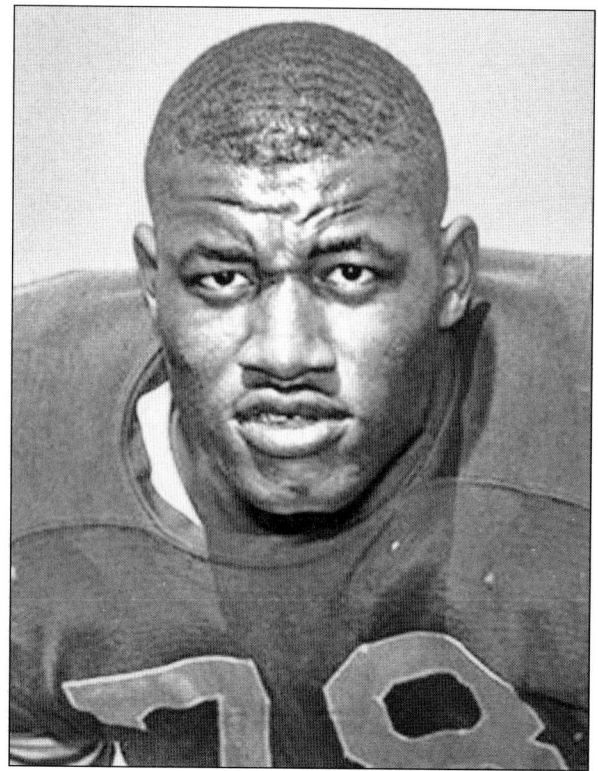

In 1962, Bobby Bell (No. 25 above) was named an All-American tackle and Outland Trophy winner at the University of Minnesota. Following college, Bell signed with the Kansas City Chiefs in the NFL. The star linebacker led the Chiefs to a Super Bowl victory in 1969 with a 23-7 victory over the Minnesota Vikings. Bell was inducted in the NFL Hall of Fame in 1983. Today Bell operates a barbecue restaurant in Kansas City.

Shelbian Jim Horn was an offensive and defensive lineman at Wake Forest University in the 1953–1955 seasons. After college, Horn returned to Shelby to join the Shelby High School Golden Lions coaching staff. (Linda Horn.)

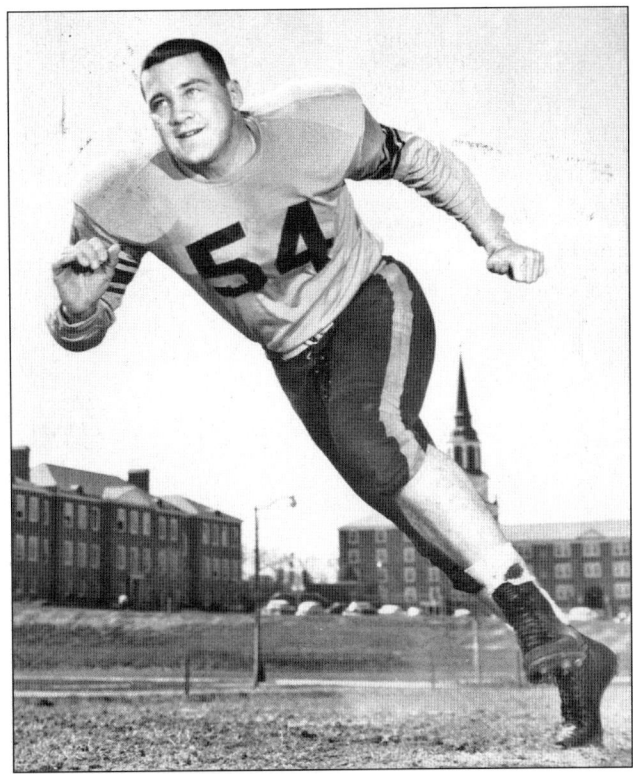

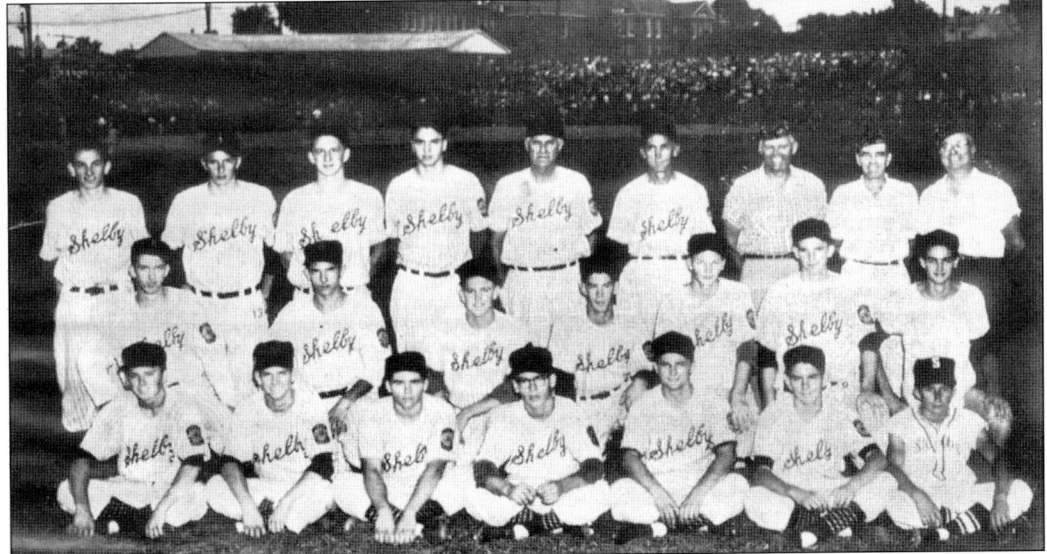

The Shelby American Legion team of 1958 earned state champion honors. Pictured from left to right are (first row) Wallace Fortenberry, Johnny Kennedy, Tom Wright Jr., Junior Queen, Ronnie Vaughn, Don Olsen, and batboy Pee Wee Trammell; (second row) Dave Chambers, Bobby Hoover, Buddy Phillips, Ken Willis, Cliff Dysart, Al Dixon, and assistant team manager "Man" Kale; (third row) Heyward Hull, Ken Hamby, Ronnie O'Shields, John Kouri, coach B. E. "Pop" Simmons, assistant coach Bill Metcalf, team manager B. F. Hamrick, athletic officer Olin Sneed, and legion commander J. C. Hardeman.

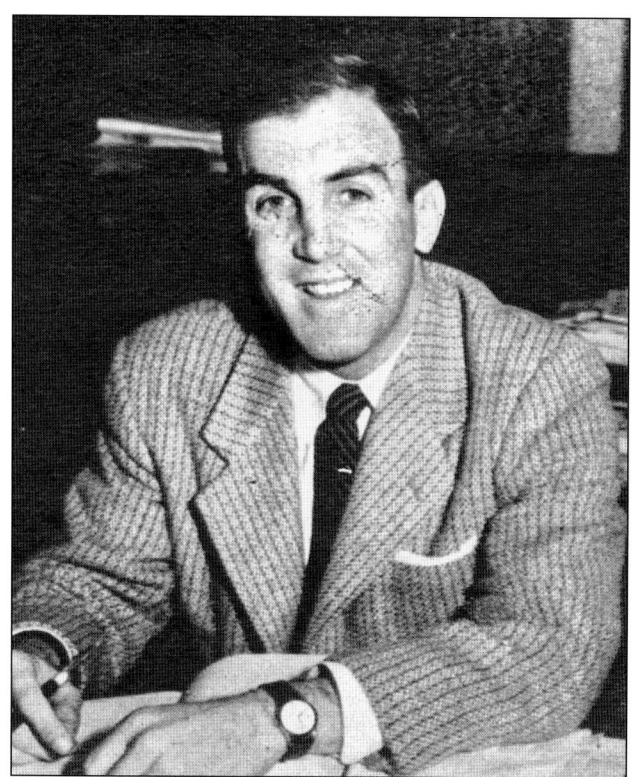

The name Buck Archer and tennis are synonymous in Shelby. Archer began playing tennis at the age of six and went on to captain the Davidson College tennis team. Archer coached many outstanding local tennis stars, including Jim Corn and Chuck Cloninger. Buck won numerous tennis titles and played on the Gordon Cup team that represented the United States against Canada. For many years, Archer was ranked No. 1 in the state for seniors' doubles.

Pete Webb and George Corn are pictured before a round of golf. Both were members of the Fellowship of Christian Athletes Hall of Fame. Webb played in two U.S. Open tournaments and won many Pro-Am tournaments in the Southeast. (The *Star*.)

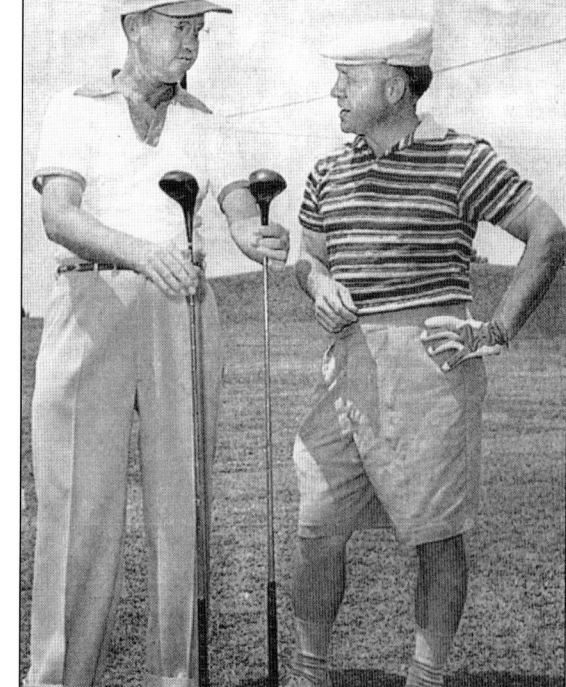

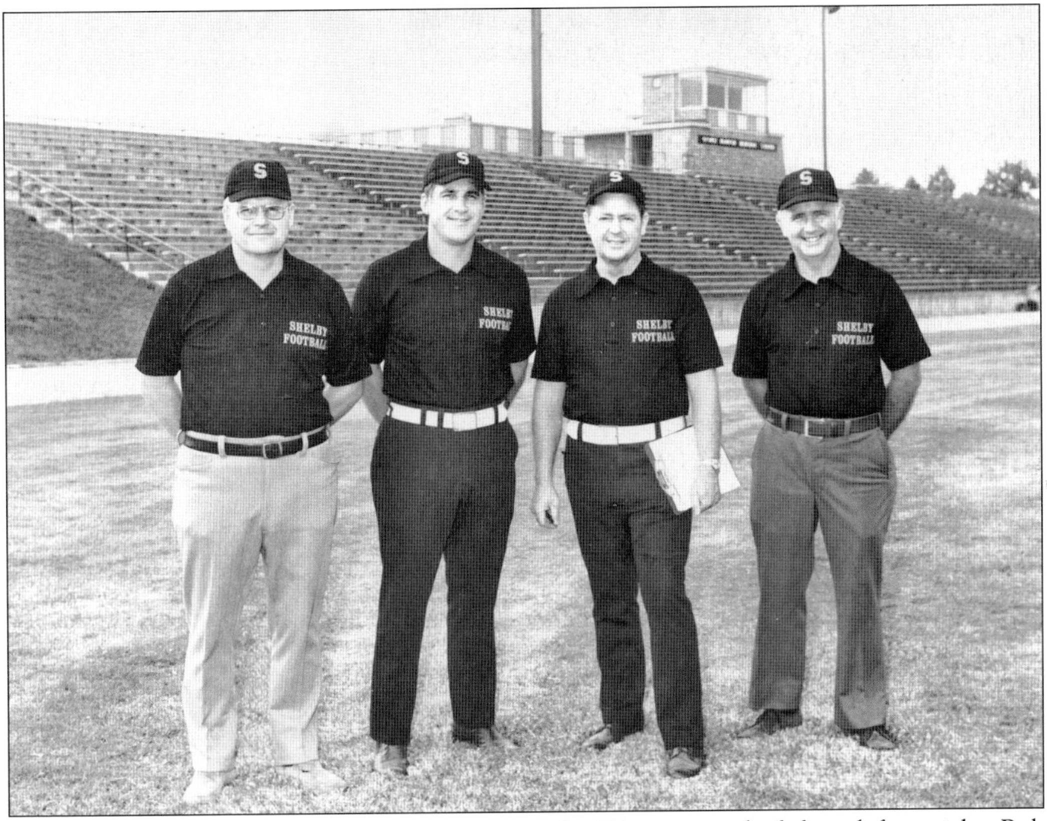

The Shelby High coaching staff in the 1960s and 1970s consisted of, from left to right, Bob Reynolds, Jim Horn, Gerald "Pearley" Allen, and Gene Kirkpatrick. This excellent coaching staff was the heart of the Shelby football dynasty and set the standard for future coaches. On countless occasions, this brain trust made adjustments to bring home the victory. Coach Allen compiled a record of 175-49-14 in 21 years as head coach. (Jim Horn.)

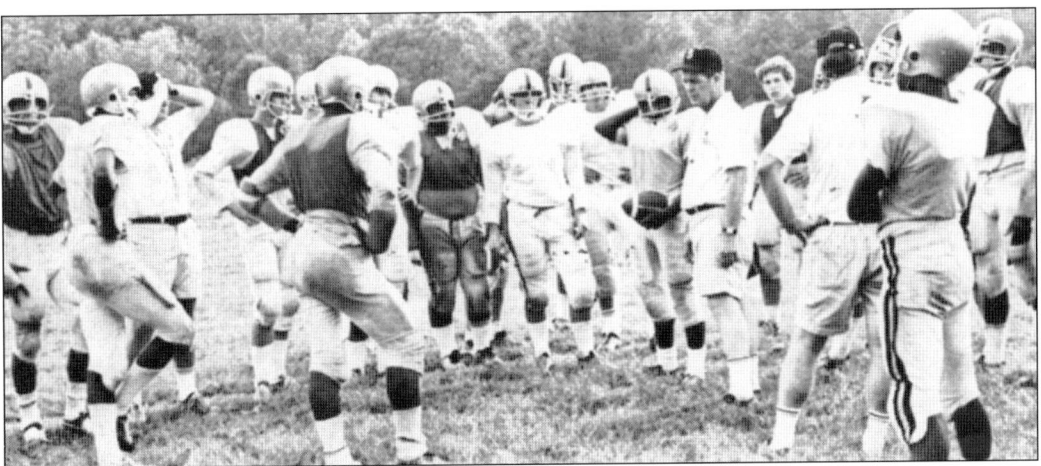

Success on the field came as a result of hours of dedicated practice. Year in and year out, the SHS coaches have produced winning teams while building a strong work ethic and developing character in their players. (*Cruiser.*)

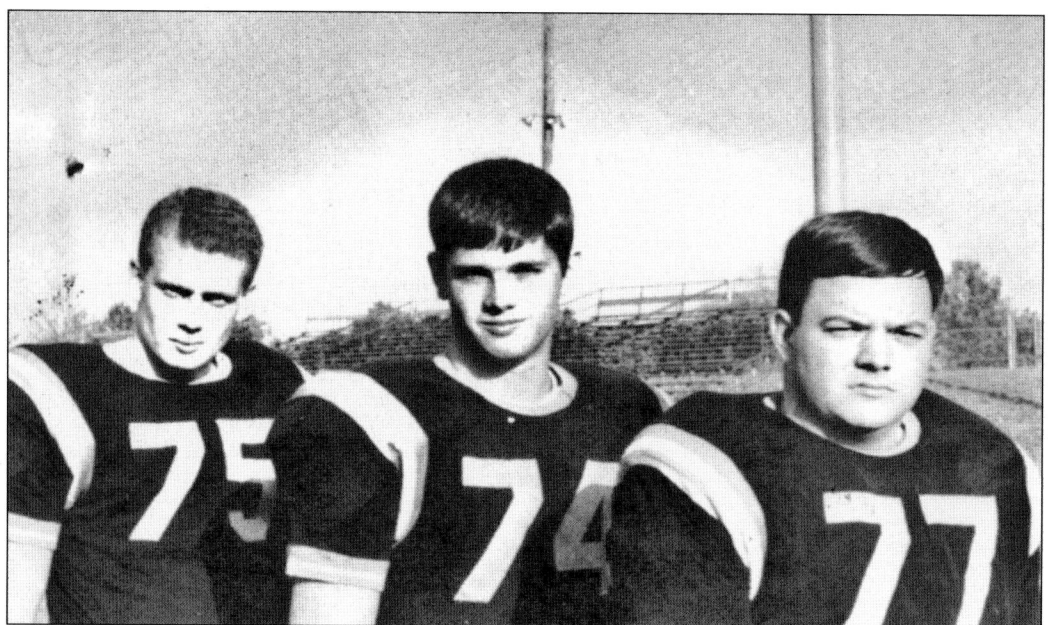

Senior tackles in 1966 included James Washburn (left), Mike Roebuck (center), and Rick Huffstetler (right). Washburn and Roebuck went on to play college football, and Washburn become a successful coach in the National Football League. (*Cruiser*.)

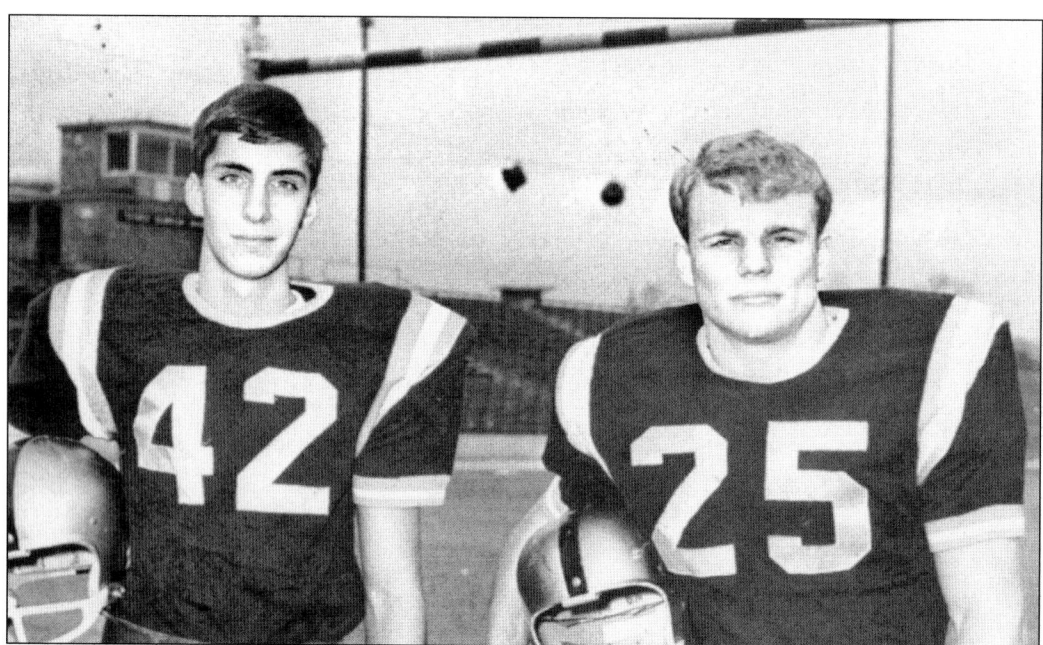

Senior halfbacks for the 1966 Golden Lions were Bee Strain (left) and David Schweppe (right). An accomplished scholar and musician, Schweppe lost his life in an automobile accident during his senior year of high school. (*Cruiser*.)

After graduating from Shelby High in 1965, pitcher Billy Champion was drafted by the Philadelphia Phillies. Making his major-league debut on June 4, 1969, Champion went on to play eight seasons of professional baseball with the Phillies and Milwaukee Brewers.

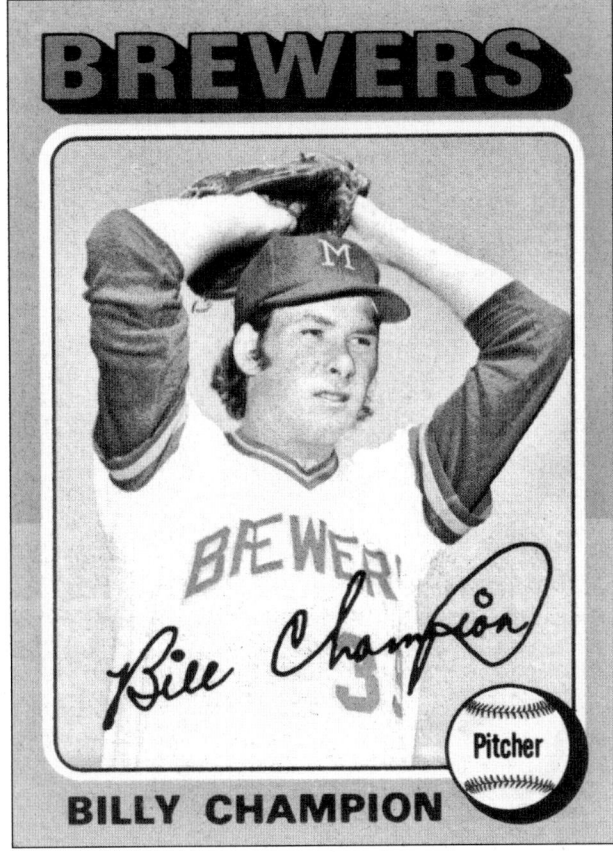

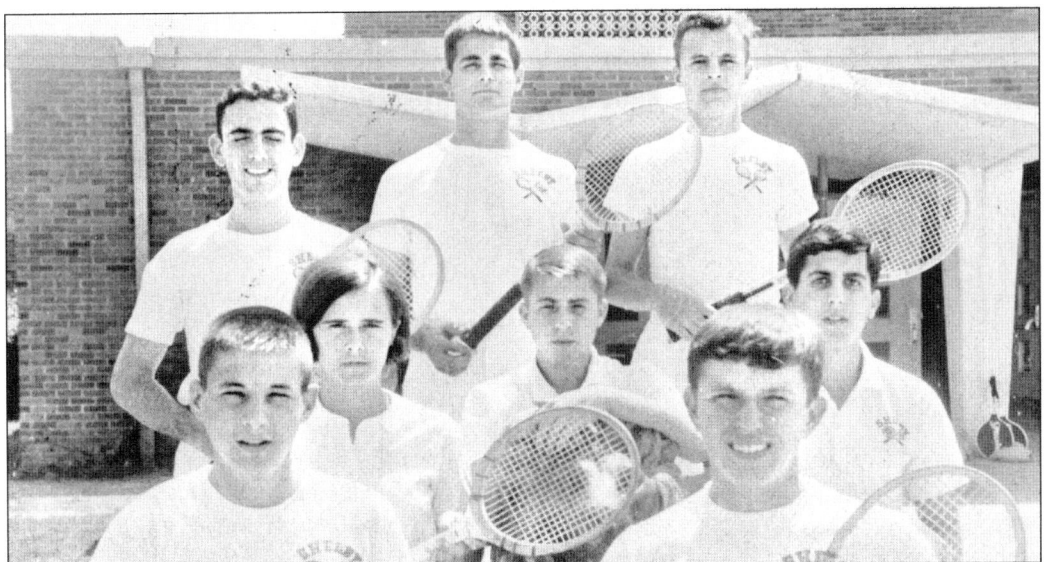

The Shelby High tennis team, led by coach Lloyd Little, won the 1966 Western North Carolina High School Athletic Association championship. Pictured from left to right are (first row) Billy Walter and Lee Wallace; (second row) Belinda Vaughn, Jim Corn, and Ali Paksoy; (third row) Ricky Tigner, Chip Cloninger, and Stuart LeGrand. (*Cruiser.*)

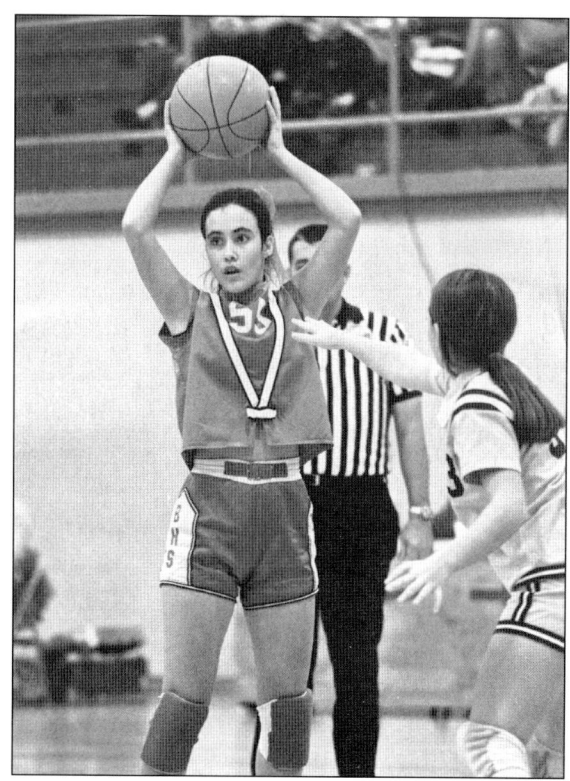

Shelby native Alison Campbell Gilbert is pictured playing basketball for Baldwin High School in Milledgeville, Georgia, where she averaged 27.3 points per game in her senior year. She went on to play college basketball at Queens College in Charlotte and at the University of Georgia in Athens. Today Gilbert is a mortgage banker with First National Bank. (Alison Gilbert.)

Shelby High standout Millie Keeter Holbrook dominated high school and college golf tournaments before joining the Ladies Professional Golf Association as a touring professional. She later played and taught golf in Japan. Today she heads the physical education department at Cleveland Community College in Shelby. (Millie Keeter Holbrook.)

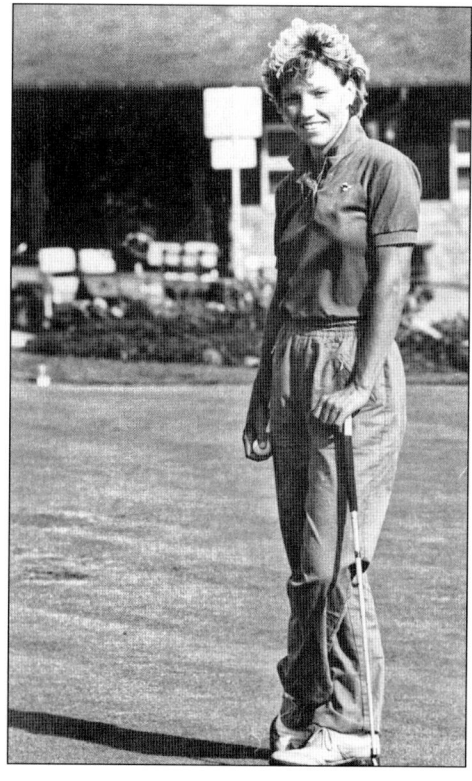

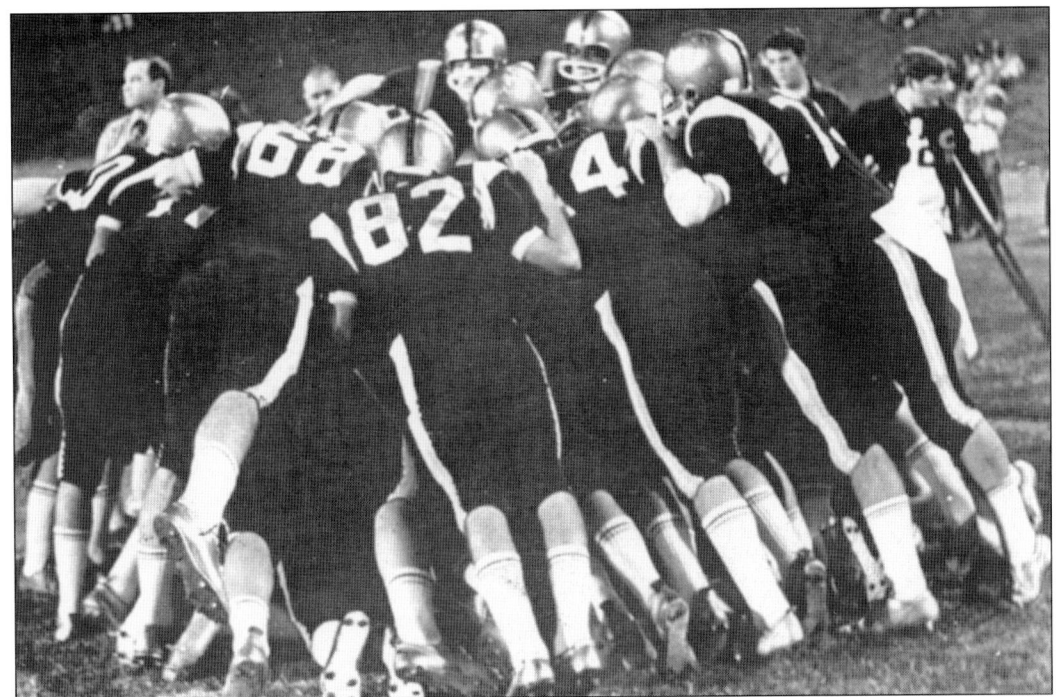

This early version of a pile-on is from the 1970 championship season. The traditional pre-game pile-on is believed to have started during the 1969 season and continues today. (*Cruiser*.)

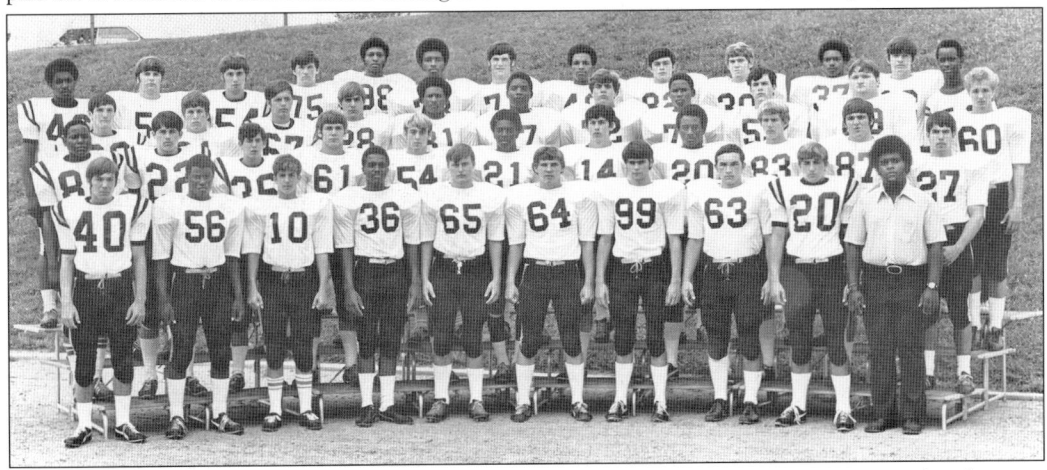

The Shelby High football team of 1972 recorded a perfect 13-0 season, winning the division championship for the third time in five years. The undefeated season was the first in Shelby's storied history. Pictured from left to right are (first row) Louie Davidson, Gregory Hopper, Brian Strain, Claude London, Weston Burgess, Harvey Ramsey, Ken Waldrop, Mark Harmon, Jeff Taylor, and manager Stacy Parrot; (second row) Dennis Laborn, Brian Shull, Joey White, Glenn McCants, Steve Kiser, Mitchell Terrell, Mike Beatty, Larry Eberhart, Kim Robinson, Frank Callahan, and Danny Miller; (third row) Roger Davis, Scott White, Billy Morehead, Bobby Noblitt, Virgil Petty, Frankie Smith, Don Peeler, James Smith, Andy McMurry, William Hullender, and Robert Howell; (fourth row) Ronald Davenport, Jim Morgan, Dusty Haynes, Jeff Peeler, Daryl Byers, Steve Ager, Mike Dover, Tommy London, Mike Mode, Chris Horne, Gerald Poston, Mike Callahan, and manager Ted Ross. (Jim Morgan.)

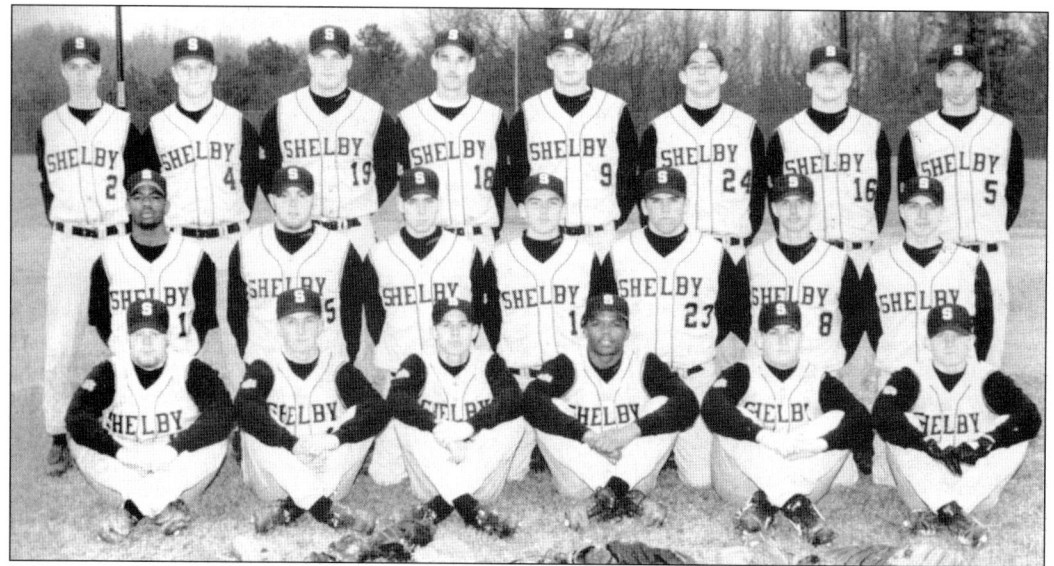

The 1998 SHS baseball team was filled with stars both on an off the field. Pictured from left to right are (first row) Bradley Willis, Zak Cox, Matt Henderson, Norris Hopper, Luke Ware, and Josh Ferree; (second row) Jarvis Harris, Jay Hollifield, Clint Franklin, Jeff Teague, Paul McMurry, Travis Glover, and Wilkes Strain; (third row) Butler Strain, Patrick Tiernan, Steven Boswell, Charlie Blanton, Brian Shuford, Hal Alexander, Chad Davis, and Rusty Blake. Today Norris Hopper is an outfielder with the major-league Cincinnati Reds. (*Cruiser.*)

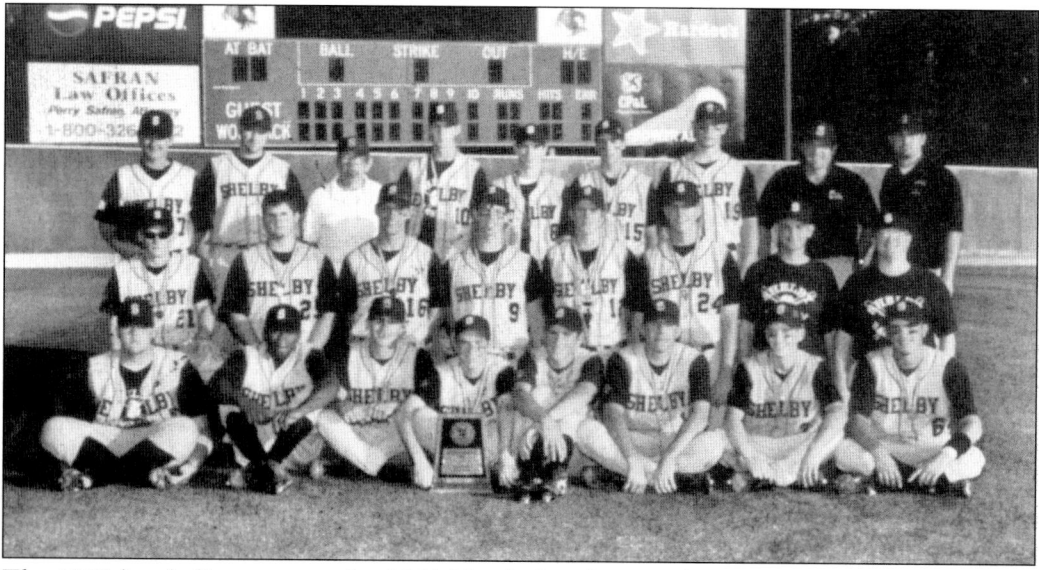

The 2001 baseball team won the 2001 North Carolina High School Athletic Association (NCHSAA) 2A state championship. Pictured from left to right are (first row) Dustin Sellers, Keith Brooks, John Turner, Brooks Greenway, Robert Taylor, Russell Forest, Michael Gross, Robbie Moss; (second row) Niles Bunting, Kelly Carpenter, Richmond Lutz, Trey Bridges, Tyler Trice, Greg Davis, and statisticians Bob Sherman and Jim Sherman; (third row) head coach Guy Suttle, assistant coach Brad Taylor, manager Gary "Zeek" Parker, Bronson Smith, Allen White, Michael Strickland, Brody Taylor, assistant coach Tommy Wease, and assistant coach Dave McDowell. (*Cruiser.*)

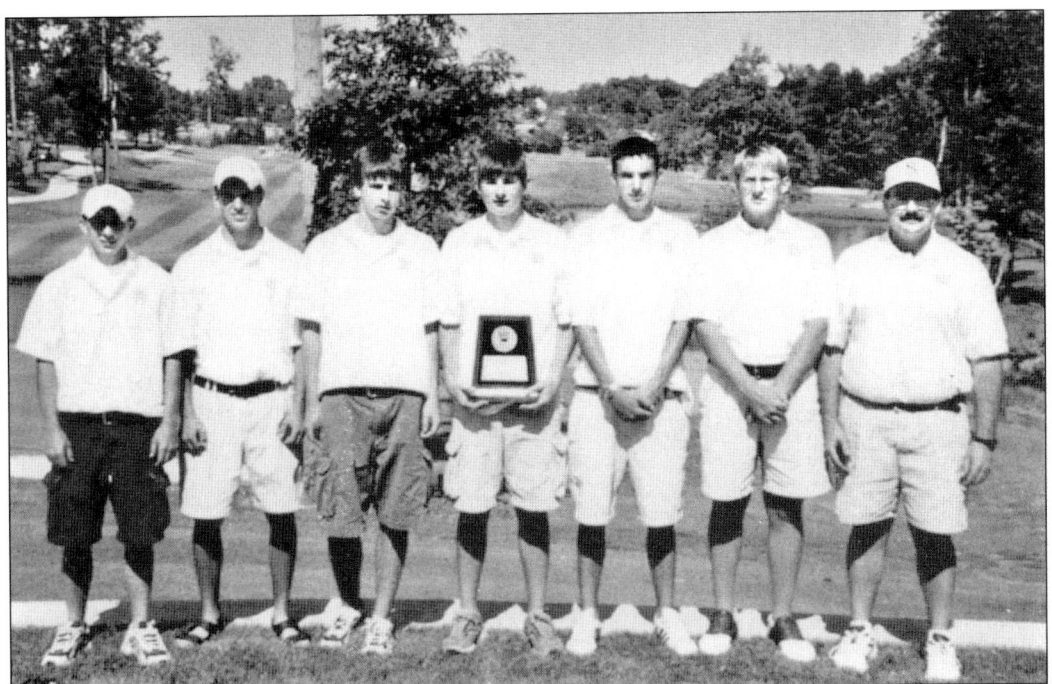

Shelby High experienced remarkable success in 2001, with the golf team bringing home the state 2A title. Pictured from left to right are David Webb, Ben Goforth, Patrick Cardell, Clay Arey, Chris Burris, Tripp Reynolds, and coach Bob Burris. (*Cruiser.*)

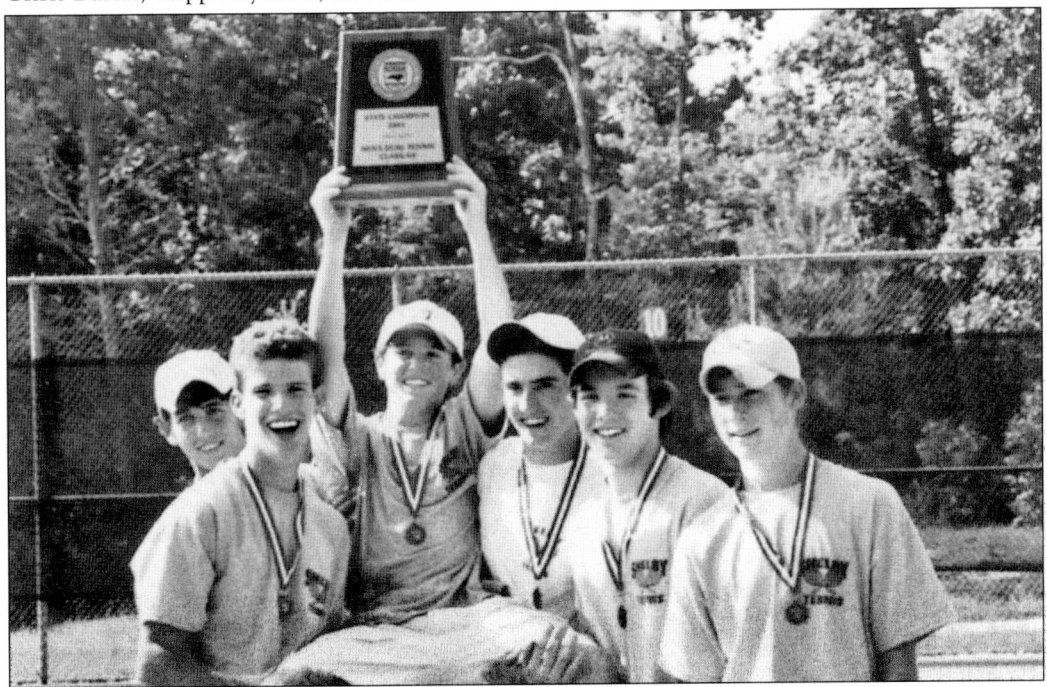

The SHS tennis team completed the 2001 season of champions winning the NCHSAA 2A tennis championship. Pictured from left to right are Perry Wright, William Noblitt, Alex Pearson, Lane Pearson, Jay Chitty, and David Rybnicek. (*Cruiser.*)

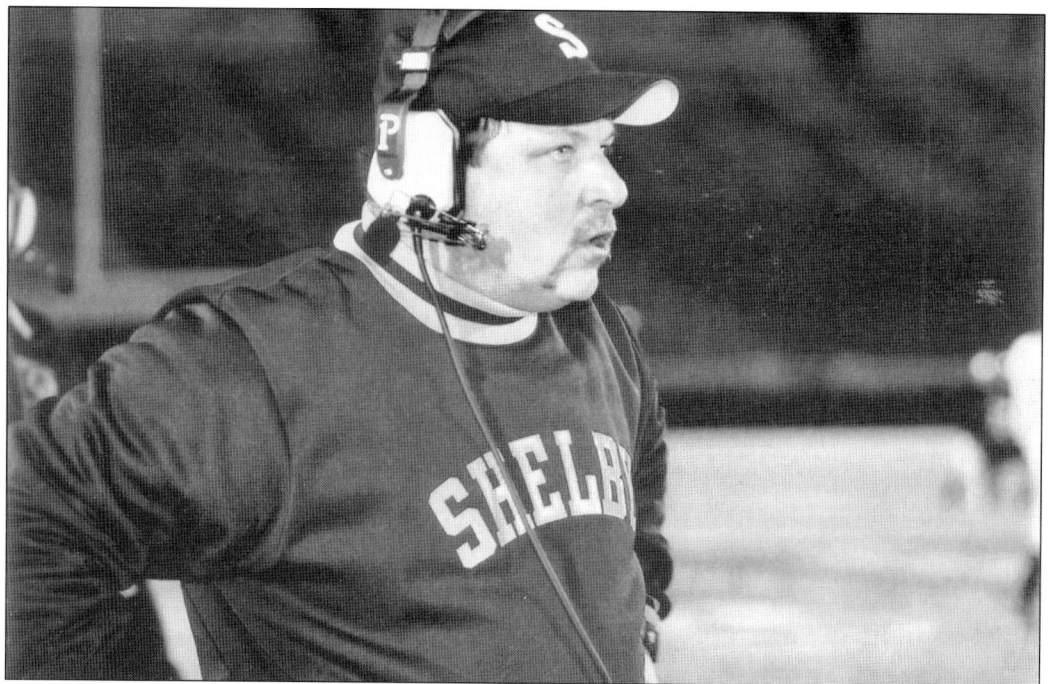

Chris Norman has compiled at impressive 80.62 winning percentage with a 104-25-1 record in 10 seasons as Shelby High Golden Lions head football coach. (Patrick McMurry.)

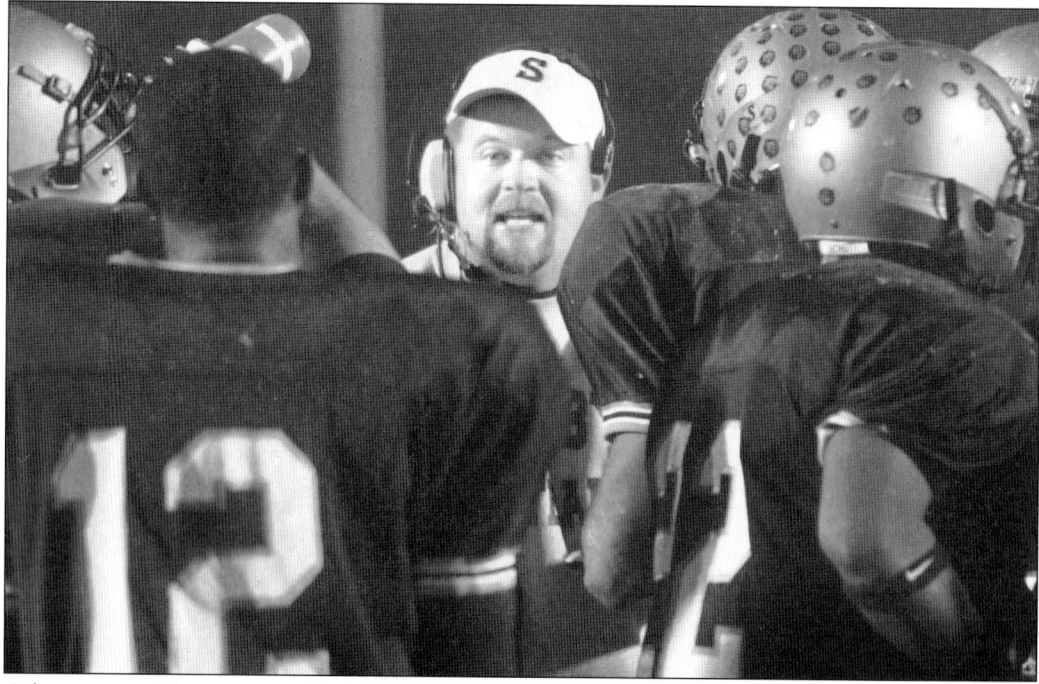

A large part of the success of the Shelby High football program can be found in the generations of quality personnel. Lance Ware played football at SHS before playing football at Appalachian State University. After college, Ware returned to Shelby to teach and coach at Shelby High. (Larry Ware.)

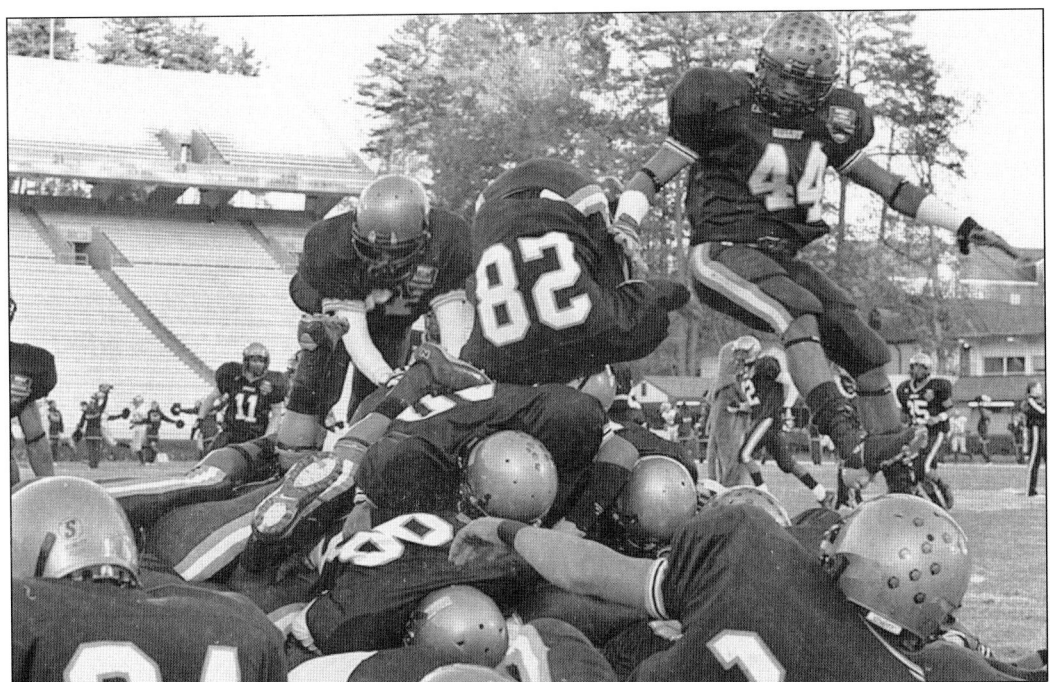

Keenan Stadium in Chapel Hill was the venue for the 2005 NCHSAA 2A state championship game. The Lions performed their pregame ritual of the pile-on on their way to winning another state championship. (Patrick McMurry.)

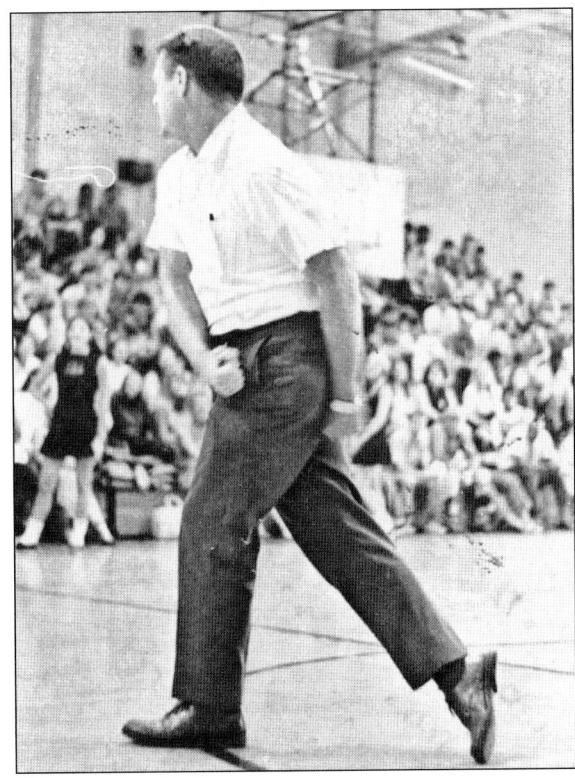

Coach "Pearley" Allen is pictured leading his favorite cheer during a SHS pep rally: "We're not ruff, we're not tuff, we're just Shelby High struttin' our stuff." (*Cruiser.*)

ACROSS AMERICA, PEOPLE ARE DISCOVERING SOMETHING WONDERFUL. THEIR HERITAGE.

Arcadia Publishing is the leading local history publisher in the United States. With more than 4,000 titles in print and hundreds of new titles released every year, Arcadia has extensive specialized experience chronicling the history of communities and celebrating America's hidden stories, bringing to life the people, places, and events from the past. To discover the history of other communities across the nation, please visit:

www.arcadiapublishing.com

Customized search tools allow you to find regional history books about the town where you grew up, the cities where your friends and family live, the town where your parents met, or even that retirement spot you've been dreaming about.

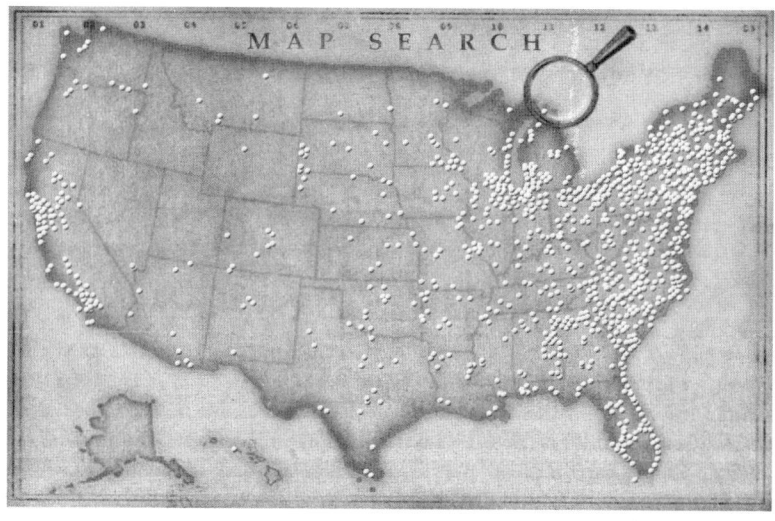